AILA's Focus on Private Bills & Pardons in Immigration

AILA TITLES OF INTEREST

AILA's OCCUPATIONAL GUIDEBOOKS

Immigration Options for Artists and Entertainers

Immigration Options for Physicians

Immigration Options for Nurses & Allied Health Care Professionals

Immigration Options for Religious Workers

Immigration Options for Academics and Researchers

Immigration Options for Investors and Entrepreneurs

STATUTES, REGULATIONS, AGENCY MATERIALS & CASE LAW

Immigration & Nationality Act (INA)

Immigration Regulations (CFR)

Agency Interpretations of Immigration Policy (Cables, Memos, and Liaison Minutes)

AILA's Immigration Case Summaries

CORE CURRICULUM

Navigating the Fundamentals of Immigration Law

Immigration Law for Paralegals*

AILA's Guide to Technology and Legal Research for the Immigration Lawyer

CD PRODUCTS & TOOLBOX SERIES

AILA's Immigration Practice Toolbox

AILA's Litigation Toolbox

FOR YOUR CLIENTS

Client Brochures (10 Titles)

U.S. Tax Guides for Foreign Persons and Those Who Pay Them, 4 volumes— (H-1Bs, L-1s, J-1s, B-1s)*

ONLINE RESEARCH TOOLS

AILALink Online

AILA's FOCUS SERIES

EB-2 & EB-3 Degree Equivalency by Ronald Wada

Waivers Under the INA by Julie Ferguson

Private Bills & Pardons in Immigration by Anna Gallagher

TREATISES & PRIMERS

Kurzban's Immigration Law Sourcebook by Ira J. Kurzban

Professionals: A Matter of Degree by Martin J. Lawler

AILA's Asylum Primer by Regina Germain

Immigration Consequences of Criminal Activity by Mary E. Kramer

Essentials of Removal and Relief by Joseph A. Vail

Essentials of Immigration Law by Richard A. Boswell

Litigating Immigration Cases in Federal Court by Robert Pauw

OTHER TITLES

David Stanton Manual on Labor Certification

AILA's Global Immigration Guide: A Country-by-Country Survey

Immigration & Nationality Law Handbook

The Visa Processing Guide

Ethics in a Brave New World

Immigration Practice Under NAFTA and Other Free Trade Agreements

GOVERNMENT REPRINTS

BIA Practice Manual

Immigration Judge Benchbook

Citizenship Laws of the World

ICE Inspector's Field Manual

Adjudicator's Field Manual

Tables of Contents and other information about these publications can be found at *www.ailapubs.org*. Orders may be placed at that site or by calling 1-800-982-2839.

*An AILA-distributed title

AILA's FOCUS ON PRIVATE BILLS & PARDONS IN IMMIGRATION

ANNA MARIE GALLAGHER

Website for Corrections and Updates

Corrections and other updates to AILA publications can be found online at: *www.aila.org/BookUpdates.*

If you have any corrections or updates to the information in this book, please let us know by sending a note to the address below, or e-mail us at *books@aila.org*.

This publication is designed to provide accurate and authoritative information in regard to the subject matter covered. It is distributed with the understanding that the publisher is not engaged in rendering legal, accounting, or other professional service. If legal advice or other expert assistance is required, the services of a competent professional should be sought.

—from a Declaration of Principles jointly adopted by a Committee of the American Bar Association and a Committee of Publishers

Copyright © 2008 by the American Immigration Lawyers Association

All rights reserved. No part of this publication may be reproduced or transmitted in any form or by any means, electronic or mechanical, including photocopy, recording, or any information storage retrieval system, without written permission from the publisher. No copyright claimed on U.S. government material.

Requests for permission to make electronic or print copies of any part of this work should be mailed to Director of Publications, American Immigration Lawyers Association, 918 F Street NW, Washington, DC 20004, or e-mailed to *books@aila.org.*

Printed in the United States of America

ISBN 978-1-57370-221-8
Stock No. 52-21

**To my sons,
Jairo and Sam**

Preface

In 2005, AILA asked me to participate in a panel along with Matt Guadagno and Royal Berg on private bills, pardons, and discretion during AILA's annual conference in Salt Lake City. I was tasked with preparing the sections on private bills, and began at that point to think quite a bit about the importance of private bills in immigration practice. As a young attorney, I was fortunate to practice at a time when there was still quite a bit of relief available to noncitizens, including those with criminal convictions. Since the passage of many restrictive immigration laws in the 1990s, I look nostalgically to those days when immigration judges considered all of the facts in my clients' cases and granted much-deserved relief to them. Attorneys practicing today must be especially creative in representing clients with complicated cases, and face many more legal obstacles than we faced in our early practices.

In preparing to write this book, I sent out an inquiry to AILA members asking them to share their experiences, and received quite a few responses. Many members told me that they had informally shared information on strategies they pursued in seeking a private bill or pardon, or in negotiating with the government for a favorable exercise of discretion. All who responded were pleased that AILA was going to publish a book on these "Hail Mary" defenses, as it provides a tool with the relevant information needed to pursue these remedies. As I have told many students who I have taught these past few years, there are great laws on the books—unfortunately, governments sometimes forget to pay attention to them. As difficult as these "Hail Mary" defenses are, there are procedures available to be studied and used in aggressively representing your client.

The book is divided into seven chapters. The first four chapters address issues relating to private bills. Chapters 5 and 6 discuss pardons. Chapter 7 focuses on deferred action and other forms of prosecutorial discretion. The appendices include rules governing private bills, statistics relating to private bills, a copy of the federal pardon application, a list of state pardon laws with contact information for practitioners to refer to in preparing their cases, and a bibliography.

Given the difficulties in obtaining relief under the Immigration and Nationality Act for many clients, it is important to consider the alternatives of private legislation, pardons, and prosecutorial discretion. These alternatives are not easy to pursue but must be considered in representing clients for whom little relief is available.

Anna Marie Gallagher
February 2008

Summary Table of Contents

AILA's Focus on Private Bills & Pardons in Immigration

Preface vii
Bibliography 175
Subject-Matter Index 177

Introduction
A Primer on Private Bills and Pardons in the Immigration Context 1

Chapter One
Private Bills 5

Chapter Two
Congressional Rules Governing Private Bills 19

Chapter Three
Role of the Executive Branch in Private Bills 31

Chapter Four
Private Bill Precedents and Advocacy Strategies 41

Chapter Five
Pardons 63

Chapter Six
Obtaining a Pardon Under Federal Law 73

Chapter Seven
Prosecutorial Discretion 85

APPENDICES

Appendix A— Senate Rules of Procedure for Introducing a Private Relief Bill (Immigration) 99

Appendix B—House Rules of Procedure for Private Immigration Bills 101

Appendix C—INS Operations Instructions on Private Bills 109

Appendix D—Petition for Pardon After Completion of Sentence 117

Appendix E—State Pardon Information 141

Appendix F—Private Immigration and Nationality Bills Introduced and Laws Enacted, 77th Through 109th Congress 165

Appendix G—9 FAM Appendix I...167

Bibliography..175

ACKNOWLEDGMENTS

As with any project I work on, this book represents not only my experiences and efforts but also those of many other colleagues and friends with whom I spoke and consulted during my writing. As always, the support of the AILA staff makes writing for them a delight. I want to recognize and thank Randy Auerbach, who first put the idea of writing this book into my head. A special thank you goes to AILA Publications Associate Director Danielle Polen, whose talent, good humor, and support made my work much easier. I would also like to thank AILA Legal Editor Richard Link and AILA Publications Director Tatia L. Gordon-Troy, for helping this project come to fruition. I want to recognize the following AILA members who graciously replied to my inquiries regarding their experiences with private bills: Angela Bean; Jessica Smith Bobadilla; Glenda Bunce; Buzz Burwell; Allen Erenbaum; Kenneth B. Hatcher; Chuck Kuck; Michael Maggio; Christine Lockhart Poarch; Jack Pinnix; Brent Renison; Kirsten Schlenger; Sherilyn Waxler; and Andrew Wizner. I especially want to thank Ben Casper for his comments and thoughts relating to congressional limitations on the effect of pardons.

I am grateful to the following people in the government who were helpful in providing hard-to-find information and practical tips on both private bills and pardons: Ur Jaddou; Janice Kaguyutan; Susan M. Cullen; Erik Ablin; and staff from USCIS Domestic Operations and the ICE Office of Congressional Relations. I also want to thank Richard Boswell and Matt Guadagno, who were kind enough to take time out of their very busy schedules and act as peer reviewers for the publication. I owe thanks as well to Dorina Balanean and Marisol Carrascal Miravalles, two good friends from my village here in Spain, whose friendship, laughter, and support helped me do my work. Last, and never least, thank you to my husband, Juan Luis Guillen, whose cooking skills, patience, and good sense of humor contributed in large part to the final product.

Anna Marie Gallagher
February 2008

Detailed Table of Contents

Chapter 1: Private Bills 5
    What Is a Private Bill? 5
    Controversy Surrounding Private Bills 6
    Historical Overview of Private Bills 7
    Quota Laws and the Preference System 8
    Exclusion Laws 11
    Naturalization 12
    How Private Bills Are Made 14
    How to Research Private Bills 16

Chapter 2: Congressional Rules Governing Private Bills 19
    Evolution of House and Senate Rules 19
    House Rules 21
    House Policy on Private Bills 22
    House Rules and Procedures 23
    Stays of Removal and Reports 24
    Special Requirements and Considerations in Certain Cases 25
        Adoption Cases 25
        Doctors and Nurses 25
        Drug and Criminal Activity 26
        Medical Cases 26
    Waiver of Grounds of Inadmissibility 27
    Naturalization Cases 27
    Senate Rules 28
    Senate Rules and Procedures 28

Chapter 3: Role of the Executive Branch in Private Bills 31
    Department of Homeland Security 33
    Introduction 33
    Work Authorization 33
    Role of ICE 34

    Legacy INS Operations Instructions and Private Bills 34
    Effect of Introduction of Private Bill on Immigration Status 35
    Implementation of an Enacted Private Bill 36
    Department of State 36
    Grounds of Ineligibility 38
    Adoption Cases 38
    Enactment of a Private Bill 39

Chapter 4: Private Bill Precedents and Advocacy Strategies 41
    Private Bill Precedents 41
    Adoption, Children, and Age-Out Cases 43
    Other Family Cases 48
    Death of Sponsor 49
    Criminal Issues 52
    Medical Issues 54
    Waiver of Naturalization and Citizenship Requirements 56
    Mistake of Law 57
    Political Cases 58
    Practice Tips and Strategies 59

Chapter 5: Pardons 63
    Full and Unconditional Pardon 65
    Constitutionality of the Immigration Pardon Provision 67
    Constitutional Arguments Before the BIA 70

Chapter 6: Obtaining a Pardon Under Federal Law 73
    Historical Background and Statistics 75
    Processing Federal Pardons 76
        Role of the Office of the Pardon Attorney 76
        Role of the U.S. Attorney 77
        Standards for the Consideration of Pardon Petitions 78
        Petition Procedures and Requirements 79
        Preparing the Pardon Application 81

Chapter 7: Prosecutorial Discretion 85
    Deferred Action 85
        Background 85
    Current Procedures 87
    Prosecutorial Discretion 88
        Legacy INS Memoranda 88
        ICE Discretion—Detention and Removal Operations (DRO) Officers and Office of Investigations (OI) Officers 90
        ICE Discretion—Chief Counsel's Offices 91
            Prosecutorial Discretion Prior to or in Lieu of Issuance of NTA 92
            Prosecutorial Discretion After Issuance and Filing of NTA 93
            Prosecutorial Discretion After Hearing 94
            After Issuance of Final Order—Motions to Reopen or Reconsider 94
    Conclusion 95

APPENDICES

Appendix A • Senate Rules of Procedure for Introducing a Private Relief Bill (Immigration) 99

Appendix B • House Rules of Procedure for Private Immigration Bills 101

Appendix C • INS Operations Instructions on Private Bills 109

Appendix D • Petition for Pardon After Completion of Sentence 117

Appendix E • State Pardon Information 141

Appendix F • Private Immigration and Nationality Bills Introduced and Laws Enacted, 77th Through 109th Congress 165

Appendix G • 9 FAM Appendix I 167

Bibliography 175

ABOUT AILA

The American Immigration Lawyers Association (AILA) is a national bar association of more than 11,000 attorneys who practice immigration law and/or work as teaching professionals. AILA member attorneys represent tens of thousands of U.S. families who have applied for permanent residence for their spouses, children, and other close relatives for lawful entry and residence in the United States. AILA members also represent thousands of U.S. businesses and industries who sponsor highly skilled foreign workers seeking to enter the United States on a temporary or permanent basis. In addition, AILA members represent foreign students, entertainers, athletes, and asylum-seekers, often on a pro bono basis. Founded in 1946, AILA is a nonpartisan, not-for-profit organization that provides its members with continuing legal education, publications, information, professional services, and expertise through its 36 chapters and over 50 national committees. AILA is an affiliated organization of the American Bar Association and is represented in the ABA House of Delegates.

American Immigration Lawyers Association
Tel: (202) 216-2400
Fax: (202) 783-7853
www.aila.org

INTRODUCTION

A PRIMER ON PRIVATE BILLS AND PARDONS IN THE IMMIGRATION CONTEXT

Over the years, thousands of noncitizens with compelling stories have been deported or excluded because their cases did not fall within the four square corners of existing immigration laws. Many have lost their immigration status and have been removed because of criminal convictions, while many others have fallen between the cracks of the law. The purpose of public immigration laws is to unite families, to provide much-needed workers for the U.S. labor market, and to protect refugees. Unfortunately, many of the amendments made to the Immigration and Nationality Act since 1990 may indicate otherwise. Many of these laws either restricted or eliminated access to previously available relief from deportation or exclusion. Administrative and federal courts often interpret the laws in ways that harm rather than protect the rights of deserving immigrants, nonimmigrants, undocumented persons, and refugees. When existing immigration laws fail to provide the necessary relief to noncitizens, their only options may be to apply for a private bill in the U.S. Congress or a pardon for those with criminal issues.

Since the beginning of the republic, Congress has passed private immigration laws in order to provide much-needed remedies that public laws cannot provide. The harsher the laws on the books at any given time, the greater the need for private immigration relief.[1] Historically, an increase in the number of private immigration bills introduced in Congress has alerted senators and representatives of the need for immigration law reform. There is less need for private bills when immigration laws are fair and take into account hardship cases.

Private bills serve a two-fold purpose. On the one hand, they provide individual relief to deserving noncitizens. On the other hand, an increase in the number of private bills involving a particular issue acts as a sort of early-warning system to advise Congress and other decision makers of flaws and inequities in existing laws. The introduction of private bills has had an impact on several types of immigration legislation, including those involving national quotas, exclusion, and naturalization. There was a noticeable increase in the number of private bill requests after the passage of the Quota Act of 1921, which continued in force until 1965.[2] The Quota Act established a system of immigration based on national origin. Hundreds of private bills were requested during these years on behalf of nationals from countries who did not receive a large number of visas allocated to them under the law. These cases resulted in Congress recognizing a need to change the law, and the quota system was ultimately abolished in 1965 by an act that established an immigration

---

[1] B. Maguire, *Immigration—Public Legislation and Private Bills* (1997), at xv.

[2] Emergency Quota Act, ch. 8, 42 Stat. 5 (1921).

system based on skills needed in the United States, family ties to U.S. citizens and lawful permanent residents, and a reformulation of the preference system based on family relations and employment skills.[3] In the area of exclusion and deportation, the large number of private bills introduced on behalf of relatives of U.S. citizens and lawful permanent residents in 1957 and in 1961 led to the passage of remedial legislation.[4] Finally, increased numbers of private bills served to reveal inequities in the naturalization laws relating to expatriating acts resulting from long periods of residence abroad.[5]

In addition to private fixes through specific legislation, federal and state pardons serve as an important form of individual relief for deserving cases. Changes relating to grounds of inadmissibility and removal included in the Antiterrorism and Effective Death Penalty Act of 1996[6] and the Illegal Immigration Reform and Immigrant Responsibility Act of 1996[7] resulted in thousands of persons with criminal convictions or past criminal activity being subject to deportation, many facing permanent expulsion. Since Congress is hesitant to provide relief through private bills in criminal cases, pardons may serve as the only alternative to removal.

This book is divided into seven chapters, with appendices. Chapter 1 addresses private bills, providing information on the history of private bills, the legal authority for private bills, and the effect of a private bill on immigration status. It also provides an overview of how private laws are made and information on how to research private immigration bills.

Chapter 2 addresses congressional rules governing private bills. It discusses the House of Representatives' rules and procedures governing private bills and the evolution of these rules during the last half of the 20th century until present. It explains the current rules and procedures in the House governing the introduction and passage of private bills in the immigration context. It also addresses the Senate's current rules and procedures governing private bills and the evolution of those rules.

Chapter 3 discusses the role of the executive branch in the private bill process. Specifically, it addresses the role of the Department of Homeland Security (DHS) and, to a lesser extent, the role of the Department of State (DOS) in the private bill process. This chapter addresses the immigration status of an applicant during the process and stays of removal. It also talks about DHS and DOS reports and responses to members of Congress. Under both the House and Senate procedures, members may request reports on the potential beneficiary or beneficiaries of private bills.

Chapter 4 provides an overview of private bill precedents in order to give the reader a better idea of the types of cases toward which Congress is favorable. As

---

[3] Immigration Act of 1965, Pub. L. No. 89-236, 79 Stat. 911.

[4] B. Maguire, *supra* note 1, at 71; Act of September 11, 1957, 71 Stat. 639 (providing for waivers of certain grounds of exclusion).

[5] B. Maguire, *supra* note 1, at 71.

[6] Pub. L. No. 104-132, 110 Stat. 1214.

[7] Pub. L. No. 104-208, div. C, 110 Stat. 3009, 3009-546 to 3009-724.

INTRODUCTION

noted in the House rules, it is the policy of the Subcommittee on Immigration, Citizenship, Refugees, Border Security and International Law to act favorably on only those private bills that meet certain precedents.[8] The term "precedent" throughout this book refers to private laws that were passed by the U.S. Congress and became law. Therefore, an understanding of those precedents is vital in order to prepare and present a request for a private bill to a member of Congress. This chapter also discusses strategies to be used by practitioners in advocating for a private bill on behalf of a client.

Chapter 5 provides an overview on the use of pardons to provide immigration relief to noncitizens with criminal convictions. It will explain what crimes may be forgiven, for immigration purposes, by a pardon. It also discusses the requirements for a pardon to be effective in resolving an immigration problem. Finally, it addresses the issue of the constitutionality of Congress's limitation on the presidential pardon power by only recognizing certain crimes that can be eliminated by a pardon for immigration purposes.

Chapter 6 provides information on the role of federal pardons as a potential remedy in immigration cases. It will discuss the rules and procedures governing executive clemency. It also gives the reader a historical overview of federal pardons approved under several administrations, highlighting both successful and unsuccessful cases.

Chapter 7 discusses the role of state pardons in resolving immigration cases. It will talk about the different state clemency models, including pardon power exercised by independent boards with no involvement of the governor, pardons approved where the governor may act only upon advice of a board, and pardons exercised solely by the governor. The chapter also includes a short state-by-state description of pardon procedures.

Although private bills and pardons are often seen as remedies of last resort, practitioners should aggressively pursue them on behalf of their clients. Hopefully, this book will serve to encourage you to consider such strategies.

---

[8] U.S. House of Representatives Committee on the Judiciary, Subcommittee on Immigration, Citizenship, Refugees, Border Security and International Law, Rules of Procedure and Statement of Policy for Private Immigration Bills, 110th Cong. (2007), at 3 (statement of policy).

CHAPTER 1

PRIVATE BILLS

What Is a Private Bill?

A private bill is an individual discretionary exception to the general law. It provides relief for one or several persons, corporations, or institutions and is distinguished from a public bill, which relates to public issues and deals with individuals only by classes.[1]

Congress has plenary power to regulate immigration.[2] Its power extends to the classification of noncitizens as a basis for determining their eligibility to enter and remain in the United States.[3] Its power also extends to the passage of private bills providing immigration benefits to noncitizens. Constitutional authority for private bills is found in the First Amendment, which provides as follows:

> Congress shall make no law respecting an establishment of religion, or prohibiting the free exercise thereof; or abridging the freedom of speech, or of the press; or the right of the people peaceably to assemble, and *to petition the Government for a redress of grievances*.[4]

The introduction of a private bill does not guarantee its enactment. The power to enact private laws is solely within the power granted to Congress under article I of the Constitution, section 8, clause 1, to pay the debts of the United States. Courts have interpreted this authority to pay debts to include moral or even honorary debt.[5] The power of Congress to pass immigration laws under the Commerce Clause[6] also can be interpreted as granting authority to Congress to enact private immigration bills.[7]

In 1896, the U.S. Supreme Court noted the following in its decision in *U.S. v. Realty Co.*, regarding the nation's debts to individuals:

---

[1] A. Hinds, *Hinds' Precedents of the House of Representatives of the United States,* Washington, D.C. U.S. Govt. Print. Off., 1907, vol. IV, at 247.

[2] *Chae Chan Ping v. U.S.,* 130 U.S. 581 (1889); *Kleindienst v. Mandel,* 408 U.S. 753 (1972); *Fiallo v. Bell,* 430 U.S. 787 (1977).

[3] *Fiallo v. Bell,* 430 U.S. 787 (1977); *Rodriguez-Silva v. INS,* 242 F.3d 243 (5th Cir. 2001); *U.S. v. Navarro,* 218 F.3d 895 (8th Cir. 2000); *Giusto v. INS,* 9 F.3d 8 (2d Cir. 1993). *See generally* G. Chin, "Is There a Plenary Power Doctrine? A Tentative Apology and Prediction for Our Strange but Unexceptional Constitutional Immigration Law," 15 *Geo. Immigr. L. J.* 257 (2000).

[4] U.S. Const., amend. I.

[5] B. Maguire, *Immigration—Public Legislation and Private Bills* (1997), at 2, n.11, citing *U.S. v. Realty Co.,* 163 U.S. 427, 440 (1896).

[6] U.S. Const., art. I, §8, cl. 3.

[7] B. Maguire, *supra* note 5, at 2, n.12, citing *The Passenger Cases, Smith v. Turner,* 48 U.S. 283 (1949), *Henderson v. Mayor of New York,* 92 U.S. 259 (1875), and *Chy Lung v. Freeman,* 92 U.S. 275 (1875).

The nation, broadly speaking, owes a 'debt' to an individual when his claim grows out of general principles of right and justice; when, in other words, it is based upon considerations of a moral or merely honorary nature, such as are binding on the conscience or the honor of an individual, although the debt could obtain no recognition in a court of law.[8]

The principal factor in determining whether a private bill is warranted in the immigration context is hardship. The circumstances in the case must be extraordinary in order to justify the passage of a private immigration bill. As explained in 1971 by Peter W. Rodino, Jr., Chairman of the House Committee on the Judiciary, a private immigration bill is an extraordinary remedy available to assist aliens with unusual problems resulting in unusual hardship.[9]

Although the first private bills enacted in Congress involved naturalization issues, they represent a relatively low number of the total enacted in the immigration context. The great majority of private bills enacted grant lawful permanent resident status by waiving certain provisions of the immigration laws relating to grounds of inadmissibility or removal, numerical limitations, definitions of eligible immigrant categories, and other provisions. The private bill process is conducted openly in both the House and the Senate, with each chamber having their own rules governing their procedures.[10]

Controversy Surrounding Private Bills

The private bill process has been subject to abuse in certain cases and therefore has come under attack. As a result of scandals and other internal controversies, such as the number of bills introduced, the role of the Senate and House committees in the process, the relationship between the House and the Senate, contempt of the private bill process by certain members of Congress, and special privileges in some cases, there has been much criticism of the private bill system over the years.[11] It should be noted that the majority of the members of Congress never introduce private bills.[12]

In recent history, there have been three major controversies involving private bills. The first controversy involved a multi-million-dollar operation to smuggle noncitizens to the United States in the 1950s. It was alleged that many had received help from innocent congressmen. According to reports in the papers, members of Congress introduced private bills because of pressure from individuals and groups in their home districts. A congressman from North Dakota, William D. Langer, introduced bills on behalf of noncitizens in New York to stay the deportation of

---

[8] *U.S. v. Realty Co.*, 163 U.S. 427, 440 (1896).

[9] B. Maguire, *supra* note 5, at 3, n.19, citing 117 Cong. Rec. 10143 (Apr. 7, 1971).

[10] U.S. House of Representatives Committee on the Judiciary, Subcommittee on Immigration, Citizenship, Refugees, Border Security and International Law, Rules of Procedure and Statement of Policy for Private Immigration Bills, 110th Cong. (2007); U.S. Senate Committee on the Judiciary, Subcommittee on Immigration, Border Security, and Citizenship, Rules of Procedure for Introducing a Private Relief Bill (Immigration), 108th Cong. (2005).

[11] For more on the internal controversies, see B. Maguire, *supra* note 5, at 231–49.

[12] *Id.* at 231.

former Nazis and members of the German-American bund. According to Langer, the stays were necessary to protect their constitutional rights. After being accused of running a smuggling racket, he withdrew a number of bills seeking relief for 75 Pakistani seamen who had jumped overboard. Another congressman had introduced a bill at the request of the Legal Aid Society and others involving a native of Italy who had been smuggled into the United States for $1,000. As a result of these cases, an investigation into private bills was carried out in 1953.[13]

The second major controversy involved allegations of misconduct by senators who introduced private bills on behalf of Chinese shipjumpers. The investigation revealed that 80 percent of the 657 private bills introduced from 1967 to 1969 had originated in the offices of four lawyers in New York City and nine lobbyists in Washington, D.C.[14] During its investigation, the Senate committee responsible for the investigation noted the increase in private bills—from 96 in the 88th Congress to 657 in the 90th and 91st Congresses—and also pointed out that high fees had been charged to the beneficiaries of the bills. Additionally, many bills were introduced without the knowledge of a senator. The committee did note, however, that no evidence was found that any senator received any money for the introduction of any private bill. In response to the investigation, the Senate changed its rules of procedures for introduction of private bills.[15]

The third major controversy surrounding private bills involved the Abscam scandal. Abscam involved the investigation and conviction of seven members of Congress suspected of accepting bribes in exchange for promising to introduce private bills on behalf of foreign businessmen.[16] The FBI sting operation began in 1978 and involved agents and informants posing as representatives of Middle Eastern sheiks who were interested in investing in the United States.[17]

Historical Overview of Private Bills

Congress has a long history of passing private laws in order to provide a remedy in cases where the public law cannot do so. Of the 108 laws passed by the first Congress in 1789, five were private laws. That number quickly grew over the years, and from 1817 through 1971, most Congresses enacted hundreds of private bills.[18] During the 49th Congress (1885–87), members passed 1,031 private laws, as compared with 434 public laws.[19] At the turn of the century, the 56th Congress enacted 1,498 private laws and only 443 public laws.[20] The highest number of private

---

[13] *Id.* at 228.

[14] *Id.* at 229.

[15] *Id.*

[16] *Id.* at 230. "Abscam" was the code name given to the operation by the FBI.

[17] *Id.*

[18] R. Beth, Private Bills: Procedure in the House (Oct. 21, 2004), CRS Report for Congress No. 98-628, available at *www.rules.house.gov/archives/98-628.pdf*.

[19] The History of the Private Calendar and the Consideration of Private Bills, 145 Cong. Rec. E713-01 (Apr. 21, 1999).

[20] *Id.*

bills was passed during the 59th Congress (1905–06), when Congress approved 6,249 bills.[21] However, the number of private bills enacted has declined significantly, as Congress has expanded the use of administrative discretion to deal with many situations that would give rise to the need for private legislative remedies.[22] In addition, the decline may be attributable to legislative action, internal chamber rules, corruption and scandal, and ignorance and neglect.[23]

From its first session in 1789, Congress has enacted over 7,000 private immigration bills.[24] From the 77th session of Congress in 1942 until the 107th session in 2003, 60,601 private immigration-related bills were introduced and 6,761 were enacted.[25] During the 101st Congress, 289 private bills were introduced, with 16 becoming law. That number, however, declined significantly by the 108th Congress, when 82 private bills were introduced with only six becoming law.[26] And although 77 private immigration bills were introduced in the 109th Congress, none became law.[27]

Quota Laws and the Preference System

As noted in the introduction, private bills have influenced changes in public immigration laws in several areas. The first major impact of private bills on influencing remedial public legislation occurred with national quotas.[28] From the passage of the Quota Act of 1921[29] and the National Origins Quota Act of 1924[30] until their abolition in 1965,[31] immigration to the United States was largely determined by national origin, with preference being granted to those of western and northern European ancestry. In addition to the original quota system, the Immigration and Nationality Act of 1952 (INA)[32] created a preference-based system, allocating visas to skilled noncitizens and to certain relatives of U.S. citizens and lawful permanent residents. A certain number of visas were allocated to countries around the world and to persons within the preference categories, some receiving much higher allocations than others. Prior to changes in the law made in 1965, thousands of

---

[21] A History of the Committee of the Judiciary 1813–2006, H. Doc. 109-158, p. 143 (2006).

[22] R. Beth, *supra* note 18, at 1.

[23] M. Mantel, "Private Bills and Private Laws," 99 *Law Libr. J.* 87 (Winter 2007).

[24] B. Maguire, *supra* note 5, at 87 (Maguire counts 7,266 private laws enacted during the first 100 Congresses); Private Immigration Legislation (Congressional Research Service 2005), p. 2, n.9 (CRS counts 55 private immigration bills enacted from the 101st Congress through the 109th Congress (2005)).

[25] U.S. Department of Homeland Security, Yearbook of Immigration Statistics, 2003 (U.S. Government Printing Office 2004), Table 51.

[26] M. Mantel, *supra* note 23, at 94.

[27] Report on the Activities of the Committee on the Judiciary of the House of Representatives during the One Hundred and Ninth Congress, H. Rep. 109-749, pp. 107, 108.

[28] To review the private bill precedents relating to quota laws, see B. Maguire, *supra* note 5, at 98–138.

[29] Emergency Quota Act, ch. 8, 42 Stat. 5 (1921).

[30] National Origins Quota Act, Pub. L. No. 43-139, 43 Stat. 153 (1924).

[31] Immigration Act of 1965, Pub. L. No. 89-236, 79 Stat. 911.

[32] Pub. L. No. 82-414, 66 Stat. 163 (1952) (also known as the McCarran-Walter Act).

private bills were introduced and enacted to grant status to applicants in oversubscribed categories.

Of the 7,266 private laws enacted into law in the first 100 Congresses, 4,728 involved issues relating to immigration quotas, representing 65 percent of all private bills passed up to that time. These private bills relating to quotas involved the following categories:

- Conferring immediate relative status on spouses, children, parents, and other close relatives of U.S. citizens (1,664 private bills). The purpose of the private bills enacted in this category was to eliminate the long visa waiting periods, to overcome age and residency requirements, or to avoid problems relating to the petition process.

- Establishing a preference for relatives or for those with certain skills, as well as conferring status on certain permanent residents (351 private bills). The purpose of private bills in this category was to generally avoid oversubscribed quotas or an inadequate preference system for either family– or skills-based immigration.

- Waiver of exclusions for those ineligible for a visa because of race, including fiancés (380 private bills). The purpose of the private bills in this category was to waive exclusions established in the National Origins Quota Act of 1924, which prohibited the entry of persons from most parts of Asia.

- Waivers for health and criminal grounds for fiancés (165 private bills). The purpose of private bills in this category was to provide private relief in the absence of public laws to permit U.S. servicemen returning home from World War II to bring their foreign-born spouses.

- Grant of immigration status for generally oversubscribed visa categories of a miscellaneous nature, including occupational reasons or separated families of U.S. citizens or lawful permanent residents (2,168 private bills). This category also included private laws to provide admission for persons excludable for medical reasons, persons whose cases were deemed in the national interest, and refugees.[33]

During and after the passage of these private bills, remedial legislation was put into place. In 1948, Congress passed legislation permitting suspension of deportation, permitting persons who did not have qualifying relatives to obtain permanent residence and persons racially ineligible to qualify for immigration relief.[34] Congress passed these provisions in order to provide relief for those not favored by private bills but who nonetheless should have had their cases considered for relief.[35] Additional

---

[33] B. Maguire, *supra* note 5, at 88.

[34] Pub. L. No. 80-864, 62 Stat. 1206 (1948); Displaced Persons Act of 1948, Pub. L. No. 80-774, 62 Stat. 1009.

[35] Sen. Rep. No. 1204, 80th Cong., 2nd Sess. (1948), at 3.

amendments to the suspension of deportation provision relieved many noncitizens from seeking relief in private bills.[36]

The INA also worked to remedy some immigration problems that were previously the subject of hundreds of private bills. Among other things, the act reordered the preferences for family and employment-based immigration. However, the act did eliminate race as a bar to admission. Despite some positive changes brought about by the act, low quotas continued to act as obstacles for immigration from those countries subject to the quotas. From 1952 until the passage of the Immigration Act of 1965,[37] a total of 160 private bills were passed relating to occupations.[38]

In addition to national quotas, a preference system was established by the INA. The system granted greater preference to skilled noncitizens and less to relatives of U.S. citizens and lawful permanent residents within quotas allocated to each country. Although the act granted a certain number of visas for those persons with certain skills, the category was oversubscribed. Other than temporary measures to clear up backlogs, the only relief for persons in this category prior to the changes made by legislation passed in 1965[39] was through private legislation.

Adoption is another area where the introduction and passage of a large number of private bills has impacted public legislation. The Displaced Persons Act of 1948 permitted the immigration of orphans[40] and the Refugee Relief Act of 1953 admitted additional orphans.[41] During debate on a law for adopted children in 1961, the chairman of the House Immigration Subcommittee noted the influence that private bills had in enacting permanent legislation.[42] While the 1961 legislation covered many of the needs for obtaining status on behalf of adopted children, this still remains an area where private bills continue to be requested, due to age limitations, petitioning requirements, and failure to comply with definitions.

Private bills also served to show the need for permanent legislation permitting the immigration of sheepherders,[43] and the need for providing immigration status through registry for long-term residents in the United States.[44] Prior to the passage of remedial legislation benefiting these populations, private bills had been the only form of relief that was pursued by individuals.

---

[36] Pub. L. No. 82-414, 66 Stat. 163 (1952); Pub. L. No. 87-885, 76 Stat. 1247 (1962); Pub. L. No. 89-236, 79 Stat. 911 (1965).

[37] Pub. L. No. 89-236, 79 Stat. 911 (1965).

[38] B. Maguire, *supra* note 5, at 92.

[39] Immigration Act of 1965, Pub. L. No. 89-236, 79 Stat. 911 (1965).

[40] Pub. L. No. 80-774, 62 Stat. 1009, as amended by Pub. L. No. 81-555, 64 Stat. 219 (1950), Pub. L. No. 82-60, 65 Stat. 96 (1951), and the Immigration and Nationality (McCarran-Walter) Act of 1952, Pub. L. No. 82-414, §402, 66 Stat. 163, 277.

[41] Pub. L. No. 83-203, 67 Stat. 400 (1953), as amended by Pub. L. No. 83-725, §1, 68 Stat. 999, 1044 (1954); extended in part by Pub. L. No. 85-316, §§4, 15, 71 Stat. 639 (1957).

[42] B. Maguire, *supra* note 5, at 92, citing to 106 Cong. Rec. 18283 (Sept. 6, 1961).

[43] *Id.* at 94.

[44] *Id.*

Exclusion Laws

As with the quota laws, exclusion laws resulted in the filing of hundreds of private bills on behalf of persons who were prohibited from entering the United States and for whom no alternative relief, including waivers, was available.[45] The number of private bills filed served to alert Congress that the laws were too harsh and public remedial legislation was necessary. From the beginning of the republic, there have been laws excluding certain categories of persons. Grounds for exclusion have been based on health, security, political activity, labor concerns, and criminal issues.

In 1940, Congress passed the Alien Registration Act,[46] or Smith Act, a law that expanded the grounds of exclusion relating to threats to the nation to include membership in certain prohibited groups, including past affiliation with such groups. In 1950, Congress passed the Internal Security Act,[47] which again expanded the grounds of exclusion to include Communist Party membership, codified certain security grounds, and added a bar to admission for those who would likely engage in espionage, sabotage, and public disorder after entry. The INA, which codified all existing immigration laws, increased and strengthened the grounds of exclusion, including those related to security, fraud, health, labor, and criminal issues. Waivers for certain grounds of exclusion—health and illiteracy, for example—were included in the act. Additional waivers for criminal and health grounds were provided for in later legislation.[48]

Despite the passage of provisions allowing waivers of certain grounds of exclusion, many people still remained subject to grounds of exclusion that resulted in the separation of families. The influence of private bills relating to public legislation can be seen with the passage of legislation in 1954 and 1957, providing for additional waivers for minor criminal offenses; legislation passed in 1961 and 1965 permitting health waivers; and legislation passed in 1981 permitting waivers for certain drug offenses.[49] In the first 100 Congresses, a total of 1,843 private laws were enacted to waive certain grounds of exclusion. This comprised 25 percent of the private laws enacted during that period of time.[50] The highest number of private bills enacted to cure grounds of exclusion occurred during the 83rd through the 85th Congresses (1953–58), when 1,355 private laws were enacted.[51] The great majority of these waived grounds based on criminal and health issues for which public law provided no

---

[45] To review private bill precedents relating to grounds of exclusion, see *id.* at 155–79.

[46] Act of June 28, 1940, 54 Stat. 670.

[47] Pub. L. No. 82-831, 64 Stat. 987 (1950).

[48] Pub. L. No. 83-777, 68 Stat. 1145 (1954) (petty-offense exception); Pub. L. No. 85-316, 71 Stat. 639 (1957) (crimes of moral turpitude, prostitution, tuberculosis, and misrepresentation); Pub. L. No. 89-236, 79 Stat. 911 (1965) (mental retardation and insanity); Pub. L. No. 97-116, 95 Stat. 1611 (1981) (single offense of 30 grams or less of marijuana).

[49] B. Maguire, *supra* note 5, at 148.

[50] *Id.*

[51] *Id.*

relief. As noted above, remedial legislation providing for waivers was passed in the years following this notable increase in private legislation.

Note: One of the more famous private bill cases seeking a waiver for a ground of exclusion involved Michael Wilding, the son of Elizabeth Taylor and stepson of Senator John Warner (R-VA). A native and citizen of the United Kingdom, he had been convicted of possession of 13.6 milligrams of cannabis when he was 21. In 1988, the U.S. Congress approved a private bill on his behalf in order to waive the ground of exclusion.[52]

Naturalization

Private bills relating to naturalization were the first type of private laws to be considered by Congress in 1839.[53] However, the total number of private bills enacted in this category is lower than the number of those seeking to avoid quota/preference or exclusion. This is so because there is a high standard for naturalization and the naturalization laws have been fairly consistent over the years, with few changes.[54] During the first 100 Congresses, 695 private bills relating to naturalization were enacted, representing 10 percent of the 7,266 private laws enacted during that period of time.[55] Private bills relating to naturalization have been filed in the following categories of cases:

- Loss of citizenship due to private acts: This category involved loss of citizenship due to marriage to a foreign national, voting in foreign elections, or renunciation of citizenship. Eighty-nine private bills were enacted in the first 100 Congresses, representing 13 percent of all citizenship bills.

- Inability to confer or derive citizenship: This category involved the inability of a person to confer or derive citizenship through parents because of insufficient residency periods in the United States. These cases totaled 43, representing 6 percent of citizenship bills passed in the first 100 Congresses.

- Failure to retain citizenship once gained: This category involved those who lost citizenship because they traveled to their home countries or another country for long periods of time after naturalization, as well as children born abroad to a U.S. citizen and noncitizen and who were required to return to the United States for a period of time to retain citizenship. Ninety-three private bills were enacted in this category, representing 13 percent of all citizenship bills passed in the first 100 Congresses.

- Inability to meet residence requirements for naturalization purpose: This category involved those persons who failed to meet the residence requirement in the United States prior to applying for naturalization.

---

[52] Priv. L. No. 100-36, 102 Stat. 4859 (1988).

[53] To review private bill precedents relating to naturalization, see B. Maguire, *supra* note 5, at 198–226.

[54] *Id.* at 193.

[55] *Id.* at 192.

- Special exemptions: This category involved draft dodgers, Communist Party members, U.S. government and English requirement cases. Thirty-eight private bills were enacted in this category, representing 5 percent of all citizenship cases.[56]

Enactment of private bills in the above categories was often followed by passage of public laws, thereby avoiding the need for future private legislation. Legislation that was passed in 1951 and 1954 repealed the prohibition against voting in foreign elections in Italy and in Japan.[57] Prior to a Supreme Court case[58] and remedial legislation passed in 1978 repealing the law, private bills were enacted to naturalize persons who lost their citizenship because of residence abroad.[59] Legislation was passed in 1934 permitting American mothers to confer citizenship to their children born abroad.[60] During hearings relating to this legislation, there was discussion concerning the number of meritorious cases resolved through private bills.[61] Legislation was passed in 1959 exempting parents of citizens from loss of citizenship due to residence abroad,[62] and additional legislation passed in 1956, 1966, 1972, and 1978 worked towards eliminating the need for any private bills relating to conferral or derivation of citizenship.[63] Few private bills were enacted relating to defector cases. However, legislation was passed in 1952[64] and in 1985 providing waivers under certain circumstances in national security cases.[65] The number of private bills enacted to provide waivers of residency requirements for Cuban nationals increased in the 1960s until the Cuban Adjustment Act of 1966 was enacted to provide permanent residence for Cubans who entered the United States during those years.[66]

How Private Bills Are Made

A private bill is introduced and referred to a committee the same way as any public bill.[67] Any member may introduce a bill at any time when Congress is in session. Permission to introduce a bill is not required. The member introducing the bill is known as the sponsor, and any members may act as cosponsors. Once the bill is printed into the *Congressional Record*, it is assigned a legislative number. Copies

---

[56] *Id.* at 194.

[57] Act of August 16, 1951, 65 Stat. 191; Act of July 20, 1954 (68 Stat. 495).

[58] *Schneider v. Rusk*, 377 U.S. 163 (1965).

[59] B. Maguire, *supra* note 5, at 192.

[60] Act of May 24, 1934, 48 Stat. 797.

[61] B. Maguire, *supra* note 5, at 194, citing Senate Committee on Immigration, American Citizenship Rights of Women, 72nd Cong., 2nd Sess., at 25.

[62] Pub. L. No. 86-129, 73 Stat. 274 (1959).

[63] Pub. L. No. 84-430, 70 Stat. 50 (1956); Pub. L. No. 89-770, 80 Stat. 1322 (1966); Pub. L. No. 92-584, 86 Stat. 1289 (1972); Pub. L. No. 95-579, 92 Stat. 2474 (1978).

[64] Immigration and Nationality (McCarran-Walter) Act of 1952, Pub. L. No. 82-414, 66 Stat. 163.

[65] Pub. L. No. 99-169, 99 Stat. 1002 (1985).

[66] B. Maguire, *supra* note 5, at 197.

[67] For more detailed information on how laws are made in the United States, see C. Johnson, How Laws Are Made, H.R. Doc. No. 108-93 (2003).

of the bill are sent to the judiciary committees of each house, which have jurisdiction over private bills. However, the subcommittees—the Senate Subcommittee on Immigration, Border Security and Citizenship and the House Subcommittee on Immigration, Citizenship, Refugees, Border Security and International Law—initiate action on private bill legislation by holding hearings and preparing reports. The rules of procedures relating to private bills are adopted by these subcommittees and then affirmed by the committees on the judiciary.

> *Note*: There is no requirement in either the House or the Senate rules relating to private immigration bills that limits the introduction of a bill only to a constituent within the member's district or state. Therefore, members can introduce private bills on behalf of noncitizens who are not residing within the areas they represent.

There are special procedures for the consideration of private bills in the House. When the private bill is reported, it is placed on the Private Calendar.[68] Consideration of private bills is on the first Tuesday of each month, and at the discretion of the Speaker, on the third Tuesday of each month. The bills are called up automatically, in the order in which they were reported, and are placed on the Calendar. Debate may be held and amendments to the bills may be considered. During the call of the Private Calendar, if two members object to the consideration of a bill, it is automatically recommitted. Each party appoints official objectors, who examine bills on the Private Calendar and object to those they consider inappropriate. In practice, however, instead of objecting, the objectors will often request that a bill be passed over without prejudice. This gives the sponsor an opportunity to discuss with them concerns relating to the bill before the next calendar call.[69]

In the Senate, when bills are considered after action by the Judiciary Committee, they are placed on a Calendar of Business.[70] They are generally taken up by unanimous consent on the Senate floor at a time convenient for the majority leader. There are no designated days or time limitations on the consideration of private bills. Although debate is permitted in the Senate, it rarely occurs in private bill legislation. A Senator may place a "hold" on any legislation to prevent its consideration on the floor. A hold can be placed anonymously and can extend through the entire Congress. Until 1969, private bills could be introduced by Senate staff. However, after the scandals involving bills introduced on behalf of Chinese crewmen, this rule changed. Private bills now must be signed and delivered by the senator endorsing them.[71]

---

[68] U.S. House of Representatives Committee on the Judiciary, Subcommittee on Immigration, Citizenship, Refugees, Border Security and International Law, Rules of Procedure and Statement of Policy for Private Immigration Bills, 110th Congress (2007), rule XIII, cl. 1.

[69] R. Beth, *supra* note 18.

[70] For a detailed review of Senate procedures, see F. Riddick, *Senate Procedure, Precedents and Practices,* United States Senate, 93rd Cong., 1st. Sess., S. Doc. No. 21. *See also* V. Heitshusen, The Legislative Process on the Senate Floor: An Introduction, CRS Report for Congress No. 96-548, available at *www.senate.gov/reference/resources/pdf/96-548.pdf.*

[71] B. Maguire, *supra* note 5, at 20.

Once the bill is approved by the House, the enrolling clerk prepares the engrossed copy of the bill as passed, and sends it to the Senate for consideration. The Senate refers the engrossed bill to the appropriate committee for its consideration. The Senate committee can approve the bill as is or submit amendments. If the Senate approves the bill, it is then returned along with any amendments to the House with a message stating the action taken by the Senate. On its return to the House, the bill and any amendments are read to the members. If there are no objections, the bill is then ready to be enrolled and presented to the president for signature.[72] If a bill originates in the Senate, it follows a similar procedure. It is sent for consideration to the House of Representatives, where it is referred to the appropriate House committee for consideration.[73]

When the bill has been agreed to in identical form by both houses, a copy of the private bill is enrolled for presentation to the president. Under the U.S. Constitution, every bill passed by the House of Representatives and the Senate must, before it becomes law, be presented to the president.[74] Once a bill has been delivered to the White House, it commences the 10-day constitutional period for presidential action.[75] If the president approves a bill, he or she will sign it. Also, a bill can become law without the president's signature if he or she does not return a bill with objections within 10 days after it has been presented.[76] However, if Congress by adjourning prevents its return, the bill does not become law.[77] Notice of the president having signed the bill is sent to the body in which the bill was initiated and that body informs the other. It is also published in the *Congressional Record*. The bill becomes law on the date of approval by the president or passage over the president's veto, unless the bill expressly provides for a different effective date.[78]

Once the president approves a bill or permits it to become law without signing it, the original enrolled bill is sent by the White House to the archivist of the United States for publication. It is then assigned a private bill number.[79]

How to Research Private Bills

Prior to the reorganization of the Immigration and Naturalization Service in 2003, the Office of Immigration Statistics within that agency tracked the number of private bills introduced and enacted, and published that information in its annual *Yearbook of Immigration Statistics*. That office no longer tracks or publishes these statistics. According to the U.S. Citizenship and Immigration Services Public Affairs Office, U.S. Immigration and Customs Enforcement (ICE) has been tasked with creating a

---

[72] C. Johnson, *supra* note 67, at 37–42.

[73] *Id.* at 50.

[74] U.S. Const., art. I, §7.

[75] C. Johnson, *supra* note 67, at 51.

[76] U.S. Const., art. I, §7.

[77] C. Johnson, *supra* note 67, at 52.

[78] *Id.*

[79] *Id.*

report on all private bills introduced and enacted.[80] ICE does maintain information on the number of private bills introduced and passed and will provide that information upon request. However, there is no formal reporting mechanism in place to share the information with other agencies.[81]

Unfortunately, because private bills apply to individuals or a family, they are rarely publicized unless there is a scandal connected to the case. It may be difficult to research and identify the number of private bills passed in a year and their content. In order to do so, practitioners may want to look at the following:

Private laws are published in the *Statutes at Large*, the official compilation of public and private acts passed during each congressional session, arranged chronologically. It is prepared and published by the Office of the Federal Register, National Archives and Records Administration.[82] Public and private laws are published in different sections of each volume.

Another helpful resource is the Congressional Information Service's *Serial Set Index*. Each volume of this multi-volume set has a list of private relief and related actions. The index is arranged alphabetically by the names of individuals who were the subject of the private bills. Although the text of private bills is not included in the set, it does provide information on congressional reports and documents relating to the private bill.

Another resource for finding private bills is through the U.S. Government Printing Office's website for legislative matters.[83] This site provides full-text browsing for all bills from the 104th Congress (1995–96) to the present.

Perhaps the best place to find information on private bills is Thomas, a research website maintained by the Library of Congress.[84] It provides free online federal legislative information. Thomas has a feature that permits you to browse for private laws beginning with the 96th Congress (1979–80). The text of the bills, however, is only available from the 101st Congress (1989–90) onward. In addition to searching on Thomas, information on which private immigration bills were introduced and passed is available in the annual reports of the judiciary committees of both the House and Senate. Copies of the House reports are available by visiting the House Committee on the Judiciary website.[85] For copies of the annual Senate reports,

---

[80] Conversation with Christopher Bentley, USCIS Public Affairs Office, Apr. 20, 2007, on file with author.

[81] Conversation with Hal Griffin, Special Assistant to the Director of the Office of Congressional Relations, ICE, Aug. 13, 2007, on file with author.

[82] For more on *Statutes at Large*, visit the Government Printing Office website at www.gpoaccess.gov/statutes/index.html.

[83] www.gpoaccess.gov/legislative.html.

[84] www.thomas.gov.

[85] www.judiciary.house.gov (Legislative & Oversight link, then Legislative Reports link). It does not appear that a .pdf for each report is easily available. Instead you will have to click on the link for the reports of the session of Congress you wish to search. The next screen will allow you to enter a search query. Enter "private bill". A list of the private bills considered by the House during that session should appear.

inquiries should be made directly to the Senate Judiciary Committee, 224 Dirksen Building, Washington, D.C. 20510. Telephone inquiries can be made by calling (202) 224-9516.

CHAPTER 2

CONGRESSIONAL RULES GOVERNING PRIVATE BILLS

Two sets of rules govern procedures relating to private bills in the immigration context, those of the House of Representatives and those of the Senate.[1] The judiciary committees of the House and the Senate have jurisdiction over private immigration bills. However, the subcommittees on immigration within the judiciary committees actually perform all of the legislative work on private bills. Rules of procedure for each chamber of Congress are, therefore, adopted by the subcommittees on immigration and then adopted by the judiciary committees for each new Congress. There are different procedures for the passage of laws in the House and the Senate. Because of the size of the House of Representatives (435 members), more comprehensive rules are necessary to govern the legislative process. The Senate, with 100 members, has fewer rules governing legislative scheduling. These differences are reflected in the rules governing processing of private bills in each chamber. The rules of procedure in the House are more detailed than those of the Senate.

As a practical matter, private bills are usually initiated when someone contacts his or her representative or senator requesting that he or she sponsor a private bill to remedy the case in question. The person seeking the private bill, and his or her attorney (if one is retained), then begin the process of gathering the relevant information required under the House or Senate rules.

Evolution of House and Senate Rules

From 1954 through 1988, significant changes relating to both House and Senate rules and procedures governing the private bill process occurred. During the 83rd Congress (1953–54), both the House and the Senate established rules and procedures governing private bills. During the 91st Congress, the House Subcommittee on Immigration tightened its rules and established expedited procedures to consider private bills. During the 96th and 97th Congresses (1979–82), both the House and the Senate outlined their revised procedures for private bills. In 1987, Senate Immigration Subcommittee Chairman Edward Kennedy (D-MA) and Ranking Member Alan Simpson (R-WY) distributed a "Dear Colleague" letter reinforcing the revised rules, reminding the members of the extraordinary nature of a private bill and that introduction of one does not act to stay deportation.[2]

---

[1] U.S. House of Representatives Committee on the Judiciary, Subcommittee on Immigration, Citizenship, Refugees, Border Security and International Law, Rules of Procedure and Statement of Policy for Private Immigration Bills, 110th Cong. (2007); U.S. Senate Committee on the Judiciary, Subcommittee on Immigration, Border Security, and Citizenship, Rules of Procedure for Introducing a Private Relief Bill (Immigration), 108th Cong. (2005).

[2] B. Maguire, *Immigration—Public Legislation and Private Bills* (1997), at 25, 26, and 33.

From 1947 until 1954, when the House issued its rules on private bills, it was the practice of the House committee to request a report from legacy Immigration and Naturalization Service (INS) when a sponsor wrote to the Subcommittee on Immigration requesting action on a private bill. The request for a report resulted in an automatic stay of deportation. In the Senate, simple introduction of a private bill acted to stay deportation. During the 83rd Congress, after being faced with an unprecedented number of private bills (2,001 introduced in the first session), the House Immigration Subcommittee adopted rules of procedures for private bills.[3] Prior to the adoption of these rules, both the House and the Senate had indicated a concern regarding delays in receiving reports from legacy INS and in deporting noncitizens whose private bills had been denied.[4]

One of the most significant changes in the private bill process made by the House rules related to stays of deportation. Under the rules, the subcommittee would not request a report from the attorney general, thus staying deportation, for those noncitizens who entered the United States as stowaways, deserting seamen, or otherwise illegally without inspection unless the subcommittee found that the purpose of the bill was to stop separation of families. This became Rule 4 of the subcommittee rules.[5] Another important change in the House rules required exhaustion of administrative remedies prior to requesting a private bill. Other changes included the fact that no bill would be deferred for hearing due to nonappearance of the sponsor and that the subcommittee would only reconsider previously tabled bills if the facts had substantially changed.[6]

The 1954 House rules remained virtually the same until the 100th Congress (1987–88), when changes were made regarding the hardship criteria for consideration of the bill and guidelines on precedents to which the committee would adhere.[7]

Although the Senate did not adopt formal rules governing private bills for many years, its process generally followed that of the House committee. In a policy statement issued during the 83rd Congress (1953–54), the Senate noted various precedents on private bills and cases that would be subject to unfavorable treatment, including those involving serious criminal acts and exchange visitors. It indicated that special needs of U.S. citizens or permanent resident relatives in the United States or abroad could result in favorable action on private bills.[8] The Senate policy also recognized a need for certain skilled workers in the United States, specifically mentioning "doctors and scientific men and women." Waivers for petty theft and for mental and physical defects involving relatives of citizens were also cited for

---

[3] *Id.* at 26.

[4] *Id.* at 27.

[5] *Id.*

[6] *Id.*

[7] *Id.* at 28. Precedents refer to private bills that have been passed by Congress.

[8] *Id.*

favorable consideration. As with the House, the Senate indicated that bills relating to exchange visitors and cases in which administrative remedies had not been exhausted would not receive favorable consideration.[9] The Senate formally adopted guidelines on private bills in 1979 and included a similar requirement of proof of hardship prior to requesting a report resulting in a stay of deportation.[10]

Shortly after the introduction of the highest-ever number of private immigration bills (7,293 during the 90th Congress (1967–68)), the House Subcommittee on Immigration changed the rules and expanded the number of prohibited categories of private bills to include visitors, exchange visitors, and students.[11] During the 92nd Congress (1971–72), the House Subcommittee on Immigration revised the rules. Under revised Rule 4, all nonimmigrants had to establish hardship in order to be eligible for a private bill. At the time, Subcommittee Chairman Peter Rodino (D-NJ) noted that the purpose of private bills was to alleviate hardships that the general laws could not remedy.[12]

The Senate adopted for the first time formal guidelines governing the processing of private bills in the 96th Congress (1979–80). The new guidelines eliminated the practice of staying deportation as a result of the introduction of a private bill and request for a report from a government agency. Instead, the sponsor had to establish hardship in order for the subcommittee to make a request for a report and stay deportation. In addition, the guidelines specifically prohibited the consideration of private bills for medical doctors who had not passed the necessary examination.[13] Policies regarding the types of cases considered and the applicable precedents paralleled those of the House.

With the formalization of rules, policies, and procedures over the years by both chambers of Congress, the number of private bills has significantly declined.

House Rules

The processing of private legislation in the House is governed by specific rules and precedents.[14] The Committee on the Judiciary and its Subcommittee on Immigration, Citizenship, Refugees, Border Security and International Law have jurisdiction over private bills in the immigration context. Once a private bill has been

---

[9] *Id.*

[10] *Id.* at 29.

[11] House Committee on the Judiciary, Rules of Procedure (91st Congress, 1969–70).

[12] 117 Cong. Rec. 101143 (Apr. 7, 1971), *cited in* B. Maguire, *supra* note 2, at 30.

[13] B. Maguire, *supra* note 2, at 31, 32.

[14] *Jefferson's Manual,* 109th Cong., H.R. Doc. 108-241; Rules of the House of Representatives, 110th Cong., 1st Sess. (May 24, 2007); House subcommittee rules, *supra* note 1; *Deschler's Precedents of the United States House of Representatives,* 94th Cong., 2nd Sess., H.R. Doc. 94-661; *Hinds' Precedents of the House of Representatives of the United States* (1907); *Cannon's Precedents of the House of Representatives of the United States* (1935).

acted upon by the committee and the subcommittee, the bill then goes to the floor of the House of Representatives for debate.

Significant changes were made in 1932 and 1935 regarding the timeframe for consideration of bills and screening for action. As a result of these changes, all private bills must be referred to a special private bill calendar after action is taken by the Committee on the Judiciary or its Subcommittee on Immigration.[15] The House rules on private bills are different than rules governing other legislation because the time limits for consideration of private bills are shorter, and there are special screening mechanisms in place prior to consideration of such bills on the House floor. All private bills in the House of Representatives are placed on the Private Calendar, which is called on the first and third Tuesdays of each month.[16] If two or more members object to the consideration of the bill, it is recommitted to the committee that brought it.[17] There are six official objectors—three on the majority side and three on the minority side—who study each private bill on the Private Calendar.[18] Rather then looking at the merits of the proposed bill, the objectors will examine the case to determine whether there are any ethical issues of concern, such as a conflict of interest.

Note: The House subcommittee often receives requests to reconsider private bills that were tabled in a prior Congress. As per its stated policy, it is reluctant to reconsider a private bill unless new evidence or information not available at the time of the initial request for the bill is presented. However, the rule does not reflect the practice. Private bills are often reintroduced in new Congresses with the hope that the sponsor(s) will be able to gather the necessary number of votes for their passage.

House Policy on Private Bills

The Subcommittee on Immigration, Citizenship, Refugees, Border Security and International Law will only review cases of such an extraordinary nature that an exception to the law is needed. It will generally only act favorably on those private bills that meet certain precedents. Precedents are similar to case law in their effect. Just as practitioners cite to certain authority in their arguments or briefs to support a position, House members will cite to precedents to support their point or to defend against one. Precedents, however, do not necessarily carry equal weight.[19] More recent precedents may carry greater weight than earlier ones, and a precedent that is part of an evolved pattern will carry more weight than an isolated one.[20]

---

[15] B. Maguire, *supra* note 2, at 12.

[16] Rules of the House of Representatives, Rule XV, cl. 5, 110th Cong., 1st Sess. (May 24, 2007).

[17] *Id.*

[18] C. Johnson, How Laws Are Made, H.R. Doc. No. 108-93, at 20 (2003).

[19] T. Carr, Parliamentary Reference Sources: House of Representatives, CRS Report to Congress RL30787, at 4 (Mar. 16, 2004), *available at www.rules.house.gov/archives/rl30787.pdf.*

[20] *Id.*

Note: Practitioners should remember, though, that just because the facts of a particular case do not fit within a prior precedent does not necessarily mean that the bill will fail. The question is whether the facts in the case are particularly compelling and generally satisfy the standard of hardship.

House Rules and Procedures

A request for consideration of a private immigration bill begins with a letter to the chairperson of the Subcommittee on Immigration, Citizenship, Refugees, Border Security and International Law from the sponsor of the bill. The letter should outline all of the relevant facts in the case and should include all supporting documents. Documents will not be accepted if filed by anyone other than the sponsor of the bill.

The following documentation must be submitted in triplicate in support of a private bill request:

- The date and place of birth of each beneficiary.
- The addresses and telephone numbers of each beneficiary presently in the United States.
- The dates of all entries (legal and illegal) and departures from the United States, along with the type of visa used for admission; the name of the consulate where each beneficiary obtained a visa for entry; the name of the consulate where the beneficiary will be seeking a visa if one is issued.
- The status of all petitions and immigration proceedings, including immigrant and nonimmigrant petitions that have been filed by the beneficiary or on his or her behalf.
- Copies of all immigration-related letters between agencies in the United States and the beneficiary.
- Copies of all administrative and judicial decisions involving the beneficiary's case.
- The names, addresses, and telephone numbers of interested parties in the United States.
- The names, addresses, dates and places of birth, and immigration or citizenship status of all close relatives.
- The occupations, recent employment records, and salaries of all beneficiaries.
- A signed statement by each beneficiary, or the beneficiary's guardian, that he or she wants the relief requested in the private bill.
- Information on how failure to obtain the relief sought in the private bill will result in extreme hardship to the beneficiary or each beneficiary's U.S. citizen spouse, parent, or child.
- A signed statement by the sponsor of the bill confirming that he or she has personally met the beneficiary or with members of the beneficiary's family.

A beneficiary of a private bill must apply for the relief requested not later than two years from the date of enactment of the private law. A private bill may not be considered unless and until all administrative and judicial remedies are exhausted.

Note: A potential beneficiary need not have a final order of removal in order to request private relief. However, practitioners should carefully advise their clients of the risk of exposure to removal proceedings once they make themselves known to the government. Of course, requesting a report from the Department of Homeland Security (DHS) or Department of State (DOS) on a beneficiary of a private bill will stay removal. But if the private bill is not passed, it is likely that the person will be placed in removal proceedings and ultimately removed if there is no alternative relief available.

Only the sponsor of a private bill may testify before the subcommittee on behalf of the private bill. Generally, there are no formal hearings on private bills in the House. If the sponsor fails to appear, action on the bill will not be deferred.

Stays of Removal and Reports

The subcommittee will not intervene in removal proceedings and will not request stays of removal from DHS's Immigration and Customs Enforcement (ICE), with one exception. Where the subcommittee requests a report from DHS on a beneficiary of a private bill, the subcommittee will request that DHS stay the removal of the beneficiary until final action is taken on the private bill. According to the House rules, only those cases designed to prevent extreme hardship to the beneficiary or the U.S. citizen spouse, parent, or child will merit a request for a report. The subcommittee can only request the report after a voice vote of its members indicating their support. Procedures for requesting a report are simpler in the Senate. The subcommittee chair can request a report on a private bill simply by sending a written request to ICE without a vote from the members.

At the beginning of a new Congress, the House Judiciary Committee sends a memorandum to ICE asking that it agree to stay the removal of beneficiaries of private bills when reports are requested.[21] Historically under legacy INS and currently under ICE, this general request to honor stays of removal pending final action on a private bill has been honored. ICE grants an automatic stay of removal, valid for the entire two-year period that Congress is in session until March 15 after the installation of the next Congress.[22] For the last several Congresses, there has been no correspondence between Congress and ICE formally requesting the stays. However, ICE continues the practice of legacy INS in granting stays in those cases in which reports have been requested.[23]

---

[21] Conversation with Susan M. Cullen, ICE Acting Director of Policy, May 31, 2007, on file with author.
[22] *Id.*
[23] *Id.*

CHAPTER 2 • CONGRESSIONAL RULES GOVERNING PRIVATE BILLS 25

The subcommittee can request reports on private bills from any federal agency or department and it will wait until receiving such reports prior to taking any final action on the bill.

Special Requirements and Considerations in Certain Cases

There are additional requirements for private bill requests in cases relating to adoption, private bills for doctors or nurses, private bills requesting a waiver of grounds of exclusion or deportation relating to criminal activity, and for private bills for persons receiving medical treatment. Practitioners should be aware that the subcommittee may also be inclined to look without favor on certain cases. For example, it will generally be unsympathetic to private bill requests on behalf of persons with deferred status or who have been paroled indefinitely into the United States.[24] However, that does not mean that private bills cannot be obtained in such cases. Rather, practitioners will have to prepare those cases aggressively and search carefully for the few precedents when the House has ruled favorably under similar circumstances.

Adoption Cases

Under current law, foreign-born children are permitted to immigrate to the United States if the adoption takes place before the child turns 16 years old and the child is an "orphan" as defined under INA §101(b)(1)(F) [8 USC §101(b)(1)(F)] or the child has resided with the adoptive parents for two years. There are many favorable precedents in which private bills have been enacted when the child is young and there has been a longstanding parent-child relationship.

In adoption cases, the following additional information must be provided:

- The home study of the prospective parents;
- Evidence of child support; and
- A statement detailing the ages and occupations of the natural parents, brothers and sisters.

Doctors and Nurses

Under the Immigration and Nationality Act,[25] doctors and nurses who have passed certain exams are permitted to immigrate to the United States through employment-based visas. Many doctors have been the beneficiary of private bills over the past years. Over the years, many entered the United States as nonimmigrants with the intention of remaining permanently. In response to this, Congress enacted laws requiring that doctors return to their home country before immigrating, with certain exceptions.[26] The subcommittee has indicated its concern that doctors who are beneficiaries of private bills often look for more lucrative employment when granted permanent residence,

---

[24] House subcommittee rules, *supra* note 1, at 5.

[25] Pub. L. No. 82-414, 66 Stat. 163 (1952).

[26] INA §212(a)(5)(B); 8 USC §1182(a)(5)(B).

thereby leaving underserved areas without any medical assistance. As a result of this concern, Congress does not view private bills for doctors sympathetically.[27]

When a private bill is filed on behalf of a doctor or a nurse, the following information must accompany the request:

- Confirmation of passage of the required licensing examination in the case of doctors, and of the Commission on Graduates of Foreign Nursing Schools exam for nurses.
- Evidence of employment by the doctor or nurse in a health manpower shortage area, or a recommendation by a U.S. government agency establishing that the doctor's or nurse's services are needed.
- Evidence of substantial community ties over a long period of time.
- Documentation as to a potential employer's efforts to recruit U.S. citizens for the position. This information should include the salary levels of other doctors or nurses on staff plus an explanation on the recruitment techniques used for employment of the beneficiary.

Drug and Criminal Activity

Where a private bill is being requested to waive grounds of exclusion or deportation relating to criminal activity, the following documents should be provided:

- Any and all records relating to the offense(s), including state and local police records; and
- An affidavit from the beneficiary explaining his or her criminal record in full.

Practitioners also should present information to the subcommittee regarding the beneficiary's conduct after the criminal conviction. Affidavits, letters of reference, bank records, and employment records are particularly helpful. The purpose of such information is to help the subcommittee determine whether a private bill would be in the best interests of the community.[28]

Medical Cases

The subcommittee is generally reluctant to schedule private bills on behalf of persons who came to the United States to seek medical treatment.[29] The subcommittee takes the position that those persons who seek medical care in the United States should return home after they receive such care. An exception to this position is when medical care is not available in a person's home country. In such a case, the subcommittee asks that an advisory opinion be requested from such organizations as the World Health Organization and the Pan American Health Organization as to the availability of adequate medical treatment in the beneficiary's home country.

---

[27] House subcommittee rules, *supra* note 1, at 4.
[28] *Id.*
[29] *Id.* at 5.

Waiver of Grounds of Inadmissibility

According to the House subcommittee rules, all private bills seeking a waiver of the grounds of inadmissibility relating to mental or physical illnesses require that a bond be posted. In order to adequately review the case, the subcommittee requests that all medical records as well as information from government agencies concerning possible public charge aspects of the case be presented.[30]

The subcommittee is reluctant to act favorably on cases involving visa fraud and will look closely to precedents to determine whether favorable consideration is warranted.[31]

Naturalization Cases

Any private bill seeking to fast-track naturalization should be accompanied by evidence to indicate that such action would be in the national interest as opposed to personal interest.[32] The subcommittee does not believe that U.S. citizenship should be granted to athletes seeking to compete in national, international, or Olympic games.

The subcommittee has noted that there have been few instances of private legislation on behalf of U.S. citizens who have renounced their citizenship.[33] There are few favorable precedents waiving any naturalization requirements or granting posthumous or honorary citizenship. The House is not inclined to favorably view such bills.[34]

Only a handful of people have received a grant of honorary citizenship since the creation of the republic. They are Mother Theresa, famous for her charitable work with the poor;[35] Raoul Wallenberg, the Swedish diplomat who saved thousands of Jews during World War II; Winston Churchill, Prime Minister of the United Kingdom during World War II; and William Penn, founder of the state of Pennsylvania, and his wife, Hannah Callowhill Penn.[36] Honorary citizenship is a symbolic gesture and does not grant any additional legal rights in the United States or in international law. Nor does it give the grantee any voting privileges.[37] Honorary citizenship is usually granted through a joint resolution of Congress enacted as a public law since it is a public honor given by the U.S. government to a deserving individual and not a private remedy waiving the application of public laws.[38]

---

[30] *Id.*

[31] *Id.* at 6.

[32] For examples of private bills involving naturalization, see chapter 4.

[33] House subcommittee rules, *supra* note 1, at 6.

[34] *Id.*

[35] Pub. L. No. 104-218, 110 Stat. 3021 (Oct. 1, 1996).

[36] H.R. 104-796 (Sept. 17, 1996).

[37] 146 Cong. Rec. H10452 (Sept. 17, 1996).

[38] For further information on honorary citizenship, see B. Torreon, Recipients of Honorary U.S. Citizenship, CRS Report for Congress RS21471 (Nov. 2, 2004).

Senate Rules

There are fewer rules to guide the Senate in the consideration of private bills than there are in the House. Unlike the House, which approves its rules on private bills at the beginning of each new Congress, the Senate has not done so since the 108th Congress.[39] As with the House of Representatives, the Senate Committee on the Judiciary and its Subcommittee on Immigration, Refugees and Border Security have jurisdiction over immigration matters. When a private bill is considered in the Senate, after the committee has taken action, it is placed on the Calendar of Business along with public bills under General Orders. The bill is then taken up by unanimous consent on the Senate floor at a time convenient to the majority leader, without the designation of days or time limits.[40] Until 1969, Senate staff often handled the introduction of private bills.[41] However, after the controversy relating to the introduction of private bills on behalf of Chinese crewmen, the majority leader of the Senate, Michael J. Mansfield (D-MT), and the minority leader, Hugh D. Scott (R-PA), wrote to the secretary of the Senate and demanded that private bills be delivered to the Senate desk, in person, and be signed by the senator introducing the bill.[42]

Senate Rules and Procedures

The Senate rules governing the introduction and processing of private bills are much less detailed than those of the House. Prior to the introduction of a private bill, the subcommittee asks senators who desire to introduce a private bill to send a letter, copying the ranking member, explaining their request and attaching a copy of the private bill. This practice is not included in the formal rules, but it is one with which most of the senators are familiar and comply.[43] The subcommittee takes no position on the private bill and moves it forward as a courtesy to the sponsoring senator.

Under the subcommittee rules, supporting information for a private bill is limited to three or four typewritten pages. This must include a detailed statement by the sponsor establishing the equities in the case and explaining why an adequate judicial or administrative remedy is not available; the alien registration number of the potential beneficiary; the Senate bill number and copy of the bill; and a request that the chair of the immigration subcommittee obtain a departmental report on the beneficiary, usually from ICE. In addition to this information, the sponsor is permitted to submit background material, including character references, employment records, school records, etc.

---

[39] Senate subcommittee rules, *supra* note 1.

[40] C. Johnson, *supra* note 18, at 39, 40.

[41] B. Maguire, *supra* note 2, at 20.

[42] Letter from Sen. Mike Mansfield, Majority Leader, and Sen. Hugh Scott, Minority Leader, to Secretary of the Senate Francis R. Valeo, dated October 1, 1969, 115 Cong. Rec. 30528 (Oct. 20, 1969), cited in B. Maguire, *supra* note 2, at 229.

[43] Conversation with Senate aides, Aug. 9, 2007, on file with author.

CHAPTER 2 • CONGRESSIONAL RULES GOVERNING PRIVATE BILLS   29

Note: When a private bill is recommended for favorable action, the supporting information is used for the Senate report and must be typewritten to be cut and pasted for printing. Originals that the beneficiary would like to retain should not be submitted. Copies are sufficient for the subcommittee.

As with House procedures, the introduction of a private bill in the Senate does not act to stay deportation unless the subcommittee requests a report from a relevant government agency, usually ICE or DOS. A sponsor's request for a report is made in writing by the subcommittee chair and sent to the relevant government agency. The request is made as a matter of course. This procedure is different than that of the House, where the members of the subcommittee must approve a request for a report by vote.

The request for a report should contain the following information:

- In the case of a beneficiary who is present in the United States—
  - Date and place of person's last entry into the United States;
  - His or her immigration status at the time;
  - The date and place of birth of the beneficiary;
  - The beneficiary's address in the United State;
  - The location of the U.S. consulate where he or she obtained a visa, if that is the case.
- In the case of a beneficiary who is physically outside the United States—
  - Date and place of birth;
  - The address of the beneficiary;
  - The location of the U.S. consulate before which his or her application for a visa is pending;
  - The address of the person in the United States primarily interested in the beneficiary's admission.
- In the case of a beneficiary who is seeking expedited naturalization—
  - The date that the person was admitted to the United States for permanent residence;
  - The beneficiary's date and place of birth and his or her address in the United States.

At times, subcommittee staff will have contact with the attorney representing the potential beneficiary. However, they correspond to a much greater extent with the staff of the sponsoring senator.

Note: When working on a private bill, it is important that the sponsoring senator and his or her staff are actively involved and pushing for its passage. The sponsoring senators need to be aggressive in order to obtain the necessary votes for passage of the bill. It is important for the attorney representing the potential beneficiary to maintain regular contact with the Senate staff to ensure they have the necessary information and to remind them of the importance of the bill.

Favorable consideration of a private bill will not occur until the relevant government agency has submitted a report as requested. After a report is received, the private bill may be scheduled for consideration by the subcommittee.

CHAPTER 3

ROLE OF THE EXECUTIVE BRANCH IN PRIVATE BILLS

The executive branch of the government plays a minimal role in the processing of private bills. It is involved in the following: (1) stays of removal and preparation of reports upon request by Congress; (2) recommendations on situations in which public laws may be an alternative; and (3) presidential veto. Prior to 1953, agencies took positions on private bills, either supporting or opposing them. However, since that time, the executive branch has rarely taken a position or shown interest in the final dispositions of requests for private bill relief.[1]

The Department of Homeland Security (DHS), per an agreement with the U.S. Congress, agrees to stay the removal of potential beneficiaries of private bills when Congress requests a report on the case. Historically, legacy Immigration and Naturalization Service (INS) agreed to stays of deportation under the same circumstances. Given the small number of private bills introduced in recent years, there is little tension between DHS and Congress regarding the granting of stays. Both DHS and the Department of State (DOS) provide reports upon request to Congress regarding the beneficiaries of private bills.

Prior to 1953, in its reports to the Senate or House judiciary committees, legacy INS generally pointed to three reasons for opposing a private bill: (1) the availability of administrative relief; (2) creation of an unfavorable precedent; and, (3) preference for public legislation.[2] Legacy INS often pointed to the fact that thousands of others similarly situated who did not have any relief to remedy their immigration status were not requesting private bills.[3] Regarding unfavorable precedents, which mostly involved waiver cases, legacy INS expressed dismay at providing status to a person who would not qualify under the law.[4] Initiatives by the executive branch resulted in major legislation in 1940, 1948, 1952, and 1965, alleviating the need for thousands of private bills.[5]

Ultimately, the executive branch has the last word on any legislation through the use of presidential veto, especially given that few bills are then overridden by Congress.[6] There have been 28 presidential vetoes of private bills based on precedent,

---

[1] B. Maguire, *Immigration—Public Legislation and Private Bills* (1997), at 35, 36.
[2] *Id.* at 41.
[3] *Id.* at 36.
[4] *Id.* at 41.
[5] *Id.* at 43.
[6] *Id.* at 48.

the character of the beneficiary, and the availability of an administrative remedy.[7] Bills vetoed based on problems relating to precedent included persons seeking to regain U.S. citizenship after relinquishing it for business reasons,[8] a deserting crewman who had worked in the Polish underground fighting the Nazis,[9] a case involving a native-born U.S. citizen who had lost her citizenship after naturalizing in Italy to marry her Italian husband,[10] and a Spanish national who possessed exceptional skills in designing furs.[11] In deciding to use veto power to reject the bill, the president often cited to the presence of hundreds of other similarly situated individuals and noted concerns that some of the cases did not present compelling reasons to provide an exception to the law.[12]

The president also vetoed bills based on the character of the beneficiaries, including many cases involving German nationals. Examples included two young natives of Germany who were fugitives and one German who had been sentenced to death for avoiding the draft under Hitler. In vetoing these bills, President Franklin Roosevelt noted that they had criminal or civil proceedings pending against them.[13] Another case involved a German who had been in the United States for 13 years, did not seek to regularize his status, but instead sought to be repatriated to Germany during the war. In vetoing the bill, President Dwight Eisenhower noted that the beneficiary had clearly shown his allegiance to Germany rather than to the United States through his conduct.[14]

The president also has vetoed bills when administrative actions could have remedied the problem. Examples of such cases include a deserting crewman and spouse of a lawful permanent resident who was eligible for adjustment under a new

---

[7] *Id.* at 48. President Roosevelt vetoed 11 bills; President Harry Truman vetoed nine; President John Kennedy vetoed one; and President Ronald Reagan vetoed one. For a list of presidential vetoes of private immigration bills, see *id.* at appx. D1.

[8] 76th Congress, H.R. 7179, Veto Message October 10, 1940 (H.R. Doc. No. 975, 3rd Sess.), cited in B. Maguire, *supra* note 1, at 49.

[9] 80th Congress, H.R. 3061, Veto Message April 12, 1948 (H.R. Doc. No. 607, 2nd Sess.), cited in B. Maguire, *supra* note 1, at 49.

[10] 81st Congress, H.R. 5016, Veto Message August 14, 1950 (H.R. Doc. No. 683, 2nd Sess.), cited in B. Maguire, *supra* note 1, at 49.

[11] 81st Congress, S. 305, Veto Message August 29, 1950 (S. Doc. No. 210, 2nd Sess.), cited in B. Maguire, *supra* note 1, at 49.

[12] B. Maguire, *supra* note 1, at 49, 50.

[13] 76th Cong., S. 1384, Veto Message May 29, 1940 (S. Doc. No. 201, 3rd Sess.), cited in B. Maguire, *supra* note 1, at 50.

[14] 83rd Cong., S. 153, Veto Message March 17, 1954 (S. Doc. No. 106, 2nd Sess.), cited in B. Maguire, *supra* note 1, at 49.

law,[15] and a native of Germany and spouse of a U.S. citizen who also could adjust under new legislation.[16]

Department of Homeland Security

Introduction

The three immigration-related agencies within DHS are U.S. Citizenship and Immigration Services (USCIS), U.S. Immigration and Customs Enforcement (ICE), and U.S. Customs and Border Protection (CBP). USCIS is responsible for administering benefits and carrying out services relating to the immigration of noncitizens to the United States through family-based petitions, employment-based petitions, and as refugees and asylees. ICE is charged with immigration-related investigations and enforcement of U.S. immigration laws. CBP is responsible for managing, controlling, and securing the borders of the United States. Although USCIS is somewhat involved, ICE is the primary agency involved in private bill issues.

Other than providing a record file when requested, USCIS has no role in the private bill process until a bill is passed and status is granted. Once that happens, USCIS takes the appropriate steps to provide documentation to the beneficiary of the bill. There is no headquarters unit in USCIS that monitors private bills.[17]

Work Authorization

USCIS is responsible for adjudicating requests for employment authorization under 8 CFR §274a.12. However, that provision does not contain a category that provides employment authorization to the potential beneficiary of a private bill solely because of the introduction of a private bill. The beneficiary of a private bill would have to qualify under 8 CFR §274a.12(c)(14). If USCIS does grant deferred action as a result of the introduction of a private bill and the applicant is provided a notice to that effect, he or she should submit a copy of that notice with the application for employment authorization. When the potential beneficiary has not received a notice of deferred action but a report has been requested from ICE and removal stayed, USCIS will have to review the noncitizen's file to confirm that a stay has been granted prior to issuing an employment authorization document.[18]

> *Note*: When a practitioner has filed an application for employment authorization, Form I-765, on behalf of a client whose removal has been stayed and USCIS delays in adjudicating the application, the practitioner should

---

[15] 76th Cong., H.R. 5640, Veto Message August 26, 1940 (H.R. Doc. No. 935, 3rd Sess.), cited in B. Maguire, *supra* note 1, at 50.

[16] 76th Cong., H.R. 5641, Veto Message August 26, 1940 (H.R. Doc. No. 936, 3rd Sess.), *cited in* cited in B. Maguire, *supra* note 1, at 51.

[17] Electronic correspondence with David G. Gulick, Domestic Operations Chief of Staff, USCIS, dated Aug. 1, 2007, on file with author.

[18] Electronic correspondence with David G. Gulick, Domestic Operations Chief of Staff, USCIS, dated Sept. 10, 2007, on file with author.

contact the member of Congress who is sponsoring the private bill and ask that they make a formal inquiry to USCIS on the status of the adjudication.

Role of ICE

ICE has an Office of Congressional Relations (OCR) that acts as a liaison between Congress and the agencies. Generally, OCR is charged with maintaining a professional liaison with members of Congress and their staff, providing timely information in response to requests from Congress, and with gathering information and preparing reports on private bills when a member or members request such a report. Once a report is requested, a designated person in charge of private bill reports at the ICE Office of Investigations at headquarters is assigned to coordinate the process. He or she will contact the relevant district office and ask them to carry out an investigation. This involves a review of the A-file and interviewing several people, including the potential beneficiary, family members, members in the community, etc. A criminal background check is also done. The investigation for the report takes between 45 and 60 days to complete. ICE then produces a one– to three-page report that includes the following information:

- Information on the introduction and content of the private bill;
- Biographic information of the beneficiary;
- Entry and immigration status issues and problems;
- Information on the beneficiary's family;
- Business and assets;
- Criminal background check.

The report is then forwarded to Congress for its review and consideration.[19]

There are no public guidelines or procedures used by ICE in carrying out its work relating to private bills. There is one internal written document issued in 2004 by the Office of the Principle Legal Advisor that sets forth ICE's understanding of current procedures in responding to congressional requests for reports on potential beneficiaries. This memorandum mentioned that another memorandum would be forthcoming to provide additional guidance, but such a memorandum has not been issued.[20]

Legacy INS Operations Instructions and Private Bills

Under legacy INS, procedures governing private bill issues were governed by Operations Instructions. The Operations Instructions have been in the process of being phased out during the last several years. It is not presently clear what DHS norms, procedures, or internal memoranda govern work relating to private bills in the agencies. However, it does appear that staff members of ICE's OCR continue to follow procedures similar to those laid out in the Operations Instructions. Therefore, it is worth describing those procedures.

---

[19] Correspondence with ICE Office of Congressional Affairs, dated Aug. 13, 2007, on file with author.

[20] Correspondence with ICE Office of Congressional Affairs, dated Aug. 13, 2007, on file with author.

Under the instructions, immigration personnel are not permitted to recommend or draft a private bill.[21] Current procedures preclude DHS from taking a position—either to recommend or oppose—private legislation.[22]

As noted in chapter 2, the House or Senate Judiciary Committee can request that any relevant government agency provide it with a report on a private bill. When so requested, ICE staff will notify the appropriate district offices and ask that information relating to the beneficiary of the private bill within their possession be forwarded to headquarters.[23] A stay of removal is generally granted in those cases in which Congress requests a report on a private bill.[24] Removal will be stayed until March 15 of the year the next new Congress is installed.[25] When a private bill is reintroduced in the following Congress and a report is requested, a stay of removal also will be granted pending the final outcome of the case.[26] Removal will not be stayed when a report is not requested by Congress.[27]

Effect of Introduction of Private Bill on Immigration Status

The Operations Instructions provide that the introduction of a private bill that seeks to adjust the status of a nonimmigrant to that of a lawful permanent resident is regarded as prima facie evidence of termination of the lawful nonimmigrant status, where it has not been previously terminated.[28] Additionally, 8 CFR §214.1(d) provides that nonimmigrant status will be considered terminated by the introduction of a private bill to confer permanent resident status on a noncitizen. If removal proceedings already have been instituted, they should be carried out until a final decision in the case. If proceedings have not been instituted, but the beneficiary indicates that he or she does not want private legislative relief, removal proceedings will be initiated.[29]

If the beneficiary of a private bill was maintaining A or G nonimmigrant status or was a treaty trader when the private bill was introduced, the beneficiary may be considered to have voluntary departure for the period of time that he or she remains in that status.[30] If removal proceedings have not been instituted, but the beneficiary had terminated his or her lawful nonimmigrant status when the private bill was

---

[21] INS Operations Instruction (OI) 107.1(a).

[22] Conversation with Susan Cullen, ICE Acting Director of Policy, dated May 31, 2007, on file with author.

[23] OI 107.1(c).

[24] *Id.*

[25] Conversation with Susan Cullen, ICE Acting Director of Policy, dated May 31, 2007, on file with author. OI 107.1(f)(2) states that the stay will be granted until February 1 of the next odd-numbered year.

[26] Conversation with Susan Cullen, ICE Acting Director of Policy, dated May 31, 2007, on file with author.

[27] *Id.*; OI 107.1(d).

[28] OI 107.1(e).

[29] *Id.*

[30] *Id.*

introduced, removal proceedings will commence and be carried out upon the expiration of any voluntary departure time.[31]

Where a beneficiary had E, F, I, J, or M nonimmigrant status at the time that the bill was introduced, removal proceedings will not be instituted.[32]

According to the Operations Instructions, removal proceedings will not be instituted in cases involving appealing humanitarian factors.[33]

Implementation of an Enacted Private Bill

When a private bill is enacted, DHS will notify the appropriate district office of its enactment. When a private bill provides that lawful permanent resident status be granted to the beneficiary, the appropriate visa fee will be paid and the field office will prepare a Form I-181 to be placed in the A file. Form I-357 will be provided to the beneficiary.[34]

When a private bill authorizes the grant of immediate relative or preference status to the beneficiary in order to obtain an immigrant visa, the field office will send Form G-388 to the appropriate party, including a notice that a visa petition should be filed, if necessary.[35]

If the private bill directs that pending removal proceedings should be terminated, the field office will notify the beneficiary that proceedings have in fact been terminated as a result of the bill. When a private bill grants some other benefit or waiver, the field office also will notify the beneficiary and offer the appropriate instructions on how to proceed.[36]

Note: ICE cannot institute removal proceedings against a beneficiary of a private law that granted him or her status or permanent residency or that terminated removal proceedings on grounds based solely on facts contained in the judiciary committees' reports on the bill.[37]

Department of State

The majority of reports requested by the Senate or House judiciary committees are generally prepared and provided by the relevant agency within DHS. However, where a beneficiary is outside of the United States, the request for a report will be made to DOS, which has its own guidelines regarding private bills.[38]

When the Senate or House Judiciary Committee requests a report from DOS, all available information regarding the beneficiary should be provided. Any report

---

[31] *Id.*
[32] *Id.*
[33] *Id.*
[34] OI 107.1(h)(2).
[35] *Id.*
[36] *Id.*
[37] *Id.*
[38] 9 *Foreign Affairs Manual* (FAM) Appendix I 500, General Guidelines Regarding Private Bills.

should explain the reasons why a visa was denied or could not be issued, include information on the merits of the case, and contain any other relevant information that may assist the committees in considering the bill.[39]

Note: Similar to DHS practice, consular posts should make no recommendation or observation on the merits of the private bill.[40]

A report prepared by a consular post can be transmitted to DOS for ultimate submission to the committee by fax, e-mail, or cable. The report should include the following information:

- The private bill number;
- Biographical information regarding the beneficiary, including the following:
  - Beneficiary's name;
  - Date and place of birth;
  - Place of residence;
  - Marital status and, if divorced, duration of marriage and previous marriage(s);
  - Children, if any, and their dates and places of birth, and current residence;
  - Background data (schooling, professional or vocational training or experience, military service, standing in the community);
  - Circumstances that led to ineligibility for visa;
  - Previous action taken on visa application, including grounds for refusal;
  - General health conditions of the beneficiary, including the date and results of the medical examination;
  - Family ties in the United States and/or abroad; and,
  - Claimed purpose of entry into the United States and length of intended stay if a nonimmigrant visa was previously issued to the beneficiary.
- Any relationship to a U.S. citizen or lawful permanent resident;
- A complete report relating to any immigrant or nonimmigrant visa application made by the beneficiary;
- Results of local police and other agency name checks;
- Any information regarding hardship of the beneficiary that might result in the denial of the visa;
- Any known grounds of ineligibility applicable to the beneficiary; and,
- Any relief that may be available to the beneficiary that would permit the granting of a visa, either currently or in the future.[41]

---

[39] 9 FAM Appendix I 502.
[40] *Id.*
[41] 9 FAM Appendix I 504.

A beneficiary of a private bill is required to undergo a medical examination. When a beneficiary refuses to comply, the consular officer must so indicate in the report. When the beneficiary does undergo a medical examination, a copy of the medical exam must be included in the report only if it shows a medical ground of ineligibility.[42]

Generally, DOS is given short notice to provide a report on a private bill. Therefore, it quickly contacts the consular post with the request and expects the post to provide it with some response immediately.[43] If a full report cannot be provided in a timely fashion, the post must advise DOS of the reasons for delay and when a full report can be delivered.[44]

Grounds of Ineligibility

When a private bill seeks relief from a ground of ineligibility, the report to the committee should state whether the requested relief would in fact remedy all known grounds for which the beneficiary might be refused a visa. When a consular officer is submitting a report on a bill that seeks to waive a drug or criminal conviction, he or she must submit the following:

- Complete transcripts of the court proceedings;
- Any other record relating to the offense, including police records;
- An affidavit from the beneficiary describing any criminal record; and,
- Any other information available at the post.

When the bill seeks relief from grounds of a drug conviction, the officer must submit a transcript indicating the exact amount of drug possessed at the time of arrest. If this information is not available, either because the beneficiary is not residing abroad or because the courts will not provide that information, the report should so indicate and state whether the documents can be obtained through a direct request to the beneficiary. Certified copies of all documents and their translations must be provided to DOS.[45]

Adoption Cases

When a private bill seeks to provide the beneficiary the status of a child for adoption purposes, the report provided to DOS should include the following information:

- A detailed statement regarding the adoption proceedings;
- The applicable adoption law in the beneficiary's country;
- Whether the adoptive parent(s) and child have met and whether the two-year period of legal custody and residence with adoptive parent(s) has been fulfilled.[46]

---

[42] 9 FAM Appendix I 508.
[43] 9 FAM Appendix I 505.
[44] *Id.*
[45] 9 FAM Appendix I 507.
[46] 9 FAM Appendix I 510(a).

Three certified copies of the foreign adoption decree with translation, where applicable, must accompany the report. Documentation confirming that the parents have provided support to the beneficiary, in the form of cancelled checks and letters, should be included in the report, as it could favorably affect congressional action on the bill.[47]

When the results of a medical examination of the beneficiary reveal a sickness or disability, the consular officer's report should indicate that this information has been provided to the adoptive parents and that the parents intend to pursue processing of the visa application until its completion.[48]

Enactment of a Private Bill

After the consular post receives notification of enactment of a private bill, the post will request the beneficiary to appear at the consular office for the final interview and issuance of the visa. Unless the bill indicates otherwise, the beneficiary must apply for and be issued a visa within two years of the date of enactment or lose the relief provided.[49] Once the visa has been issued, the consular post must inform interested members of Congress.[50]

---

[47] 9 FAM Appendix I 510(b).
[48] 9 FAM Appendix I 510(c).
[49] 9 FAM Appendix I 512(a).
[50] 9 FAM Appendix I 512(b).

CHAPTER 4

PRIVATE BILL PRECEDENTS AND ADVOCACY STRATEGIES

Private Bill Precedents

Advocates representing individuals seeking private bill relief should carefully review precedents to determine if similar cases were considered and approved in the past. Although the Senate subcommittee rules[1] do not expressly address the issue of precedents, the House subcommittee rules provide that, "It is the policy of the Subcommittee generally to act favorably on only those private bills that meet certain precedents."[2] In addition to the hardship factor, the most important factor considered by the subcommittee is whether a private immigration bill falls within precedents in which relief has been granted.

Historically, the great majority of private immigration bills have granted lawful permanent resident status to the following categories of persons: (1) individuals excluded under the quota system that was in effect from 1921 through 1965; (2) individuals needing waivers from requirements of family– or employment-based immigration; (3) war brides and children of U.S. citizen military personnel who did not meet the requirements under the law; (4) displaced persons and refugees after World War II; and (5) individuals in need of waivers of certain grounds of exclusion.[3]

A small number of private bills have granted citizenship, either through waiving certain requirements for naturalization or providing an outright grant in certain cases.[4] The cases in which citizenship was directly granted involved women who had lost their citizenship through marriage to a foreigner, children born abroad to U.S. citizens, and persons born U.S. citizens but who lost their citizenship because of retention requirements.[5]

After the scandals involving private bills in the 1970s, a decline in private bills began to occur. This trend has reached a low point in the past several years with only four private bills enacted in the 108th Congress and none in the 109th Congress.[6]

---

[1] U.S. Senate Committee on the Judiciary, Subcommittee on Immigration, Border Security, and Citizenship, Rules of Procedure for Introducing a Private Relief Bill (Immigration), 108th Cong. (2005).

[2] U.S. House of Representatives Committee on the Judiciary, Subcommittee on Immigration, Citizenship, Refugees, Border Security and International Law, Rules of Procedure and Statement of Policy for Private Immigration Bills, 110th Congress (2007) (statement of policy).

[3] *See* B. Maguire, *Immigration—Public Legislation and Private Bills* (1997) at 73–83.

[4] *Id.* at 192.

[5] *Id.* at 195–96.

[6] *See* Report on the Activities of the Committee on the Judiciary of the House of Representatives (108th Congress), H.R. Rep. No. 108-805; Report on the Activities of the Committee on the Judiciary of the House of Representatives (109th Congress), H.R. Rep. No. 109-749.

During the past 10 years, the beneficiaries of private immigration bills have been individuals who generally were unable to receive lawful permanent resident status through no fault of their own. Despite compliance with filing requirements, many individuals have been denied immigrant status or rendered ineligible for adjustment of status because of delays or errors on the part of the government. The two most common situations involve orphan adoptees aging out before the adoption and immigrant petition process can be finalized and conditional permanent resident applications not being approved before the death of the U.S. citizen spouse.[7] However, there have been other types of cases that have resulted in successful private immigration relief. These include the case of the high-profile human rights activist Wei Jingsheng;[8] Persian Gulf War evacuees with U.S. ties;[9] and an individual married to a U.S. citizen who had been convicted of possession of a controlled substance.[10]

The House subcommittee rules contain a statement of policy that lists certain types of bills, the criteria used to review them, and whether there are favorable precedents for those categories, which include the following:

- Waivers for requirements for adopted children: Generally, these are favored if the child is young and there has been a long-term relationship between the parent and the child.
- Waivers permitting doctors and nurses to adjust status are disfavored.
- Waivers permitting persons who entered the United States for medical treatment to remain permanently are generally disfavored and require an advisory opinion from an international health organization explaining the availability of medical care in the home country.
- Waivers permitting persons with deferred action or parole status to adjust status are disfavored.
- Waivers of health grounds are generally disfavored and require the posting of a bond.
- Waivers for those seeking lawful resident status to avoid military service in their home country are disfavored.
- Waivers for visa fraud are disfavored.
- Expedited naturalization for athletes seeking to compete as U.S. citizens, waivers of naturalization requirements, restoration of U.S. citizenship for those who have renounced their citizenship, and posthumous citizenship are generally disfavored.

---

[7] M. Lee, Private Immigration Legislation (Aug. 9, 2005, updated Feb. 28, 2007), CRS Report for Congress RL33024.

[8] Priv. L. No. 106-14 (2000)

[9] Priv. L. No. 106-8 (2000).

[10] Priv. L. No. 105-6 (1998).

Both the House and Senate subcommittee rules favor cases involving extreme or unusual hardship to U.S. citizen or lawful permanent resident family members. In addition to reviewing and arguing past precedents, advocates must establish hardship in any cases in which they seek private immigration relief. Below are precedents listed by category to guide you in drafting your case for private relief.

Adoption, Children, and Age-Out Cases

Private relief for Min-Zen Lin.[11] The beneficiary, a 1-year-old native and citizen of China, was adopted by a U.S. citizen couple. The natural parents gave up their child for economic reasons. After the adoption, the adoptive mother resided with the child for six months. The private law held that the beneficiary was a child under INA §101(b)(1)(F) [8 USC §1101(b)(1)(F)] relating to immigration of adopted children as immediate relatives.

For the relief of Juan Esteban Ramirez.[12] The beneficiary, a native and citizen of Ecuador, entered the United States as a visitor with the help of an American doctor who met him during a visit to a missionary hospital in Ecuador. The beneficiary had been treated for malnutrition and had surgery on his legs to correct the effects of polio. He was one of seven children born out of wedlock and was sold to restaurant owners to work. After coming to the United States, he was placed in a foster home and attended a school for the physically handicapped. The private bill granted him lawful permanent residence.

Private relief for Ok-Boon Kang.[13] The beneficiary, a 21-year-old native and citizen of Korea, an orphan, and alleged child of a U.S. citizen soldier and a Korean woman, entered the United States as a visitor with prospective adoptive parents. The couple had already adopted five other Korean children. The private bill held that the beneficiary qualified for relief as an adopted child under INA §101(b)(1)(E) [8 USC §1101(b)(1)(E)].

Private relief for Andre Bartholo Eubanks.[14] The beneficiary, a 6-year-old native and citizen of Brazil who entered the United States as a visitor, was given up by his parents for adoption by a U.S. citizen uncle and a lawful permanent resident aunt when he was 5. The couple had been married for 15 years and had no children. The adoptive mother did not comply with the two-year residence period required by law prior to the immigration of adopted children. The private bill held the beneficiary to be within INA §101(b)(1)(E) [8 USC §1101(b)(1)(E)] for purposes of immigration of adopted children.

Private relief for Gladys Belleville Schultz.[15] The beneficiary, a 17-year-old native and citizen of Haiti, was adopted at the age of 15 by a U.S. citizen couple. She

---

[11] Priv. L. No. 96-99, S. Rep. No. 806 (1980).

[12] Priv. L. No. 97-26 (1982).

[13] Priv. L. No. 97-34 (1982).

[14] Priv. L. No. 97-17 (1982).

[15] Priv. L. No. 97-7 (1981).

had lived in an orphanage since the age of 9 and met her adoptive parents during a visit with a church group to the United States a year before the adoption. The private bill classified the beneficiary as an adopted child under INA §101(b)(1)(F) [8 USC §1101(b)(1)(F)] for purposes of immigrating to the United States.

Private relief for Shinji Oniki.[16] The beneficiary, a 19-year-old native and citizen of Japan, entered the United States as a visitor and resided with his natural mother. He had been born out of wedlock and his mother had given him to her mother for adoption 30 days after his birth. She left her child at age 6, went to the United States with her U.S. citizen husband, and subsequently received immigrant status. The mother kept in touch with her son through the years. The private bill granted the beneficiary lawful permanent residency.

Private relief for Samuel Joseph Edgar.[17] The beneficiary, a 19-year-old native of Scotland and citizen of England, entered the United States as a visitor. He had been a ward of the Scottish government since birth because his father was in prison and his mother could not care for him. At the age of 12, he had been placed in a foster home and later accompanied the foster family to the United States. After a breakdown in that relationship, he was placed with another foster family, who adopted him. The private bill granted the beneficiary lawful permanent residence status.

Private relief for Edwin Marcos Rios and Geovanna Rios.[18] The beneficiaries, siblings who were 21– and 18-year-old natives and citizens of Bolivia, entered the United States as visitors. They were the nephew and niece of U.S. citizens, who adopted them in the United States. Their mother died of cancer in March 1981 and their father died that same year. The private bill held that the beneficiaries were adopted children of U.S. citizens under INA §101(b)(1)(F) [8 USC §1101(b)(1)(F)].

Private relief for Sueng Ho Jang and Sueng Il Jang.[19] The beneficiaries, 24– and 20-year-old siblings, natives and citizens of Korea, entered the United States with their parents as dependents of treaty traders. Their parents and two brothers died aboard a Korean Airlines flight that was sabotaged in 1983. The father had been employed with the airline for seven years. The private bill granted the beneficiaries lawful permanent resident status.

Private relief for Jose Maria Vas.[20] The beneficiary, a 23-year-old native and citizen of Hong Kong, was over 21 when his family adjusted their status to permanent residency. A second-preference petition was approved. The private bill provided that the beneficiary could be considered a child for purposes of INA §202(b)(1) [8 USC §1152(b)(1)].

---

[16] Priv. L. No. 97-36 (1982).
[17] Priv. L. No. 98-25 (1984).
[18] Priv. L. No. 99-5 (1986).
[19] Priv. L. No. 99-19 (1986).
[20] Priv. L. No. 100-4 (1987).

Private relief for Heraclio Tolley.[21] The beneficiary, a native and citizen of Mexico, was orphaned when his mother died and his father abandoned him at age 2. He was raised by his maternal grandparents in Mexico. An uncle who visited him several years later brought him to the United States. The uncle was killed in an auto accident. The family for whom the uncle worked adopted the beneficiary but the adoption proceedings were not complete until after his 16th birthday. The private bill held that the beneficiary was an adopted child under INA §101(b)(1)(F) [8 USC §1101(b)(1)(F)].

For the relief of Nuratu Olarewaju Abeke Kadiri.[22] The beneficiary, a native and citizen of Nigeria, born in 1978, was brought to the United States as a minor child by her parents, who later separated and left her with cousins, who raised her as guardians. The mother's whereabouts were unknown. Prior to returning permanently to Nigeria, the father filed and received temporary resident status for his daughter under the Immigration Reform and Control Act of 1986,[23] but never completed adjustment of status for her. Neither the daughter nor the guardians knew this, and the deadline for completing the process had passed. The private bill granted the beneficiary lawful permanent residence.

For the relief of Kerantha Poole-Christian.[24] The beneficiary, a native and citizen of Jamaica, was living in the United States with her mother. Prior to returning to Jamaica for an immigrant visa interview, the mother left her daughter with friends. The visa was denied. The mother and father gave up their daughter for adoption to friends. However, the adoption was not finalized until the beneficiary was 17. During the process, her natural mother had died. The beneficiary was granted lawful permanent resident status.

For the relief of Sepandan Farnia and Farbod Farnia.[25] The beneficiaries, native and citizens of Iran, had come to the United States as young children with their mother. The mother and her two sons had fled Iran after her husband had been executed and they had been in hiding for a year. Their applications for asylum were denied. In the meantime, the sons had grown up and their mother had died. At the time of the request for private relief, they were employed college students living with extended family members and had no ties to their native country. The private bill granted the beneficiaries lawful permanent resident status.

For the relief of Guy Taylor.[26] The beneficiary, a native and citizen of Canada, was an orphan. His father died before his birth and his mother, a U.S. citizen, died of a drug overdose after his 16th birthday. He had been raised primarily in the United

---

[21] Priv. L. No. 105-5 (1998).
[22] Priv. L. No. 105-9 (1998)
[23] Pub. L. No. 99-603, 100 Stat. 3359.
[24] Priv. L. No. 106-7 (2000).
[25] Priv. L. No. 106-10 (2000).
[26] Priv. L. No. 106-21 (2000).

States, first by his mother, and then later by his maternal grandmother as a guardian. The beneficiary wished to enlist in the U.S. military but could not do so without lawful immigration status. He had been paroled into the United States after his mother died. The private bill granted him lawful permanent residency. It is unclear from the legislative history why he was not considered a U.S. citizen at birth through his mother.

For the relief of Tony Lara.[27] The beneficiary, a native and citizen of El Salvador, had been brought to the United States illegally as a young child. His mother drowned after attempting to re-enter the United States after deportation. He lost contact with his father, who had been deported after several drug arrests. The beneficiary and his sister were taken in by U.S. citizen family friends who could only afford to adopt the sister. He later moved in with the family of his high school wrestling coach and became a champion wrestler. Although he could have obtained immigration status as a special immigrant juvenile, he was provided wrong advice by an attorney and never applied. The beneficiary had no ties to El Salvador, stayed in contact with his sister, and was supported by his coach and the coach's wife. The private bill granted the beneficiary lawful permanent residency.

For the relief of José Guadalupe Tellez Pinales.[28] The beneficiary, a native and citizen of Mexico, was brought to the United States illegally by a great uncle when he was a young child. He was raised by his great uncle and his first wife, believing that they were his parents. Before the beneficiary came to the United States, his father had been killed in an accident and his mother could not raise him along with another child. No formal adoption proceedings had been carried out prior to the beneficiary's 16th birthday. The private bill granted the beneficiary lawful permanent resident status.

For the relief of Rita Mirembe Revell.[29] The beneficiary, a native and citizen of Uganda, lived with her adoptive parents since the age of 8. Her adoptive parents are Dennis Revell and the now-deceased Maureen Reagan, daughter of President Ronald Reagan. Because of her adoptive mother's terminal cancer, it was impossible for her and her husband to adopt the beneficiary under the adoption laws of Uganda. The favorable factors that supported a grant of relief were the fact that Ms. Reagan's illness prohibited the adoption of the beneficiary, the couple had provided support for her since the age of 3 and she had lived with them since the age of 8. The private bill granted her lawful resident status. Ms. Reagan died on August 8, 2001, only a few weeks after the enactment of the private bill.

For the relief of So Hyun Jun.[30] The beneficiary, a native and citizen of South Korea, was born on September 16, 1984. When the beneficiary was 17, her mother was permanently injured in a car accident and was unable to care for her. Her father

---

[27] Priv. L. No. 106-22 (2000).

[28] Priv. L. No. 106-24 (2000).

[29] Priv. L. No. 107-1 (2001).

[30] Priv. L. No. 107-6 (2002).

had a history of alcohol abuse and had been both physically and mentally abusive to the beneficiary. The beneficiary's aunt and uncle, John and Ok Sun Thornton, and her mother agreed that the Thorntons would adopt the beneficiary. The Thorntons began the process to adopt the beneficiary, but their efforts were thwarted for many years because the beneficiary's father had disappeared and they could not proceed without his consent. In February 2000, the beneficiary first came to the United States to live with her aunt and uncle. Formal adoption proceedings were instituted in 2000 and finalized on March 6, 2001, seven months after the beneficiary's 16th birthday. The private bill classified the beneficiary as a child under INA §101(b)(1)(F) [8 USC §1101(b)(1)(F)], thereby permitting the adoptive parents to file the necessary papers to adjust her status.

For the relief of Lindita Idrizi Heath.[31] The beneficiary was born on March 25, 1984, in the former Yugoslavia. She was a 7-year-old Kosovo refugee living in Germany when she met Dennis and Mary Jo Heath. Mr. Heath was stationed in Germany. Several years later, when Mr. Heath was again stationed in Germany, the couple decided to adopt the beneficiary. She entered the United States on July 2, 2001, under a grant of humanitarian parole. The adoption had been completed on June 1, 2001. The private bill classified the beneficiary as a child under INA §101(b)(1)(F) [8 USC §1101(b)(1)(F)], permitting her to adjust her status to lawful permanent residence.

For the relief for Richi James Lesley.[32] The beneficiary was born in February 1977 to an unknown U.S. serviceman and Korean mother, who gave him up for adoption. In August 1977, he was adopted by U.S. Air Force Sergeant James Doyle Lesley and his wife in Korea. The couple had previously adopted another Korean child who was four years older than the beneficiary. On April 29, 1978, Sergeant Lesley was killed in a fishing accident. His wife, 20 years older, was unable to care for the children. The Air Force sent the beneficiary and his older sister to the United States to be placed with the sergeant's mother. The beneficiary lived with his grandmother until her death, and then with other family and friends, from the time he was 1 year old until he went to college. He did not know that he was not a U.S. citizen until deportation proceedings were brought against him in 2000. The beneficiary did not speak Korean and had no ties to his birth country. The private bill granted him lawful permanent residence in the United States.

For the relief of Tanya Andrea Goudeau.[33] The beneficiary, a native and citizen of Sri Lanka, was born on December 6, 1984. Her natural father abandoned her and her mother when she was 3 years old. Her mother later moved to Italy, leaving her with her elderly grandmother. The adoptive parents became aware of her difficulties when she was 6 years old. When they found out that there was little food for her and that she was no longer attending school, they began adoption proceedings. Although

---

[31] Priv. L. No. 108-1 (2004).
[32] Priv. L. No. 108-3 (2004).
[33] Priv. L. No. 108-6 (2004).

they became her formal guardians prior to her 16th birthday, the adoption was not finalized until afterwards. The private bill classified her as a child under INA §101(b)(1)(E) [8 USC §1101(b)(1)(E)] for purposes of approval of an immediate relative visa petition.

Other Family Cases

For the relief of Madeleine Mesnager.[34] The beneficiary, an 81-year-old native and citizen of France, wanted to come to the United States to live with her adoptive U.S. citizen daughter. The beneficiary had raised her adoptive daughter, who is also her niece, since she was 2 years old when her natural mother had become paralyzed. The adoptive mother supported her daughter for 29 years, then adopted her when she was 31 years old. The adoption had been delayed for many reasons, including the war. The adoptive daughter wanted to care for her mother in her final years. The private bill classified the adoptive mother as an immediate relative under INA §201(b) [8 USC §1151(b)].

For the relief of Zohreh Farhang Ghahfarokhi.[35] The beneficiary, a native and citizen of Iran, came to the United States with her husband and their oldest daughter in 1984. While they were in the United States, a second daughter was born. In 1994, the husband filed an application for adjustment of status for himself, his wife, and their older daughter. Later, the couple began to have marital problems. In 1996, the family traveled to Iran for a visit. The wife and older daughter obtained advance parole to travel. During the visit, the beneficiary gave her passport and other documents to her husband for safekeeping. The husband later told her that he would not permit her or their two daughters to return to the United States so that she could not divorce him and take half of his assets. The beneficiary applied for a replacement passport but the husband had revoked her and her daughter's permission to leave the country under the laws of Iran. He also threatened to kill her if she returned to the United States. When the older daughter turned 18 and the revocation no longer was binding, she applied for a passport. Soon thereafter, the beneficiary became aware of a provision of the law that stated that if the husband is not residing in the country, the woman could petition for review of the case. She did so and was granted a passport. The beneficiary and her older daughter were paroled into the United States in 1996. The older daughter later adjusted under her father's application for adjustment of status. The private bill granted the beneficiary lawful permanent resident status so that she could stay in the United States and care for her U.S. citizen daughter.

For the relief of Mina Vahedi Notash.[36] The beneficiary, a native and citizen of Iran, was brought to the United States illegally by her former U.S. citizen husband. The husband did not apply for immigration benefits for her, and during their seven-year marriage, he physically and verbally abused her. He threatened to have her

---

[34] Priv. L. No. 97-4 (1981).
[35] Priv. L. No. 106-11 (2000).
[36] Priv. L. No. 106-18 (2000).

immediately deported if she reported the abuse. After the birth of her two children, her husband told her she had to return to Iran in order to obtain her immigrant status. After she returned to Iran, her husband divorced her under Iranian law, which meant she could not challenge the divorce or the custody issues. The beneficiary stayed in Iran from 1994 until 1999, when she re-entered the United States on a fiancée visa. The wedding was called off after her fiancé discovered that she wanted to regain custody of the children. The beneficiary's ex-husband refused to allow her access to the children. The private bill granted the beneficiary lawful permanent resident status, permitting her to remain in the United States and challenge the custody arrangement.

Death of Sponsor

For the relief of Hanife Frantz.[37] The beneficiary, a 31-year-old native and citizen of Turkey, entered the United States as a visitor. She had been married to a U.S. citizen who was employed by Boeing Services International under contract to the U.S. Air Force. He was killed in an ambush with three other Americans in Turkey in 1979. The couple had one U.S. citizen child, age 3. The private bill classified the beneficiary as an immediate relative for purposes of obtaining an immigrant visa.

For the relief of Mishleen Earle.[38] The beneficiary, an 18-year-old native and citizen of Lebanon, was married to a U.S. citizen who had served in the army and was killed in the 1983 bombing of the U.S. Marine headquarters in Beirut. They had only been married for seven days, and the husband had completed the forms for her immigration. The private bill granted her lawful permanent residency.

For the relief of Rosa Pratts.[39] The beneficiary, a 27-year-old native and citizen of Honduras, entered the United States in 1986 on a diplomatic visa. She married a U.S. citizen, who filed an immigrant petition on her behalf, but he committed suicide before she could adjust status. They had a 4-year-old U.S. citizen child. The private bill classified her as an immediate relative for purposes of obtaining an immigrant visa.

For the relief of Gillian Lesley Sackler.[40] The beneficiary, a 48-year-old native and citizen of England, was married to Arthur M. Sackler, renowned philanthropist and a U.S. citizen. He filed a petition on her behalf 14 days prior to his death. The private bill granted her lawful permanent status.

For the relief of Mai Hoa "Jasmine" Salehi.[41] The beneficiary married Cyrus Salehi in March 1995. In June 1995, her husband filed an immigrant visa on her behalf. Because of a backlog in applications, they were scheduled for their interview in August 1996. In February 1996, her husband was shot and killed at a Denny's restaurant of which he was part owner. When the beneficiary appeared for her interview in August, she was denied status. Because of a request filed by the

---

[37] Priv. L. No. 97-9 (1981).
[38] Priv. L. No. 99-1 (1986).
[39] Priv. L. No. 100-38 (1988).
[40] Priv. L. No. 100-35 (1988).
[41] Priv. L. No. 105-7 (1998).

prosecutor in charge of prosecuting her husband's case, she was granted advance parole to participate in the trial. The private bill granted her lawful permanent resident status.

For the relief of Mercedes Del Carmen Quiroz Martinez Cruz.[42] The beneficiary married her husband, John Francisco Cruz, a U.S. citizen, in December 1993. Mr. Cruz filed a relative petition on her behalf in 1994 in Germany. Legacy Immigration and Naturalization Service (INS) had no record of the petition being processed. However, Mr. Cruz had a copy of the petition as well as a copy of the Frankfurt office receipt. In November 1994, the couple had a child in Germany. Mr. Cruz, a 20-year Army veteran, worked as a consultant for the military in Germany. On November 1, 1995, Mr. Cruz died of a heart attack in his sleep. He and the beneficiary had been married one year, 10 months, and 28 days. The beneficiary and her son entered the United States on a visitor visa for the funeral. She filed a petition as a widow of a U.S. citizen in January 1996, but the petition was denied because they had not been married for the required two-year period. The private bill classified her as an immediate relative, permitting her to petition as a widow.

For the relief of Suchada Kwong.[43] Suchada Vasanaarchasakul, a native and citizen of Thailand, married her U.S. citizen husband, Jimmy Kwong, on September 23, 1995. He filed an immediate relative petition on her behalf at that time. The beneficiary's medical exam revealed that she tested positive for tuberculosis. Therefore, the adjustment process had to be delayed so that she could have further tests. At that point, she was pregnant and advised to wait until after the baby's birth to have the required chest x-ray. Legacy INS scheduled her interview for conditional residence for August 15, 1996. In May 1996, the beneficiary gave birth to her son. Less than three weeks later, Mr. Kwong was killed in a car accident. The private bill granted the beneficiary lawful permanent resident status.

For the relief of Sergio Lozano.[44] On January 22, 1997, Sergio Lozano and his two siblings were granted immigrant visas as children of a lawful permanent resident, their mother. While their mother was preparing to bring them to the United States, she died as a result of typhoid fever. Their father's whereabouts were unknown. Soon thereafter, at the direction of their U.S. citizen grandmother, they took a flight to the United States. When they arrived, the immigration officials held that the immigrant visas were invalid because of their mother's death, but paroled them in to the United States. They remained in the United States, attending school and living with their grandmother. The beneficiary's two siblings were young enough to obtain visas as special immigrant juveniles. The beneficiary could not obtain such a visa because of his age. Taking into account that there was no one in El Salvador to care for him and that it would cause extreme hardship for him and his siblings to be separated, a private bill was approved, granting him lawful resident status.

---

[42] Priv. L. No. 105-8 (1998).

[43] Priv. L. No. 106-3 (1999).

[44] Priv. L. No. 106-16 (2000).

For the relief of Elizabeth Eka Bassey, Emmanuel O. Paul Bassey, and Mary Idongesit Paul Bassey.[45] The beneficiary and her husband, Paul Bassey, Nigerian natives and citizens, were career employees with the U.S. Department of State. Mr. Bassey, who began work with the U.S. government in 1961, received special immigrant status in 1991 in recognition of his service to the U.S. government, and was approved for a fourth-preference visa petition. During that same year, civil war erupted and the American embassy began evacuating Americans and embassy employees. As a result of the emergency situation, the embassy was working with a skeleton staff and needed help. Officials asked Mr. Bassey to delay his planned retirement for a year to help them. He agreed. In May 1992, Mr. Bassey died of a heart attack before he could immigrate to the United States. The beneficiary and her children were advised that they were ineligible for special immigrant status. The only other relief was through private legislation. The beneficiary and her daughter, Mary, were paroled into the United States on December 18, 1993, and remained in the country. Her son, Jacob, entered the United States on August 14, 1991, with an F-1 visa and also remained. Her other son, Emmanuel, entered the United States on January 8, 1989, as an F-1 student. The beneficiary had worked in the U.S. embassy for 12 years and had received a distinguished honor award for her work there. The private bill granted her and her children lawful permanent resident status.

For the relief of Malia Miller.[46] The beneficiary, a native and citizen of Tonga, met her husband, Todd Miller, in 1995 when he was working in American Samoa. They came to the United States in 1996 so that she could meet his parents. In April 1997, they had a son, and they married in July 1997. The beneficiary's husband returned to American Samoa to work temporarily while she remained in the United States to care for their son. In January 1998, they filed papers to obtain her residency. The beneficiary's husband was later killed in a helicopter crash in American Samoa before they could attend the interview to obtain her conditional residency. The private bill granted lawful permanent residency to the beneficiary.

For the relief of Anisha Goveas Foti.[47] The beneficiary, a native and citizen of India, worked as a travel agent for World Travel Service in Bahrain and was assigned to the travel office in the American embassy in June 1999. She met her husband, Seth Foti, a diplomatic courier for the Department of State, while working there. They married on June 3, 2000, and completed the paperwork to request the beneficiary's immigrant visa shortly thereafter. On August 23, 2000, the beneficiary's husband was killed in an airplane crash. The private bill granted the beneficiary lawful permanent resident status.

For the relief of Durreshahwar Durreshahwar, Nida Hasan, Asna Hasan, Anum Hasan, and Iqra Hasan.[48] In 1993, Mr. Waqar Hasan came to the United

---

[45] Priv. L. No. 106-19 (2000).
[46] Priv. L. No. 106-23 (2000).
[47] Priv. L. No. 107-5 (2002).
[48] Priv. L. No. 108-4 (2004).

States. A year later, his wife and four daughters joined him. On September 15, 2001, in response to the events of September 11, a man killed Mr. Hasan. At the time of his murder, Mr. Hasan had a pending application for adjustment of status for him and his family based on his employment. Because he was the principal applicant, his petition for adjustment of status for him and his family became invalid upon his death. The private bill granted lawful permanent residence to the beneficiary and her four daughters.

Criminal Issues

For the relief of Kevin Patrick Saunders.[49] The beneficiary, a native and citizen of England, and spouse of a U.S. citizen, was ineligible for a visa to enter the United States because of a conviction when he was 23 for possession of three grams of cocaine, 161.8 grams of heroin, and morphine. The private bill waived the ground of exclusion relating to the drug conviction.

For the relief of Bernard Julian Phillips.[50] The beneficiary, a native and citizen of England and spouse of a U.S. citizen, was found ineligible for a visa because of a conviction for possession of 19.8 grams of marijuana. The beneficiary's spouse wanted him to accompany her to the United States because of her parents' illnesses. One suffered from cancer and the other from Parkinson's disease. The private bill waived the ground of exclusion relating to the drug conviction.

For the relief of Sun Pok Winer.[51] The beneficiary, a native and citizen of Korea and the spouse of a U.S. citizen serviceman, was excluded from entry into the United States because of a conviction for possession of 120 grams of marijuana that occurred six years prior to her application for a visa. The private bill waived the ground of exclusion relating to the drug conviction.

For the relief of Lester Bruce Priday.[52] The beneficiary, a native and citizen of Australia, the spouse of a U.S. citizen and father of one U.S. citizen child, was excluded from entering the United States because of two convictions for possession of cannabis and hemp seeds that occurred five years prior to his application for a visa. The private bill waived the ground of exclusion relating to the drug conviction.

For the relief of Kwi Sok Buckingham.[53] The beneficiary, a native and citizen of Korea and spouse of a U.S. citizen serviceman, was excluded from entering the United States because of a conviction for giving 69 valium tablets to two individuals. The private bill waived the ground of exclusion relating to the drug conviction.

---

[49] Priv. L. No. 94-66 (1976).
[50] Priv. L. No. 94-116 (1976).
[51] Priv. L. No. 95-63 (1978).
[52] Priv. L. No. 95-64 (1978).
[53] Priv. L. No. 95-35 (1978).

For the relief of Monika Grantz.[54] The beneficiary, a native and citizen of Germany and the wife of a U.S. citizen serviceman, was ineligible for a visa because of a conviction for trafficking in narcotics (hashish), fraud, forgery, and tax evasion. The court gave her a six-month probationary sentence because of extenuating circumstances and her help in investigating others involved in the crimes. The private bill waived the ground of exclusion relating to the drug conviction.

For the relief of Roland Karl Heinz Vogel.[55] The beneficiary, a native and citizen of Germany, was excludable from the United States because of a conviction for assault with a deadly weapon that happened during a jealous rage of a friend. The beneficiary had been supported by his U.S. citizen mother until he joined the German Navy at age 17. His mother wanted him to come live with her in the United States. The private bill waived the ground of exclusion relating to his conviction for a crime of moral turpitude.

For the relief of Hyong Cha Kim Kay.[56] The beneficiary, a native and citizen of Korea, resided in Korea with her 11-year-old daughter and 7-year-old son. She was married to a U.S. citizen serviceman, who filed a petition on her behalf but was later killed. She later was engaged to another U.S citizen. In 1975, she was convicted of possession of 50 grams of marijuana and found to be excludable from the United States. A private law was passed that provided a waiver of the conviction, but first provided for suspension of deportation for two years, during which she had to show good moral character, rehabilitation, and that she would accrue no other convictions.

For the relief of Michael Wilding.[57] The beneficiary, the son of actress Elizabeth Taylor, was a native-born U.S. citizen who renounced his citizenship in 1971. The beneficiary was married to a U.S. citizen. He was excludable from the United States due to a conviction for cultivating 10 milligrams of marijuana. The private bill waived exclusion due to the drug conviction and suspended deportation for a period of three years, with a requirement that the beneficiary perform community service.

For the relief of Larry Errol Pieterse.[58] The beneficiary married his first wife, a lawful permanent resident, and came to the United States in November 1981 as a second-preference spouse of an alien resident. He resided in the United States from that time until the passage of the private bill. In 1983, after the marriage began to fall apart, the beneficiary's wife asked him to move out. Shortly thereafter, she began to stalk him and slashed the tires of a woman he was seeing. The beneficiary told his wife he wanted to divorce. She asked him to go to his home to talk, at which time she planted cocaine in his house. A call was made to the police, who came, arrested him, and charged him with drug possession. Because of financial difficulties, the

---

[54] Priv. L. No. 95-74 (1978).
[55] Priv. L. No. 97-3 (1981).
[56] Priv. L. No. 100-23 (1988).
[57] Priv. L. No. 100-36 (1988).
[58] Priv. L. No. 105-6 (1998).

beneficiary could not go to trial and instead made a plea agreement. After being assured by legacy INS that he would not be deported because of a misdemeanor conviction, the beneficiary agreed to plead guilty to possession of drug paraphernalia. Adjudication of guilt and imposition of sentence was withheld. However, after his conviction, a new provision in the law was enacted that resulted in his being deportable. In 1990, the beneficiary remarried and since that time had been the sole support for his wife, who had a chronic illness, and helped support four children from a previous marriage. In 1991, the Florida Parole and Probation Commission's Office of Executive Clemency found that the ex-wife had planted the drugs found in the beneficiary's home and that the beneficiary was not guilty of any crime. The State of Florida granted him a full pardon. The pardon, however, did not erase the drug conviction for immigration purposes. The private bill granted a waiver of deportation and removal for any departure from the United States and also provided that the offense could not be used as evidence of bad character to render the beneficiary ineligible for citizenship.

Medical Issues

For the relief of Wilhelm Jahn Schlechter, Monica Pino Schlechter, Ingrid Daniela Schlechter, and Arturo David Schlechter.[59] The beneficiaries, parents and two children, natives and citizens of Chile, first entered the United States in 1981 and last entered in 1984. The parents sought medical care for their child, Daniela, who had a rare birth defect called bladder exstrophy, a condition where the bladder forms outside of the body. The private bill granted the family lawful permanent resident status.

For the relief of Oscar Salas-Velazquez.[60] The beneficiary, a native and citizen of Mexico, entered the United States on a visitor's visa in 1984. In 1986, he married a U.S. citizen, Jennifer Brady, to obtain his green card. In 1989, both parties admitted to marriage fraud during an interview. Legacy INS initially held the beneficiary but then later released him. Shortly after, he met his current wife, a U.S. citizen. The beneficiary later divorced his first wife and remarried. He and his second wife had two children. The beneficiary went to legacy INS to speak with them about his situation and file papers for his residency. At that point, legacy INS placed the beneficiary in deportation proceedings and he was deported based on the marriage fraud. During the time that the beneficiary was in deportation proceedings, the family discovered that his wife and possibly one of his children were carriers of the HLA-27 antigen, which predisposed them to developing Reiter's syndrome (reactive arthritis). This syndrome is triggered by intestinal infection by certain organisms that are widespread in the food and water supplies of Mexico. It is a severe disabling arthritic disease with no cure. A private bill waived the grounds of exclusion relating to his prior marriage fraud and deportation.

---

[59] Priv. L. No. 100-48 (1988).
[60] Priv. L. No. 104-3 (1996).

For the relief of Saeed Rezai.[61] The beneficiary, a native and citizen of Iran, first entered the United States as a student in 1986. In 1987, he married his first wife and received conditional permanent residence. The marriage ended shortly thereafter prior to the conditional residence status being lifted. The beneficiary filed for a waiver of the conditional status along with an application for asylum. In 1991, prior to a decision on his applications, he married his current wife, a U.S. citizen, who filed an immigrant visa petition on his behalf. The petition was denied because of suspicions of marriage fraud in the beneficiary's first marriage, but he was granted voluntary departure. Legacy INS did consider his second marriage to be valid. In the meantime, the beneficiary's wife had been diagnosed with multiple sclerosis. According to her physician's report, stress would cause her health to seriously deteriorate. The private bill granted the beneficiary lawful permanent resident status.

For the relief of Marina Khalina and Albert Mifakhov.[62] The beneficiaries, mother and child, natives and citizens of Russia, entered the United States in October 1989 at the invitation of a doctor from Salem, OR to receive medical attention for the son's severe cerebral palsy. Expenses to cover his treatment over the years were donated by Shriner's Hospital in Portland, OR. After several extensions of their nonimmigrant visas, in 1991, the beneficiary mother married a U.S. citizen, who filed for her adjustment of status. The beneficiary's husband felt unable to care for her disabled son, and the marriage ended prior to her obtaining her residency. Soon thereafter, legacy INS commenced deportation proceedings against the beneficiaries. They were granted voluntary departure, which was extended several times because of the son's condition. Because of changes in the law, further extensions could not be granted. The private bill granted lawful permanent resident status to both beneficiaries.

For the relief of Jacqueline Salinas, Gabriela Salinas, Alejandro Salinas, and Omar Salinas.[63] In March 1996, the beneficiary Gabriela Salinas and her father, Omar, entered the United States at New York to seek treatment at Mt. Sinai Medical Center for the beneficiary's rare bone cancer, Ewing's sarcoma. She was denied treatment because her family could not pay. However, the family went to Memphis for treatment at St. Jude Children's Research Hospital, which accepted her case at no cost. Shortly after her chemotherapy treatment began, her mother, Jacqueline, and her three siblings joined her and her father. On April 14, 1997, before the end of Gabriela's treatment, the father and Gabriela's 3-year-old sister were killed in a car accident. The mother, Jacqueline, who was pregnant at the time, was paralyzed from the waist down. She later gave birth to a health baby boy. St. Jude Hospital offered to care for the family and made a commitment to provide full financial support for Jacqueline and her children to live permanently in the United States. The private bill granted the family members lawful permanent residency status.

---

[61] Priv. L. No. 106-13 (2000).
[62] Priv. L. No. 106-15 (2000).
[63] Priv. L. No. 106-20 (2000).

Waiver of Naturalization and Citizenship Requirements

For the relief of Viktor Ivanovich Belenko.[64] The beneficiary, a native and citizen of the former Soviet Union and lawful permanent resident of the United States, had defected in 1976 by flying a Soviet MiG-25 Foxbat interceptor to Japan. According to the Central Intelligence Agency, the beneficiary gave the United States the most advanced aircraft in the Soviet inventory and also provided vital information regarding Soviet arms, technology, and strategies. The private bill held that he possessed the residence requirements for naturalization and waived the bar relating to naturalization of former members of the Communist Party.

For the relief of Christina Boltz Sidders.[65] The beneficiary, a native of Bolivia, entered the United States as a visitor. She derived citizenship through her U.S. citizen father but had forfeited that citizenship because she failed to return to the United States between the ages of 14 and 28. The beneficiary's father had been an employee of the U.S. embassy for four years and died when the beneficiary was four months old. She maintained relations with her father's relatives in the United States from the age of 14 and stated that she was not aware of the retention requirements. The private bill granted her lawful permanent residency status rather than restoring her citizenship. The committee, in its report, noted that there were few precedents for restoring or conferring citizenship. However, given her father's service to the United States, it felt a grant of lawful permanent residency was appropriate.

For the relief of Nery De Maio.[66] The beneficiary, a native of Colombia and lawful permanent resident of the United States for 23 years, was denied citizenship because she could not respond to questions regarding U.S. history and government. She had suffered a stroke. The private bill held that the beneficiary satisfied the requirements relating to knowledge of U.S. history and government and relating to taking an oath of allegiance.

For the relief of Audun Endestad.[67] The beneficiary, a native of Norway and permanent resident of the United States, wanted to compete in the 1984 Winter Olympics as a member of the U.S. ski team. He was eight months short of the period necessary to meet the naturalization requirements. In agreeing to a private bill, the committee noted that the beneficiary had contributed to the development of one of the strongest cross-country teams in U.S. history. The bill held that he satisfied the residency requirements for naturalization purposes.

For the relief of Marina Kunyavsky.[68] The beneficiary, a native and citizen of the former USSR, entered the United States as a permanent resident. She was a gymnast and member of the U.S. national gymnastics team and placed fourth during

---

[64] Priv. L. No. 96-62 (1980).
[65] Priv. L. No. 97-24 (1982).
[66] Priv. L. No. 98-41 (1984).
[67] Priv. L. No. 98-7 (1984).
[68] Priv. L. No. 98-13 (1984).

the 1983 USA National Championships. The beneficiary wanted to participate in the 1984 Olympics but could not qualify because she was not a U.S. citizen. The private bill held that the beneficiary satisfied the residency requirements for naturalization purposes, permitting her to obtain her citizenship.

For the relief of Jean Willhelm Willrich.[69] The beneficiary, a native of Germany and lawful permanent resident of the United States, was a soccer player. He was also married to a U.S. citizen. He wished to become a U.S. citizen but did not have the requisite residency in the country. The private bill held that he satisfied the residency requirements for purposes of naturalization of persons married to U.S. citizens.

For the relief of Chong Ho Kwak.[70] The beneficiary, a permanent resident for seven years, passed his citizenship test and was approved for naturalization on January 23, 1996, and scheduled to take the oath on June 14, 1996. On February 4, 1996, while he and his wife were closing their shop for the day, they were robbed. One of the robbers shot the beneficiary in the head. Although he was in a stabilized, semi-comatose state, the beneficiary never regained consciousness after the shooting. Legacy INS refused to naturalize the beneficiary because he was unable to take and understand the oath. The private bill ordered the attorney general to naturalize the beneficiary without the requirement of taking the oath. In 2000, the law changed to permit the waiving of the oath for a person who is unable to understand or communicate that he or she understands the oath because of a physical, developmental, or mental impairment.

Mistake of Law

For the relief of Belinda McGregor.[71] The beneficiary, a citizen of the United Kingdom (U.K.), and her husband, a citizen of Ireland, filed separate applications for the 1995 diversity visa program. As the spouse of an Irish citizen, she was eligible for the program. Her application was selected to receive a visa in 1995. When the National Visa Center received the application, the clerk mistakenly assumed that she was ineligible because she was a citizen of the U.K. The clerk tried to resolve the problem by replacing her name with that of her husband. Upon notice that he was accepted for the diversity program, the husband provided additional documents as requested. When the National Visa Center received the information, it was discovered that his wife's name had been replaced with his, so the application was placed back in her name. The National Visa Center never advised her that she had been selected, and therefore she never sent in the necessary information prior to the September 1995 deadline. Her visa was given to another applicant. Because the National Visa Center did not have the legal authority to remedy the situation, a private bill was needed. The bill deemed the beneficiary to have been selected for a diversity visa under the fiscal year 2000 diversity visa program.

---

[69] Priv. L. No. 98-15 (1984).

[70] Priv. L. No. 105-10 (1998).

[71] Priv. L. No. 106-4 (2000).

For the relief of Luis A. Leon-Molina, Ligia Pardon, Juan Leon Padron, Rendy Leon Padron, Manuel Leon Padron, and Luis Leon Padron.[72] The Padron family entered the United States with visitor visas and applied for asylum in 1994. The legacy INS service center denied their application and they were placed in deportation proceedings. On July 26, 1995, the father was selected for an immigrant visa under the diversity visa program for fiscal year 1996. In December 15, 1995, the Padrons' applications for adjustment of status based on the diversity visa grant were approved by the immigration judge, and proceedings were terminated. On that same day, the Department of State informed the immigration judge in writing that visa numbers had been reserved for the Padron family based on the judge's order. However, this notice did not constitute an allocation of the visa numbers, which could only be allocated upon completion of the decision on the applications for adjustment of status. On December 16, 1995, the U.S. federal government shut down and the Padrons' file was forgotten. On September 30, 1996, the diversity visa program for fiscal year 1996 expired along with the Padrons' eligibility for the visas. As a result of this mistake, legacy INS placed the family in deferred action. The private bill deemed the family to have been selected for diversity visas under the fiscal year 2001 diversity visa program.

Political Cases

For the relief of Michel Christopher Meili, Giuseppina Meili, Mirjam Naomi Meili, and Davide Meili.[73] The beneficiaries, natives and citizens of Switzerland, entered the United States as visitors under the visa waiver program. The beneficiary father worked as a security guard in a Swiss bank. One night in January 1997, as he was working, he discovered Holocaust-era documents in the shredding room. Shortly before that, the Swiss parliament had passed a law that specifically prohibited the destruction of documents that could assist in the identification of assets that had belonged to Holocaust survivors. Mr. Meili, realizing the importance of the documents, took some and turned them into the Swiss authorities. He was later fired for stealing the documents, and was refused other employment based on the negative recommendation by his former employer. After publicity on the case, the beneficiaries began to receive death threats. Based on these threats and the father's inability to obtain work, they requested a private bill. The private bill granted lawful permanent residency to the family. In granting it, the House report notes that it was necessary under the circumstances.[74] They did not have immediate family who could petition for them. Although the father had been offered a job by the World Jewish Congress, the labor certification process would have taken many years and would not have permitted him to stay in the United States.

For the relief of Wei Jingsheng.[75] The beneficiary, a native and citizen of the People's Republic of China, was an internationally recognized pro-democracy activist.

---

[72] Priv. L. No. 106-12 (2000).

[73] Priv. L. No. 105-1 (1997).

[74] H.R. Rep. No. 105-129, at 2 (1997).

[75] Priv. L. No. 106-14 (2000).

He had spent 29 years in prison and labor camps because of his activism. In 1997, he was released and permitted to travel to the United States for medical treatment. He entered the United States in November 1997 on a visitor visa. In 1998, Columbia University filed a petition for a change of status to exchange visitor, which was granted but expired in June 2000. The private bill granted the beneficiary lawful permanent resident status.

For the relief of certain Persian Gulf evacuees.[76] From September 2, 1990, through December 14, 1990, the U.S. government airlifted thousands of persons from Kuwait who either had U.S. citizen children or who were secretly protected U.S. citizens during the Iraqi invasion. The evacuees—141 beneficiaries—were initially paroled into the United States. This was extended until December 31, 1991, when legacy INS told them that their parole would not be renewed. Their situation was especially concerning because the Kuwaiti government refused to permit many of them, especially Palestinians, to return, arguing that they had been disloyal during the Iraqi occupation. Several members of Congress urged the attorney general to grant temporary protected status to the approximately 1,500 persons of Palestinian background airlifted to the United States. On November 14, 1991, President Bush directed the attorney general to grant the evacuees a deferral of enforced departure until January 1, 1996. That deadline was later extended until January 1, 1997, by President William Jefferson Clinton. Legacy INS refused to grant any further extensions beyond that time. At the time of the deadline, most evacuees had been able to become lawful permanent residents through employment-based visas or other means. However, there were a number who were not able to do so. The private bill granted lawful permanent resident status to those beneficiaries.

Practice Tips and Strategies

Unfortunately, many members of Congress are reluctant to sponsor private legislation, for a variety of reasons. There is a general reluctance in Congress to pass bills that benefit individuals rather than the public. At times, members refuse to sponsor a bill, fearing possible political costs if the case later turns out to be controversial. Also, there are hundreds if not thousands of persons with equally compelling stories. When such is the case, public legislation is the better route to pursue.

Prior to representing a client who seeks private relief, an attorney should determine if he or she is required to register as a lobbyist in order to present the case. Lobbying at the federal level is regulated by the Lobbying Disclosure Act of 1995.[77] The act applies to lobbying activities, which are defined as any oral or written communications with a government official, including research and planning activities. Those persons who spend 20 percent or more of their time over a six-month period participating in lobbying activities for one client are required to register

---

[76] Priv. L. No. 106-8 (2000).

[77] Pub. L. No. 104-65, 109 Stat. 691 (1995), codified at 2 USC §1605.

as a lobbyist.[78] The great majority of attorneys involved in private immigration bills do not register as lobbyists. Given that the bulk of the work on private bill cases is actually done by the staff of the subcommittee, it is unlikely that the work of an attorney would reach the necessary threshold requiring registration as a lobbyist.

In seeking private legislation, the attorney should approach either a senator or a representative, depending on which one will be more willing to sponsor private legislation. Generally, those persons seeking private relief will contact a member of Congress within their state or district. However, an attorney should not discard the possibility of targeting a senator or representative from another district or state when feasible. When a member seems reluctant to sponsor a private bill, supporters from the community should call the member's office, urging him or her to do so. Those supporters can include neighbors, friends, church leaders and members, teachers, and any others from the community who know the client and are willing to come forward and support the bill. Barraging a member with calls has proved effective in some cases.

Attorneys should remember that generally only the most unusual and compelling cases will be sponsored for private legislation. Therefore, when presenting the facts to a member to seek his or her support, the attorney should differentiate the case from others. As previously noted, members look to precedents in making decisions on private bills before them. Thus, it is important for an attorney to research precedents and identify, if possible, similar cases in which private relief was granted. The House or Senate report on the bill provide background information on the case as well as reasons why the legislation was approved, often citing to past precedents.

In working with a client on a private bill, in addition to supplying the required information as per the Senate and House rules, the attorney should focus his or her efforts on gathering as much information as possible to establish the hardship factors. The attorney should seek supporting letters and affidavits from all those in the community who know the client. This includes employers, coworkers, church leaders and members, neighbors, family, and friends. If the case involves children, school records should be submitted along with letters from teachers and other school personnel. If seeking relief through the House of Representatives, the attorney should be familiar with the House rules, which require additional information for cases involving adoption, doctors or nurses, persons with criminal convictions, and medical cases.

In addition to gathering and submitting the required paperwork, the attorney also should garner as much public support for the bill as possible. Community members should call members of the subcommittee and the judiciary committee, asking them to support the bill. Additionally, it is important to get the support of the entire state congressional delegation to guarantee their votes once the bill goes for a vote. Press coverage may be particularly influential in obtaining private relief. It is important for

---

[78] For additional guidance on the Lobbying Disclosure Act of 1995, visit the Senate webpages at *www.senate.gov/pagelayout/legislative/g_three_sections_with_teasers/lobbyingdisc.htm.*

an attorney to maintain good press contacts and to urge the press to do human interest pieces on the client's story.

Even when a private bill is not passed, its introduction may work to the benefit of a client. When a member of Congress requests a report from the Department of Homeland Security on a potential beneficiary of a private bill, the removal of the client is stayed. Aside from the stay, the introduction of the bill may work to change the government's position on contesting any available relief for the client. This is especially so in cases in which a client may be eligible for cancellation of removal. If the attorney is particularly assertive in fighting for the client, including seeking a private bill, such a strategy may work to convince the government that the case will not go away.

CHAPTER 5

PARDONS

A state or federal pardon may defeat the grounds of removal for a noncitizen convicted of certain offenses. At one time, both legislative and executive pardons served to defeat deportability based on criminal convictions.[1] Additionally, no distinction was made between narcotics and other types of convictions for pardon purposes. The Immigration and Nationality Act of 1952[2] eliminated legislative pardons as grounds to avoid deportation. Shortly thereafter, Congress passed the Narcotic Control Act of 1956,[3] which eliminated the availability of pardons to persons convicted of narcotics offenses under former INA §241(a)(11) [8 USC §1251(a)(11)].[4] The trend over the years has been to limit the effect of pardons in immigration proceedings.

Noncitizens subject to removal based on certain convictions may avoid removal if granted a full and unconditional pardon by the president, a governor, or a constitutionally recognized executive.[5] A pardon will only waive the grounds of removal specified in INA §237(a)(2)(A)(vi) [8 USC §1227(a)(2)(A)(vi)]: crimes of moral turpitude; multiple criminal convictions; aggravated felonies; and high-speed flight from an immigration checkpoint.[6] Under a plain reading of the statutory provision, a pardon will not waive, for example, the following grounds of removal:

- INA §237(a)(1) [8 USC §1227(a)(1)] (inadmissibility at time of admission);[7]
- INA §237(a)(2)(B) [8 USC §1227(a)(2)(B)] (controlled substances);
- INA §237(a)(2)(C) [8 USC §1227(a)(2)(C)] (firearms offenses);
- INA §237(a)(2)(E) [8 USC §1227(a)(2)(E)] (domestic violence crimes);
- INA §237(a)(4)(A) [8 USC §1227(a)(4)(A)] (security and related grounds).

A pardon will not waive any other grounds. However, there appears to be an inconsistency in the law. Pardons are applicable to aggravated felonies[8] as defined under INA §101(a)(43) [8 USC §1101(a)(43)], which includes persons convicted of illicit trafficking in firearms[9] and illicit trafficking in controlled substances.[10] When a

---

[1] Immigration Act of 1917, §19, 39 Stat. 874.
[2] Pub. L. No. 82-414, 66 Stat. 163.
[3] Pub. L. No. 84-728, 70 Stat. 567.
[4] *See Matter of Lindner*, 15 I&N Dec. 170 (BIA 1975).
[5] INA §237(a)(2)(A)(vi); 8 USC §1227(a)(2)(A)(vi).
[6] *Matter of Suh*, 23 I&N Dec. 626 (BIA 2003).
[7] *Balogun v. U.S. Att'y Gen.*, 425 F.3d 1356, 1362 (11th Cir. 2005).
[8] INA §237(a)(2)(A)(vi); 8 USC §1227(a)(2)(A)(vi).
[9] INA §101(a)(43)(C); 8 USC §1101(a)(43)(C).
[10] INA §101(a)(43)(B); 8 USC §1101(a)(43)(B).

person is convicted of such crimes, receives a pardon, and is placed in removal proceedings based on such convictions, the pardon should under a strict reading of the statute eliminate the convictions for immigration purposes. Therefore, a person who receives a full and unconditional pardon for a drug trafficking crime would not be deportable under INA §237(a)(2)(A)(iv), the aggravated felony deportation ground. However, he or she may be deportable under INA §237(a)(2)(B)(i), the controlled substances deportation ground. In a case illustrative of this issue, the Board of Immigration Appeals (BIA) has held that a pardon that served to eliminate a sexual battery offense as grounds for removal as an aggravated felony did not eliminate deportability under the ground for domestic violence for the exact same offense.[11]

Note: A practitioner who represents a client who has been convicted of an aggravated felony offense and who has received a full and unconditional pardon should consider making a constitutional challenge to the immigration pardon provision if the government charges the client as removable under another ground. Arguments to support such a challenge are explained in the next section.

Pardons can also ameliorate other immigration consequences. For example, President Jimmy Carter granted a pardon in 1977 to persons who resisted the draft during the Vietnam War.[12] The scope of the pardon specifically included noncitizens who would be otherwise excludable under former 8 USC §1182(a)(22) (violation of the Military Selective Service Act). Executive Order No. 11967, which implements the pardon, states as follows:

Any person who is or may be precluded from reentering the United States under 8 USC §1182(a)(22), or under any other law, by reason of having committed or apparently committed any violation of the Military Selective Service Act shall be permitted as any other alien to reenter the United States.[13]

The terms of the Carter pardon also constitute a defense in proceedings based in inadmissibility at time of entry, under former 8 USC §1182(a)(22), for avoiding the draft.[14] The Carter pardon does not apply to deserters.[15]

---

[11] *Matter of Suh*, 23 I&N Dec. 626 (BIA 2003).

[12] Proclamation No. 4483, 42 Fed. Reg. 4391 (1977). The pardon covered the time period between August 4, 1964, and March 28, 1973.

[13] Exec. Order No. 11967, 42 Fed. Reg. 4393 (1977).

[14] *Matter of Rahman*, 16 I&N Dec. 579 (BIA 1978).

[15] *Matter of Muller*, 16 I&N Dec. 637 (BIA 1978).

A noncitizen will not be statutorily precluded from establishing good moral character within the meaning of INA §101(f) [8 USC §1101(f)] if he or she has received a pardon for a conviction.[16]

Under INA §237(a)(2)(A)(vi) [8 USC §1227(a)(2)(A)(vi)], the pardon must be issued by the president of the United States or by the governor of a state. The BIA has interpreted this provision to mean that the pardon, to be valid, must be issued by the supreme authority of the jurisdiction empowered to extend a pardon for a conviction under the law of the locality.[17] This can and does include state boards of pardons and other organizations that have been designated to be the supreme authority in the state to issue pardons.

Only domestic pardons, as made clear in the language of the statute, function to waive certain grounds of removal. Foreign pardons, no matter how clear in their effect abroad, do not act to waive any grounds of removal.[18] A pardon eliminates the immigration consequences of the pardoned offense for future entries.[19]

Full and Unconditional Pardon

In order for a pardon to be effective in curing the relevant grounds of removal, it must be full and unconditional.[20] This means that it must release the person from all legal consequences flowing from the conviction and it must not be dependent on the fulfillment of any condition.[21] Additionally, the pardon must be executively, as distinguished from legislatively, granted.[22] In *Matter of Nolan*,[23] the BIA held that an automatically issued pardon to a first-time felony offender under the constitution of Louisiana was not a full and unconditional pardon for immigration purposes. As noted by the BIA, states at times have two different categories of pardons: those granted by the governor and those awarded automatically to first-time offenders by

---

[16] *Matter of H–*, 7 I&N Dec. 249 (BIA 1956); *see Giambanco v. INS*, 531 F.2d 141 (3rd Cir. 1976) (within JRAD context legacy INS could not use conviction to deny discretionary relief); *Matter of Gonzalez*, 16 I&N Dec. 134 (BIA 1977).

[17] *Matter of Tajar*, 15 I&N Dec. 125 (BIA 1974); *Matter of C–R–*, 8 I&N Dec. 59 (BIA 1958); *Matter of D–*, 7 I&N Dec. 476 (BIA 1957).

[18] *Matter of B–*, 7 I&N Dec. 166, 169 (BIA 1955); *Matter of F–Y–G–*, 4 I&N Dec. 717 (BIA 1952); *Mullen-Cofee v. INS*, 976 F.2d 1375, 1377 (11th Cir. 1992); *Marino v. INS*, 537 F.2d 686, 691 (2d Cir. 1976); *Sohaiby v. Savoretti*, 195 F.2d 139, 140 (5th Cir. 1952); *U.S. ex rel. Consola v. Karnuth*, 108 F.2d 178, 179 (2d Cir. 1939); *Mercer v. Lence*, 96 F.2d 122, 125 (10th Cir. 1938).

[19] *Matter of H*, 6 I&N Dec. 90 (BIA 1954); *see Rasmussen v. Robinson*, 163 F.2d 732 (3d Cir. 1947).

[20] *Matter of Nolan*, 19 I&N Dec. 539 (BIA 1988).

[21] *Matter of Tajar*, 15 I&N Dec. 125 (BIA 1974); *Matter of L–*, 6 I&N Dec. 355 (BIA 1954); *Matter of T–*, 6 I&N Dec. 214 (BIA 1954); *Matter of C–*, 5 I&N Dec. 630 (BIA 1954); *Matter of S–*, 5 I&N Dec. 10 (BIA 1953).

[22] *Matter of Nolan*, 19 I&N Dec. 539 (BIA 1988) (citing *Matter of K–*, 9 I&N Dec. 336 (BIA 1961); *Matter of D–*, 7 I&N Dec. 476 (BIA 1957); *Matter of R–*, 6 I&N Dec. 444 (BIA 1954); and *Matter of R–*, 5 I&N Dec. 612 (BIA 1954)).

[23] *Id.* at 543–44.

operation of law upon the completion of the sentence. Those valid for immigration purposes are those granted by a governor or his or her designee.

When the pardon does not release a noncitizen from all legal consequences of a conviction, the pardon is not considered full and unconditional. Under federal law and the law of many states, a conviction for a felony has consequences that may continue long after a sentence has been served. These consequences, or disabilities, include the loss of the right to vote, the loss of the right to hold state office, and the loss of the right to sit on a jury. Additionally, many felons may have their ability to obtain certain employment or professional licenses restricted. Under federal gun control laws and many state laws, felons also may lose their right to own and use firearms. Restoration of these rights can occur automatically after a certain amount of time has passed, through the occurrence of a specific event such as the completion of a sentence, or through a judicial or executive act such as a pardon.

The laws imposing disabilities for a felony conviction vary among the states, especially those laws relating to restoration of civil rights and rights to possess firearms. For example, in many states, persons convicted of federal felony offenses cannot avail themselves of state procedures to restore their civil rights either because the law only applies to state offenders through a state pardon—which is not available to federal offenders—or because state procedures are generally unavailable to federal offenders.[24] Because of the wide differences in the availability of state remedies to restore rights to federal offenders, the only mechanism in federal law to restore rights, aside from firearms privileges, is through a presidential pardon. Therefore, federal felons residing in states that provide no restoration remedies for federal crimes must obtain a presidential pardon in order to exercise certain political rights, including the right to vote, to hold state office, and to sit on a jury.

The area of state laws relating to firearms disabilities is complicated. There are federal and state regulations concerning loss of the right to bear arms upon conviction of certain offenses and restoration of the right to do so. At the state level, in addition to state statutes and regulations, municipal and county rules also may be in place. There is considerable variation among the states on the definition of the term "firearm privilege."

The controlling case in the federal system relating to firearms disability is *Beecham v. United States*.[25] In that case, the U.S. Supreme Court addressed the issue of whether the firearms disability imposed upon convicted federal felons can be removed by the restoration of rights under state law. The Court said no, holding that federal felons remain subject to the firearms disability under 18 USC §922(g)(1) until their rights are restored by federal procedures. Therefore, the disability continues to apply even if the federal felon's civil rights were restored under a state procedure.

---

[24] For a state-by-state summary of disabilities and applications to remove such, see U.S. Department of Justice, Office of the Pardon Attorney, *Civil Disabilities of Convicted Felons: A State-by-State Survey* (Oct. 1996). Readers are cautioned that this publication is dated and the laws in many states may have been revised. Therefore, the best source is to research current individual state law.

[25] 511 U.S. 368 (1994).

The only means for a federal felon to regain firearms privileges is through a presidential pardon or through the restoration process as provided under 18 USC §925(c) through the Bureau of Alcohol, Tobacco and Firearms (ATF). Since October 1992, however, ATF's annual appropriation has prohibited the use of any funds to investigate or act upon applications for relief from federal firearms disabilities.[26] Therefore, as long as this prohibition remains in place, ATF cannot process applications for restoration.

Constitutionality of the Immigration Pardon Provision

INA §237(a)(2)(A)(vi) [8 USC §1227(a)(2)(A)(vi)] provides as follows:

Clauses (i), (ii), (iii) and (iv) [of INA §237(a)(2)(A)] shall not apply in the case of an alien with respect to a criminal conviction if the alien subsequent to the criminal conviction has been granted a full and unconditional pardon by the President of the United States or by the Governor of any of the several states.

Clauses (i), (ii), (iii) and (iv) are grounds of deportability for crimes of moral turpitude, multiple criminal convictions, aggravated felonies, and violations related to the crime of high-speed flight, respectively. The pardon provision excludes, by omission, the many other crimes that may subject a noncitizen to deportation. There is a question as to whether Congress, through enacting this particular provision, can limit the president's pardon power under the U.S. Constitution. The statute limits the effect of a pardon to those specific crimes endorsed by Congress. It does not to apply to crimes referred to in INA §237(a)(2)(B) [8 USC §1227(a)(2)(B)] (controlled substance offenses), INA §237(a)(2)(C) [8 USC §1227(a)(2)(C)], (certain firearms offenses), INA §237(a)(2)(E) [8 USC §1227(a)(2)(E)] (certain crimes of domestic violence), INA §237(a)(4) [8 USC §1227(a)(4)] (national security and related grounds), or to the criminal-related grounds of inadmissibility. In addressing this limitation, the BIA and some federal courts have upheld the provision, finding that pardons do not defeat removal, for example, for persons convicted of controlled substances offenses.[27]

Assistant Attorney General Walter Dellinger, in charge of the U.S. Department of Justice Office of Legal Counsel (OLC) during the Clinton administration, issued a memorandum in 1995 stating that a presidential pardon removes all punishments, penalties, and disabilities that attach by reason of a federal offense.[28] The memorandum responded to a request for an opinion concerning the following issues: (1) whether a full and unconditional presidential pardon precludes the exercise of the authority to deport a convicted felon; (2) whether a full and unconditional presidential pardon removes a state firearm disability arising as a result of a conviction of a federal crime; and (3) whether a full and unconditional presidential pardon extends to the

---

[26] *See* Pub. L. No. 107-67, 115 Stat. 514 (2001); *see also www.atf.gov/firearms/faq/faq2.htm.*

[27] *Matter of Lindner, supra* note 4; *see Mullen-Cofee v. INS, supra* note 18, at 1377; *U.S. ex rel Vermiglio v. Butterfield,* 223 F.2d 804, 809 (6th Cir. 1955).

[28] Effects of a Presidential Pardon, 19 Op. Off. Leg. Counsel 160 (1995), 1995 WL 861618.

remission of a court-ordered criminal restitution not yet received by the victim of the pardoned offender. The opinion responded in the affirmative to all three queries.

In reaching its conclusions, the opinion notes that its interpretation is supported by English common law, from which the framers of the U.S. Constitution drew their understanding of the scope of the pardon power being granted to the president. The pardoning power of the English monarchy was fairly broad.[29]

In addressing the first question, the opinion found that although the statute only addresses the effect of a pardon with respect to certain limited convictions, congressional legislation cannot define or limit the effect of a presidential pardon.[30] In reaching this conclusion, the opinion cites to the U.S. Supreme Court decision in *Ex Parte Garland*,[31] finding that the pardon power of the president is not subject to legislative control. The Supreme Court summarized the extent of a presidential pardon as follows:

> A pardon reaches both the punishment prescribed for the offence and the guilt of the offender; and when the pardon is full, it releases the punishment and blots out of existence the guilt, so that in the eye of the law the offender is as innocent as if he had never committed the offence. If granted before conviction, it prevents the penalties and disabilities consequent upon conviction from attaching; if granted after conviction, it removes the penalties and disabilities, and restores to him all his civil rights; it makes him, as it were, a new man, and gives him a new credit and capacity.[32]

Congress can neither limit the effect of a presidential pardon nor exclude from its exercise any class of offenders.[33] This broad interpretation of the presidential pardon was affirmed by the U.S. Supreme Court 10 years later in *Knote v. U.S.*, which noted as follows:

> A pardon is an act of grace by which an offender is released from the consequences of his offense, so far as such release is practicable and within control of the pardoning power, or of officers under its direction. It releases the offender from all disabilities imposed by the offense, and restores to him all his civil rights.[34]

The second question in the memorandum asked the Office of Legal Counsel to determine whether a full and unconditional pardon removes firearms disabilities imposed by a state as a result of a conviction for a federal crime. The opinion concluded that a pardon does remove state firearms disabilities based solely on a federal offense.[35] In reaching this conclusion, the opinion noted that the president's power to

---

[29] For more on the British Model, see A. Steiner, "Remission of Guilt or Removal of Punishment? The Effects of a Presidential Pardon," 46 *Emory L. J.* 959 (Spring 1997).

[30] *Id.*

[31] 71 U.S. (4 Wall.) 333, 380 (1866).

[32] *Id.* at 380–81.

[33] *Id.* at 380.

[34] *Knote v. U.S.*, 95 U.S. 149 (1877).

[35] Effects of a Presidential Pardon, *supra* note 28.

pardon extends beyond federal consequences to include consequences imposed by a state, citing to the U.S. Supreme Court decision in *Carlesi v. New York*.[36] In that case, the Court was asked to decide whether the fact that the plaintiff had received a presidential pardon for a federal offense prevented the state from treating him as a "second offender" for purposes of punishment for a subsequent state offense. In its decision, the Court stated the following:

> It may not be questioned that the States are without right directly or indirectly to restrict the National Government in the execution of its legitimate powers. It is therefore to be concluded that if the act of the State in taking into consideration a prior conviction of an offense committed by the same offender against the laws of the United States despite a pardon was in any just sense a punishment for such crime, that the act of the State would be void because destroying or circumscribing the effect of the pardon granted under the Constitution and the laws of the United States.[37]

The Supremacy Clause of the Constitution[38] provides further support for the conclusion that a presidential pardon relieves a federal offender of a state firearms disability by reason of a federal conviction.[39] Article II, section 2 of the Constitution authorizes the president "to grant Reprieves and Pardons for Offenses against the United States, except in Cases of Impeachment." The Pardon Clause gives the President exclusive jurisdiction over pardons for offenses against the United States.[40] The U.S. Supreme Court has repeatedly noted that Congress may not act in such a way as to limit the full legal effect of a presidential pardon. It has held that a presidential pardon eliminates both the conviction and the guilt, placing the offender in the same position as if he or she had not committed the offense in the first place.[41]

> *Note*: Although this discussion has focused on the effect of presidential pardons, practitioners should determine whether similar arguments can be made that gubernatorial pardons deserve the same deference and respect as do presidential pardons. Of course, the effect of a gubernatorial pardon may vary state to state depending on the language of the state constitution and any relevant case law. There are several different types of state pardons. A pardon may be full or partial, absolute or conditional. A pardon is considered to be full when it unconditionally absolves the person from all the legal consequences of a crime and of the person's conviction, similar to a presidential pardon as discussed above. A pardon may be partial when it eliminates only a portion of the pun-

---

[36] 233 U.S. 51 (1914).

[37] *Id.* at 128.

[38] U.S. Const., art. VI, cl. 2.

[39] *Harber v. Deukmejian,* 173 Cal. Rptr. 89 (Cal. Ct. App. 1981) (state firearm disability does not apply to person who received a pardon).

[40] *Schick v. Reed,* 419 U.S. 256, 266–67 (1974).

[41] *Knote v. U.S., supra* note 34; *U.S. v. Klein,* 8 U.S. (13 Wall.) 128, 148 (1871); *Ex Parte Garland,* 71 U.S. (4 Wall.) 333 (1866). For a detailed discussion of federal courts' approach to the scope of federal pardons, see A. Steiner, *supra* note 29.

ishment or absolves only a portion of the legal consequences of a criminal conviction. Many states grant both full and partial pardons.

In *Kwai Chiu Yuen v. INS*,[42] the U.S. Court of Appeals for the Ninth Circuit addressed the effect of a state pardon for a narcotics conviction on the deportability of the petitioner. The petitioner in that case relied heavily on the U.S. Supreme Court's decision in *Ex Parte Garland*,[43] arguing that the gubernatorial pardon was similar to a presidential pardon in effect. According to the petitioner, Congress could not fix punishment beyond the reach of the executive clemency power, or attach consequences beyond the release of executive clemency. The court rejected the argument, simply stating it did not apply in the state context. The court went on to say that even accepting as true the position that a pardon, full and unconditional, federal or state, exempts a person from punishment, it does not therefore exempt him or her from deportation.[44] In reaching this position, the court cited the U.S. Supreme Court's decision in *Mahler v. Eby*,[45] in which it held that although deportation may be burdensome and severe for the alien, it is not punishment.[46]

In another case involving a narcotics-related offense, the U.S. District Court for the Eastern District of New York addressed the issue of whether a state pardon could eliminate the petitioner's aggravated felony narcotics conviction, thereby permitting him to apply for asylum. The court interpreted the plain language of former INA §241(a)(2)(A)(iv) (pardon provision, now INA §237(a)(2)(A)(vi)) to exclude narcotics offenses, and upheld the BIA's decision denying the petitioner's request to stay exclusion proceedings pending the outcome of his application for a pardon.[47] The U.S. Court of Appeals for the Eleventh Circuit also addressed the effect of a pardon on narcotics offenses, reaching the same conclusion, that a pardon does not eliminate the conviction for immigration purposes.[48] Arguments regarding the constitutionality of the pardon provision itself were not raised or discussed in either of the cases.

Constitutional Arguments Before the BIA

Generally, the BIA will not consider or rule on the constitutionality of statutes or regulations that it administers.[49] However, it does consider and rule on issues of due process and fundamental fairness challenges to procedures as applied.[50] Despite the

---

[42] 406 F.2d 499 (9th Cir. 1969).

[43] 71 U.S. (4 Wall.), 333 (1866).

[44] *Kwai Chiu Yuen v. INS*, 406 F.2d 499, 502 (9th Cir. 1969).

[45] 264 U.S. 32 (1924).

[46] *Id.* at 39, as cited in *Kwai Chiu Yuen, supra* note 44.

[47] *Eskite v. District Director*, 901 F. Supp. 530 (E.D.N.Y. 1995).

[48] *Mullen-Cofee v. INS*, 976 F.2d 1375 (11th Cir. 1992).

[49] *Matter of L–S–J–*, 21 I&N Dec. 973; *Matter of U–M–*, 20 I&N Dec. 327 (BIA 1991); *Soberanes v. Comfort*, 388 F.3d 1305, 1310 (10th Cir. 2004); *Liu v. Waters*, 55 F.3d 421, 426 (9th Cir. 1995); *Ravindran v. INS*, 976 F.2d 754 (1st Cir. 1992); *Vargas v. INS*, 831 F.2d 906 (9th Cir. 1987); *Baques-Valles v. INS*, 779 F.2d 483 (9th Cir. 1985).

[50] *Matter of Toro*, 17 I&N Dec. 340 (BIA 1980).

BIA's general practice of not addressing constitutional issues, practitioners should still present constitutional arguments before both the immigration court and the BIA in representing clients with pardons who the government argues are not eligible for relief. Such arguments combined with statutory and regulatory authority may serve to tip a decision in a client's favor.

The BIA has never addressed issues relating to the constitutionality of the pardon provision. It was not part of its analysis in *Matter of Suh*,[51] in which it found that a full and unconditional pardon could only cure those crimes included in INA §237(a)(2)(A)(vi) [8 USC §1227(a)(2)(A)(vi)]. In reaching its decision, the BIA noted that when the plain language of the statute is clear, it will give effect to that language.[52]

In urging the BIA to address the constitutional argument relating to pardons—that Congress does not have the authority to limit the presidential pardon power—practitioners should consider Judge Richard Posner's dicta in *Pasha v. Gonzales*[53]:

> Why agencies refuse to pass on constitutional questions—why indeed they might lack jurisdiction to do so—has never been adequately explained. The Federal Trade Commission thinks the refusal inconsistent with Article VI of the Constitution, which both makes the Constitution, along with federal statutes and treaties, "the supreme Law of the Land" and requires all federal and state officers to take an oath to "support this Constitution." In re Verrazzano Trading Corp., 91 F.T.C. 888, 952-53 (1978). But the "law of the land" provision in the Constitution is intended merely to confirm the supremacy of federal law, and the oath is a pledge of fealty to that supremacy; these are not delegations to every subordinate official to indulge his private interpretations of the Constitution." The BIA is a subordinate unit in the Department of Justice, and the Attorney General may simply want to reserve to himself, or to the courts, any judgment as to the constitutionality of the Board's procedures. See Oestereich v. Selective Service System Local Bd. No. 11, 393 U.S. 233, 242-43 (Harlan, J., concurring).

Although the BIA maintains it has no jurisdiction over constitutional arguments, the separation of powers issue presented here could present a fundamental question about the competing powers of Congress and the president, and the BIA's responsibility to each. Such an issue may be ripe to certify to the attorney general, asking for his or her opinion on the issue.

---

[51] *Matter of Suh*, 23 I&N Dec. 626 (BIA 2003).

[52] *Id.* at 628, citing *Matter of Rojas,* 23 I&N Dec. 117 (BIA 2001).

[53] 433 F.3d 530, 536 (7th Cir. 2005).

CHAPTER 6

OBTAINING A PARDON UNDER FEDERAL LAW

The number of noncitizens convicted of federal crimes and incarcerated in federal facilities has risen dramatically over the past 20 years. Between 1984 and 1994, the number of noncitizens serving a federal sentence increased an average of 15 percent annually—from 4,088 to 18,929.[1] According to a press release from the Department of Justice (DOJ), the number of noncitizens detained in federal facilities for federal convictions as of June 30, 2004, was 91,789.[2] As the number of detained noncitizens has risen, so has the number of noncitizens removed based on criminal convictions. In 1984, only 1,000 noncitizens were deported based on criminal grounds. In 2005, the Department of Homeland Security removed 89,406 noncitizens because of prior criminal convictions.[3] Given that many noncitizens with criminal convictions face removal with little likelihood of relief, a pardon may be the only avenue available for them to pursue.

No one has a right to a presidential pardon.[4] A person seeking a pardon has no due process rights in the process.[5] Decisions to grant clemency are rarely subject to judicial review.[6] In order for a petition for executive clemency to be subject to judicial review, there must be a procedural or fundamental constitutional right that creates a protected interest in clemency.[7] The rights giving rise to a claim that may be subject to judicial review must be based on the statutes or rules defining the scope of the clemency power and the obligations of the office responsible for exercising that power.[8]

Pardon power is vested exclusively with the president. The Constitution of the United States grants the president this power in the following terms:

> The President shall have the power to grant reprieves and pardons for offenses against the United States, except in cases of impeachment.[9]

---

[1] Department of Justice, Bureau of Justice Statistics, "Noncitizens in the Federal Criminal Justice System, 1984–94" (Aug. 1996), available at *www.ojp.usdoj.gov/bjs/abstract/nifcjs.htm*.

[2] Department of Justice, Bureau of Justice Statistics, "Nation's Prison and Jail Population Grew by 932 Per Week, Number of Female Inmates Reached More Than 100,000" (Apr. 24, 2005), available at *www.ojp.usdoj.gov/newsroom/2005/pjim04pr.htm*.

[3] Department of Homeland Security, Office of Immigration Statistics, *2005 Yearbook of Immigration Statistics* (2006), Table 41.

[4] *In re Hansard,* 123 F.3d 922 (6th Cir. 1997).

[5] *Brinion v. U.S. Dep't of Justice,* 695 F.2d 1189 (9th Cir. 1983).

[6] *Connecticut Bd. of Pardons v. Dumschat,* 452 U.S. 458, 464 (1981).

[7] *Id.*

[8] *Id.* at 465.

[9] U.S. Const., art. I, §2.

There have been attempts by members of Congress to limit the president's power. For example, shortly after President Gerald Ford's controversial pardon of Richard Nixon in 1974, Senator Walter Mondale (D-MN) proposed the following amendment to the Constitution:

> No pardon granted an individual by the President under section 2 of Article II shall be effective if Congress by resolution, two-thirds of the members of each House concurring therein, disapproves the granting of the pardon within 180 days of issuance.[10]

Other amendments also have been proposed, including limiting pardons to convicted persons only[11] and providing victims of crimes of violence the right to notice of and an opportunity to submit a statement concerning proposed pardons.[12] However, none of the proposals has been successful.

As noted in chapter 5, the U.S. Supreme Court has consistently interpreted the president's pardon powers in broad terms.[13] Once a pardon is granted, it cannot be reversed. However, Congress can hold hearings to investigate the president's use of the pardon power, as was done in the case of President William Jefferson Clinton's 1999 commutation of the sentences of 16 FALN Puerto Rican nationalists.[14] Testimony provided during those hearings cautioned Congress against taking action to limit the president's power, noting that a few questionable pardons granted in the history of the United States does not warrant changing a system that generally works.[15]

A presidential pardon serves as an official statement of forgiveness for the commission of a federal crime and serves to restore basic civil rights.[16] A pardon does not result in expungement of a criminal record. In *U.S. v. Noonan*,[17] the U.S. Court of Appeals for the Third Circuit addressed this issue of first impression. In that case, the petitioner had been convicted and sentenced to three years' imprisonment in 1969 for failure to submit for induction to serve in the Vietnam War, a violation of the Mili-

---

[10] Statement of Professor Ken Gormley Before the Senate Judiciary Committee Concerning Possible Constitutional Amendments to the President's Pardon Power (Feb. 14, 2001).

[11] H.J. Res. 18, 101st Cong. (Jan. 3, 1989).

[12] U.S. Senate Republican Policy Committee, Legislative Notice, No. 54 (Apr. 17, 2000), available at *http://senate.gov/~rpc/releases/1999/L54jd041700.htm*.

[13] *U.S. v. Wilson*, 32 U.S. 150, 160 (1833); *Ex Parte Garland*, 71 U.S. (4 Wall.), 333, 380–81 (1866); *U.S. v. Klein*, 8 U.S. (13 Wall.) 128, 148 (1871); *Knote v. United States*, 95 U.S. 149 (1877); *Ex Parte Grossman*, 267 U.S. 87, 120 (1925).

[14] News Release, Judiciary Committee, Statement of Senator Orrin G. Hatch, Senate Committee on the Judiciary, Oversight Hearing of the Department of Justice and Clemency Process (Oct. 20, 1999).

[15] Statement of Professor Ken Gormley, *supra* note 10; Statement of Margaret Colgate Love, Hearing on Presidential Pardons, Senate Judiciary Committee (Feb. 14, 2001).

[16] *See* Testimony of Roger C. Adams, Pardon Attorney, Before the Committee on the Judiciary, United States Senate (Feb. 14, 2001).

[17] 906 F.2d 952 (3d Cir. 1990).

tary Selective Service Act.[18] The petitioner was a beneficiary of a pardon issued on January 21, 1977, by President Jimmy Carter, pardoning draft resisters. In 1988, the petitioner moved to expunge the record of his conviction based on the pardon. The court held that while expungement may be justified when an arrest or conviction was constitutionally infirm, there was no precedent for expungement being granted on the basis of a pardon. According to the court, a pardon did not "blot out guilt" or restore the offender to a state of innocence in the eyes of the law.[19]

Historical Background and Statistics

Since the creation of the republic, presidents have regularly exercised their pardon power. George Washington, who issued only 16 pardons during his tenure, granted a pardon in 1795 to the leaders of the Whiskey Rebellion in Pennsylvania. President Thomas Jefferson pardoned deserters from the Continental Army. He also pardoned a number of his own political supporters who had been convicted of treason for publishing anti-Federalist political materials. Presidents James Madison and Andrew Jackson pardoned pirates. During the Civil War, President Abraham Lincoln pardoned many Confederate sympathizers in return for oaths of loyalty. After the Civil War ended, President Andrew Johnson pardoned thousands of Confederates in order to heal a divided country. It is worth noting that despite congressional challenge to Johnson's acts, the pardons remained viable.[20]

During the 20th century, presidents granted pardons in even greater numbers— more than 13,000.[21] The president who granted the most pardons was Franklin D. Roosevelt (3,687).[22] Two presidents—James Garfield and Benjamin Harrison— granted no pardons.[23] President George H. Bush granted 77 pardons.[24] It is thought that his son, President George W. Bush, is likely to grant only a small number as well by the end of his second term in 2008.[25] During his tenure as governor of Texas, Bush granted fewer pardons than any Texas governor since the 1940s. His predecessors, Ann Richards, Bill Clements, and John Conally, granted 70, 822, and 1,048 pardons respectively.[26] During the first three years of his administration, Bush granted

---

[18] Act of June 24, 1948, ch. 625, 62 Stat. 604, designated the Military Selective Service Act by Pub. L. No. 92-129, tit. I, §101(a)(1), 85 Stat. 348 (1971).

[19] *Id.* at 958.

[20] Statement of Professor Ken Gormley *supra* note 10.

[21] *See* http://jurist.law.pitt.edu/pardons5a.htm.

[22] *See id.*

[23] *See id.*

[24] *See* the website of the Department of Justice, Office of the Pardon Attorney, *www.usdoj.gov/pardon*, for clemency statistics. The Office of the Pardon Attorney provides general statistics on presidential clemency actions. However, there are no comprehensive, public historical records of presidential grants of clemency, with names, offenses, date of grant, etc. *See* Prof. P. S. Ruckman, Jr., "Keys to Clemency Reform: Knowledge, Transparency" (Mar. 7, 2001), at *http://jurist.law.pitt.edu/pardonop5.htm*. Nor do the statistics that are publicly available contain information on the requester's immigration status.

[25] *See* http://jurist.law.pitt.edu/pardons0a.htm.

[26] *See id.*

11 pardons and no commutations.[27] During this same time period, he denied 580 requests for pardons and 2,400 requests for commutations.[28]

Administration	Petitions Pending	Petitions Received	Granted	Denied or No Action Taken
Richard M. Nixon	4,350	1,699	863	1,650
Gerald E. Ford	894	978	382	435
Jimmy Carter	2,129	1,581	534	1,057
Ronald Reagan	3,970	2,099	393	1,581
George H.W. Bush	1,854	731	74	896
William J. Clinton	4,546	2,001	396	1,008

Processing Federal Pardons

Role of the Office of the Pardon Attorney

In 1898, President William McKinley promulgated regulations directing all petitioners seeking presidential clemency to submit their petitions to the attorney general, and provided information on how the applications would be processed. These regulations have been reissued over the years but have remained remarkably similar to the original ones.[29] The Office of the Pardon Attorney, with a 12-person staff within the DOJ, is responsible for advising and assisting the president in executing his clemency powers under article II, section 2, of the Constitution.[30] Clemency can take the form of a pardon, a commutation of sentence, a remission of fine or restitution, or a reprieve.

The Office of the Pardon Attorney, under the direction of the deputy attorney general, receives and reviews all clemency petitions, initiates and supervises any necessary investigations, and prepares a report and recommendation for the president's consideration. It also acts as a liaison with the public while petitions are pending, responding to correspondence and inquiries.[31] The Office of the Pardon Attorney operates under regulations and standards that govern its procedures in processing petitions for clemency, including pardons.[32]

> *Note*: The regulations governing procedures before the Office of the Pardon Attorney do not bind the president. He or she retains the authority under the Constitution to consider a pardon request from a person who may be ineligible

---

[27] American Bar Association, Justice Kennedy Commission, Reports with Recommendations to the ABA House of Delegates, at 72, n.17 (Aug. 2004).

[28] *Id.*

[29] Statement of Margaret Colgate Love, *supra* note 15.

[30] 28 CFR §§0.35, 0.36. For additional information on the Office of the Pardon Attorney, visit its website at *www.usdoj.gov/pardon*.

[31] United States Attorney's Manual, Standards for Consideration of Clemency Petitions, §1-2.110.

[32] 28 CFR §1.1 *et seq.*; United States Attorney's Manual, *supra* note 31.

to apply under the regulations or who has not applied at all, and to grant a pardon if he or she believes it is appropriate.[33]

When the Office of the Pardon Attorney receives a pardon petition, the petition is screened to determine that the petitioner is in fact eligible to seek a pardon. For example, the petitioner's crime must be a federal offense, and he or she must satisfy the five-year waiting period. The office will also determine if any additional information is needed from the petitioner on the application. If the petitioner is ineligible to apply under the regulations, he or she will be informed. If the application is incomplete, the office will notify the petitioner that additional information is needed.[34]

Role of the U.S. Attorney

The Office of the Pardon Attorney will only ask for the views of the U.S. attorney whose office prosecuted the case in certain situations, including cases in which the application appears to have some merit, cases in which it needs more information about the underlying criminal case or the pardon applicant, and cases involving a particularly well-known applicant or offense if the grant or denial of the pardon is likely to receive significant public attention.[35]

How much weight the opinion of the U.S. attorney will be given depends on many factors, including how well-reasoned the view is and the specific facts of the case.[36] The recommendations of the U.S. attorney will be included in the report given to the president. Generally, the correctness of the underlying conviction is assumed and, therefore, the question of guilt or innocence is not an issue. However, when a petitioner refuses to accept guilt or raises a claim of innocence, the U.S. attorney will be asked by the Office of the Pardon Attorney to address these issues.[37] The U.S. attorney will also be asked to comment—if he or she is aware—on the petitioner's post-conviction behavior.[38] The Office of Pardon Attorney also may request the U.S. attorney to seek the views and recommendation of the sentencing judge.[39]

The U.S. attorney can support, oppose, or take no position on the request for a pardon.[40] The U.S. attorney opinion is one factor considered among many by the Office of the Pardon Attorney in addressing the request. The office will generally request a response from the U.S. attorney within 30 days, unless additional time is required.[41]

---

[33] *See* Testimony of Roger C. Adams, *supra* note 16.

[34] *See id.*

[35] E-mail correspondence between the author and the Office of the Pardon Attorney, October 15, 2007.

[36] *Id.*

[37] United States Attorney's Manual, *supra* note 31, at §1-2.111.

[38] *Id.*

[39] *Id.*

[40] *Id.*

[41] *Id.*

Standards for the Consideration of Pardon Petitions

In general, a pardon may be granted after the petitioner has demonstrated good conduct for a significant period of time after the conviction and service of sentence. The regulations require a petitioner to wait five years after completion of sentence before seeking a pardon.[42] The following factors are taken into account when considering a pardon:

- postconviction conduct, character, and reputation;
- seriousness and relative recentness of the offense;
- acceptance of responsibility, remorse, and atonement;
- need for relief; and,
- official recommendations and reports.[43]

A petitioner's ability to lead a responsible and productive life for a substantial period of time after conviction and release supports a finding of rehabilitation and indicates that the pardon may be meritorious. The background investigation, which is generally done by the Federal Bureau of Investigation (FBI), looks into the petitioner's financial and employment stability, family obligations, ties to the community, participation in community service or other activities and, where relevant, military service. The circumstances of each petitioner are considered in their totality.[44]

When an offense is very serious, for example, a crime of violence, major drug trafficking charge, breach of public trust, or white-collar fraud involving large sums of money, a petitioner should wait an appropriate amount of time in order to avoid minimizing the seriousness of the offense or undermining the deterrent effect of the conviction. In cases of a well-known person or notorious crime, the effect on law enforcement interests and the general public should be taken into consideration. The impact on the victim may also be relevant. When an offense is very old and relatively minor, the equities may weigh in favor of a positive recommendation for a pardon, assuming the petitioner satisfies the other factors.[45]

The extent to which a petitioner has accepted responsibility for his or her own criminal conduct and made restitution to the victims are important factors in determining whether to recommend a pardon. Petitioners who seek a pardon based on innocence or a miscarriage of justice bear a heavy burden of persuasion.[46]

The purpose for which a pardon is sought may influence the final decision on the petition. For example, when a person demonstrates a specific employment-based need for a pardon, such as licensure or bonding, it may provide a strong basis for a

---

[42] 28 CFR §1.2.

[43] United States Attorney's Manual, *supra* note 31, at §1-2.112.

[44] *Id.*

[45] *Id.*

[46] *Id.*

pardon assuming the petitioner is otherwise suitable for consideration.[47] In the immigration context, this may be a particularly easy factor to establish. The petitioner can argue that the pardon is needed in order to avoid long-term exile and separation from family and community in the United States, which is often the case for those individuals convicted of aggravated felonies.

Finally, the opinions and recommendations of officials involved in the case, especially the U.S. attorney who prosecuted the case and the sentencing judge, will be carefully considered in making the final report and recommendation to the president.[48]

Petition Procedures and Requirements

A person seeking a pardon is required to wait until five years after the date of release from confinement, or, if no prison time was imposed, until five years after the date of the conviction.[49] Generally, a person who is on probation, parole, or supervised release should not submit a petition.[50]

A petition for a pardon can only relate to violations of laws of the United States.[51] Petitions relating to violations of the laws of possessions of the United States or territories subject to the jurisdiction of the United States should be submitted to the appropriate official or agency in the concerned territory or possession.[52]

A person seeking a pardon is required to complete a form, Petition for Pardon After Completion of Sentence.[53] This form asks for biographical information of the applicant, employment history of the applicant, any substance abuse or mental health problems experienced by the applicant, civil and financial information, any military record, offenses for which the pardon is sought, any prior or subsequent criminal record, information on restoration of civil rights and occupational licensing, charitable and community activities, and the applicant's reasons for seeking the pardon. The pardon petition must be completed and sent along with supporting documentation to:

Office of the Pardon Attorney
U.S. Department of Justice
1425 New York Ave., N.W.
Suite 11000
Washington, D.C. 20530

Once a petition is filed with the Office of the Pardon Attorney, an investigation will be initiated.[54] As an initial matter, the Office of the Pardon Attorney will contact

---

[47] *Id.*

[48] *Id.*

[49] 28 CFR §1.2.

[50] *Id.*

[51] 28 CFR §1.4.

[52] *Id.*

[53] This form is reproduced in Appendix D. It is available on the Office of the Pardon Attorney website at *www.usdoj.gov/pardon/pardon_petition.htm.*

[54] 28 CFR §1.6(a).

the U.S. Probation Office for the federal district in which the petitioner was prosecuted and request copies of the presentence report and judgment of conviction, as well as information relating to the petitioner's compliance with court supervision.[55] It also will request the Probation Office's opinion on the pardon request.[56]

Generally, the FBI carries out the investigation, but it will not make a recommendation regarding a pardon request. Instead, it gathers factual information about the petitioner, including criminal history, records relating to the offense forming the basis of the request, employment and residency history, and the petitioner's reputation in the community. The FBI will then prepare a report and submit it to the Office of the Pardon Attorney. If the report suggests that a pardon is meritorious, or in cases of particular importance or when factual questions arise, the Office of the Pardon Attorney contacts the U.S. attorney and the sentencing judge to seek their views concerning the merits of the request. If the case warrants input from other government agencies, such as the Internal Revenue Service or the Department of Homeland Security, the Office of the Pardon Attorney also will make that contact.[57]

The regulations provide that when a crime involved a victim, the Office of the Pardon Attorney may contact the victim. Contact with victims is governed by 28 CFR §1.6(b)(2), which provides that in deciding whether to contact a victim, the office should consider the seriousness and recency of the offense, the nature and extent of the harm to the victim, the defendant's overall criminal history and history of violent behavior, and the likelihood that clemency could be recommended in the case. In practice, the Office of the Pardon Attorney does not contact a victim unless it believes that the request for a pardon has some merit. In addition, in a large number of cases, there are no victims to contact. Common examples include the majority of drug offenses and most regulatory offenses, in which the victim is society at large rather than an individual victim.[58]

When a petition for pardon is granted, the petitioner will be notified and the warrant of pardon will be mailed.[59] Where a petition is denied, the Office of the Pardon Attorney will notify the petitioner of the decision and close the case.[60] When the office makes a recommendation to the president that a pardon should be denied, if the president does not disagree or take other action relating to the adverse recommendation within 30 days, it will be assumed that the president concurs in the recommendation and the case will be closed.[61]

---

[55] *See* Testimony of Roger C. Adams, *supra* note 16.

[56] *See id.*

[57] *See id.*

[58] E-mail correspondence between the author the Office of the Pardon Attorney, October 15, 2007.

[59] 28 CFR §1.7.

[60] 28 CFR §1.8(a).

[61] 28 CFR §1.8(b).

Preparing the Pardon Application

As indicated above, in order to request a pardon, the petitioner must complete the Petition for Pardon After Completion of Sentence form. In addition to the application, the petitioner also should submit supporting documentation addressing the equities of the request and providing detailed information to the Office of the Pardon Attorney in order to facilitate processing. The list below follows the order of information requested in the petition for pardon and offers suggestions for supporting materials to attach.

- *Offenses for which the pardon is sought*: This section of the application requests detailed information on the conviction, including the date of conviction, dates of service of sentence, appeal information, and a complete and detailed statement of the offense for which your client is seeking a pardon. If possible, include a copy of the judgment of conviction with the application. If an appeal was taken, you also should attach a copy of the final decision (if unpublished) or the citation to the published decision. When responding to the question asking for a detailed account of the offense, the information you provide should not just mirror that contained in the indictment or presentence report. Your client should explain in his or her own words what happened. Make sure your client does not minimize his or her culpability for the offense. Your client should include a strong statement accepting responsibility for the offense and expressing remorse.

- *Prior and subsequent criminal record*: Your client must provide information for any other offenses for which he or she has been arrested, taken into custody, held for investigation or questioning, charged by any law enforcement authority, or convicted in any court, either as a juvenile or adult. In responding to this question, your client must provide detailed information for each incident, including the date, the nature of any charges, the facts surrounding the incident (in the client's own words), the law enforcement authority involved, the location, and the final disposition of the matter. It is important that your client explain the facts for each incident. This request to provide criminal information may raise Fifth Amendment concerns. If there are serious concerns that by applying for a pardon and submitting this information you may be exposing your client to additional prosecution, you should consider not applying.

- *Biographical information*: This section requests information on marital status, whether your client has children, and information relating to your client's education. Make sure to attach, where relevant, a marriage certificate and birth certificates for your client's children. If your client pays child support, make sure to include a copy of the court order and proof that your client complies with his or her obligations. If your client has failed to pay, make sure to explain why and to include information on any payment plan agreed to by your client and his or her ex-spouse. If your client has completed a General Educational Development (GED) program, or participated in college classes, include the GED certificate and a copy of his or her school registration. Where your client has completed educational training programs, make sure to include documents proving such. If your client has obtained any college degrees, make sure to include a copy of them as well.

- *Residences*: This section asks for a complete history of all the places where your client has lived since the conviction or release from imprisonment. If there is an issue about your client's place of residence during any period of time, you should include a copy of the rental agreement or mortgage document.

- *Employment history*: This section of the application requests information on all periods of employment and unemployment since the date of conviction or release from imprisonment. In support of your answer to this question, you should consider obtaining a job letter from each employer that confirms the dates of employment and includes a statement on your client's performance while employed and the employer's support for the pardon petition.

- *Substance abuse and mental health history*: This section asks for information relating to whether your client has abused drugs, been involved in the sale or manufacture of drugs, has participated in rehabilitation or counseling for drug or alcohol abuse, or has ever consulted with a mental health professional concerning a mental-health condition.

- *Civil and financial information*: This part of the application requests information on delinquent payments, loans, liens, whether the applicant has been involved in civil litigation, and whether he or she has filed for bankruptcy.

- *Military record*: This section requests the applicant to provide information on any service in the U.S. military.

- *Civil rights and occupational licensing*: This section requests information on the restoration of civil rights, whether the applicant has requested restoration, and whether the applicant has ever been licensed in an occupation and had that license revoked.

- *Charitable and community activities*: This section asks the applicant to describe in detail any charitable and community activities in which the applicant has been involved since conviction. It asks for the names and contact information of persons familiar with the applicant's involvement in the activities. You should consider obtaining letters confirming these activities and include them in the application packet.

- *Reasons for seeking the pardon*: This section asks the applicant to state why he or she is applying for a pardon. Remember, it is important that the applicant indicate remorse for his or her past actions.

In addition to the information above, you should submit supporting affidavits from family, friends, community members, employers, church members, pastors, and other individuals who support the pardon application. There is no limit on the number of affidavits that an applicant may submit. However, the Office of the Pardon Attorney does ask that the applicant designate three affidavits as primary affidavits.[62]

---

[62] E-mail correspondence between the author and the Office of the Pardon Attorney, October 15, 2007.

The pardon application asks for detailed, personal information on a wide variety of issues. All material relating to a pardon application is treated with a high degree of confidentiality and is shared with only a few people in the DOJ and in the White House Counsel's Office.[63] DOJ's recommendation and other key documents in a pardon file are not available to members of the public. Even years later, when some documents might become publicly available, DOJ is aware that persons who may still be alive have significant privacy interests in matters pertaining to mental health and substance abuse and will not release the documents to the public.[64]

---

[63] *Id.*
[64] *Id.*

CHAPTER 7

PROSECUTORIAL DISCRETION

The Department of Homeland Security (DHS) can exercise prosecutorial discretion on a wide range of enforcement activities, including deciding not to initiate proceedings against your client. It also has the discretion to defer a noncitizen's removal from the United States. These are alternatives that you should consider in representing a client with a particularly compelling case.

Deferred Action

Background

Deferred action is an exercise of prosecutorial discretion that defers the removal of a noncitizen, thereby making the case a low priority for the government.[1] Procedures relating to deferred action have to a great extent been shrouded in secrecy. Prior to 1975, the legacy Immigration and Naturalization Service's (INS) Operations Instructions (OI) governing deferred action were not publicly available. Only after litigation under the Freedom of Information Act was instituted by attorney Leon Wildes on behalf of John Lennon, seeking access to information on the program, did legacy INS finally decide to release them to the public.[2] The original OI provided as follows:

> In every case where the district director determines that adverse action would be unconscionable because of the existence of appealing humanitarian factors, he shall recommend consideration for nonpriority.[3]

Whether the OI conferred a substantive benefit or right on a noncitizen to seek deferred action was addressed by federal circuit courts of appeals, with differing results. The U.S. Court of Appeals for the Ninth Circuit found that the OI conferred a substantive benefit upon a noncitizen.[4] In reaching this decision, the Ninth Circuit was guided by the position taken by the U.S. Court of Appeals for the Eighth Circuit, which held that the granting of deferred action was more than just an act of administrative convenience.[5] The U.S. Court of Appeals for the Fifth Circuit reached the opposite conclusion, finding that the decision to grant nonpriority status was within the

---

[1] U.S. Immigration and Customs Enforcement, Office of Detention and Removal Operations, *Detention and Deportation Officer's Field Manual*, ch. 20.8 (2005).

[2] *Lennon v. INS*, 527 F.2d 187 (2d Cir. 1975); *see* L. Wildes, "The Deferred Action Program of the Bureau of Citizenship and Immigration Services: A Possible Remedy for Impossible Immigration Cases," 41 *San Diego L. Rev.* 819 (2004); L. Wildes, "United States Immigration Service v. John Lennon, The Cultural Lag," 40 *Brook L. Rev.* 279 (1973).

[3] INS Operations Instruction (OI) 103.1(a)(1)(ii) (as amended 1975).

[4] *Nicholas v. INS*, 590 F.2d 802, 807 (9th Cir. 1979).

[5] *See Vergel v. INS*, 536 F.2d 755 (8th Cir. 1976); *David v. INS*, 548 F.2d 219 (8th Cir. 1977).

discretion of the INS and that it was not required to notify the noncitizen that such status was applicable in her case.[6] The U.S. Supreme Court finally addressed the issue, finding that deferred action is a purely administrative act and not subject to review.[7]

In 1975, the decision-making process governing deferred action cases was changed. Legacy INS headquarters was no longer directly involved in considering and deciding cases. Instead, the decision was taken by a district director and reviewed by the regional commissioner. This decision-making process remains intact under current policy.

In 1981, the Operations Instructions for nonpriority status—deferred action—were revised. The new OI provided as follows:

> A Service director may, in his or her discretion, recommend deferral of action, an act of administrative choice to give some cases lower priority and in no way an entitlement, in appropriate cases.[8]

According to informal U.S. Citizenship and Immigration Services (USCIS) estimates, the great majority of cases in which deferred action is granted involve medical grounds.[9] USCIS has designated certain categories of noncitizens eligible for deferred action. For example, prior to the issuance of regulations governing procedures for adjudication of "U" visa requests,[10] potential beneficiaries who could establish that they suffered substantial physical or mental abuse as a result of having been a victim of a crime or similar activity involving rape, torture, trafficking, incest, or domestic violence were eligible to receive deferred-action status.[11] USCIS also has granted deferred action to foreign academic students affected by Hurricane Katrina.[12]

USCIS does not publish any statistics on the number of deferred action requests, grants, and denials. It also does not review deferred action grants or denials among the regions. Concerned with the lack of information and transparency, the CIS Ombudsman in his 2007 report recommended that USCIS do the following: (1) post general information on deferred action on its website; (2) maintain statistics on the issuance and denial of deferred action requests; and (3) designate a headquarters official

---

[6] *Soon Bok Yoon v. INS*, 538 F.2d 1211 (5th Cir. 1976); *see Pasquini v. Morris,* 700 F.2d 658 (11th Cir. 1983) (OI conferred no substantive right on noncitizen).

[7] *Reno v. American-Arab Anti-Discrimination Committee,* 525 U.S. 471 (1999); *see Matter of Bhata*, 22 I&N Dec. 1381 (BIA 2000) (BIA has no authority to review prosecutorial discretion).

[8] OI 242.1(a)(22) (removed June 24, 1997).

[9] *See* "USCIS Ombudsman Outlines FY 2007 Priorities and Makes Recommendations Regarding Deferred Action and Advance Notice of Policy Changes," 84 *Interpreter Releases* 1047 (May 7, 2007).

[10] *See* 72 Fed. Reg. 53014 (Sept. 17, 2007).

[11] *See* USCIS Interoffice Memorandum, W. Yates, "Assessment of Deferred Action in Requests for Interim Relief from U Nonimmigrant Status Eligible Aliens in Proceedings" (May 6, 2004), *published on* AILA InfoNet (*posted* Apr. 19, 2007); USCIS Memorandum, W. Yates, "Centralization of Interim Relief for U Nonimmigrant Status Applicants" (Oct. 8, 2003), *published on* AILA InfoNet at Doc. No. 03101420 (*posted* Oct. 14, 2003).

[12] *See* www.uscis.gov/files/pressrelease/F1Student_11_25_05_FAQ.pdf.

to review grants and denials of requests on a quarterly basis to ensure consistency of decision-making nationwide.[13]

Current Procedures

Although OI 242.1(a)(22), which established procedures for deferred action cases, was withdrawn in 1997, the relief remains available.[14] Deferred action is an administrative function of the Department of Homeland Security (DHS) and cannot be granted by an immigration judge.[15] There is no formal application for deferred action. Requests for deferred action should be made to the district director with jurisdiction over your client. The factors that a district director may consider in making a decision on whether to grant deferred action include the following:

- The likelihood of ultimately removing the noncitizen;
- The likelihood that because of sympathetic factors a large amount of adverse publicity will be generated;
- The noncitizen's continued presence is desired by law enforcement for an on-going investigation or review;
- Whether the noncitizen is a member of a class of deportable noncitizens whose removal has been given high enforcement priority, such as terrorists or drug traffickers.[16]

If the district director decides that a recommendation should be made, he or she will refer the case to the appropriate regional director for review. There is no appeal of a refusal to grant deferred action.[17]

Deferred action does not confer any immigration status on a noncitizen. A case can be considered for deferred action at any stage of the administrative immigration process. Where a noncitizen's case is approved for deferred action, no action will be taken to remove him or her from the United States. Deferred action, however, does not prevent DHS from initiating removal proceedings at any time. A grant of deferred action acts as an informal stay of removal that has no effect on deportability.[18] The period of time during which deferred action is in effect is considered to be a stay authorized by the attorney general for purposes of the three– and ten-year bars to ad-

---

[13] *See* CIS Ombudsman, *Annual Report 2007*, at 88.

[14] *See* INS Memorandum, D. Meissner, "Exercising Prosecutorial Discretion" (Nov. 17, 2000), at n.1, *published on* AILA InfoNet at Doc. No. 00112702 (*posted* Nov. 27, 2000), *reprinted in* 77 *Interpreter Releases* 1661 (Dec. 4, 2000), citing to legacy INS's *Standard Operating Procedures for Enforcement Officers: Arrest, Detention, Processing, and Removal*, pt. X.

[15] *Johnson v. INS*, 962 F.2d 574, 579 (7th Cir. 1992); *Velasco-Gutierrez v. Crossland*, 732 F.2d 792 (10th Cir. 1984) (regional commissioner [director] possesses discretion in deferred action determinations); *Matter of Medina*, 19 I&N Dec. 734 (BIA 1988).

[16] *See* "USCIS Ombudsman Outlines FY 2007 Priorities and Makes Recommendations Regarding Deferred Action and Advance Notice of Policy Changes," *supra* note 9.

[17] *Reno v. American-Arab Anti-Discrimination Committee*, *supra* note 7.

[18] *Siverts v. Craig*, 602 F. Supp. 50, 53 (D. Haw. 1985).

mission under INA §§212(a)(9)(B)(i)(I) and (II) [8 USC §§1182(a)(9)(B)(i)(I), (II)] for unlawful presence.[19] Persons granted deferred status may apply for employment authorization under 8 CFR §274a.12(c)(14).

Prosecutorial Discretion

Prosecutorial discretion refers to the authority of an agency charged with enforcing the law to decide whether to enforce the law against a particular person. Prosecutorial discretion does not apply to acts of approval, or grants of immigration benefits under statutes, regulations, or other laws that establish requirements for how approval should be given.[20] It cannot be used in contravention of the law. For example, the government cannot consent to an aggravated felon receiving cancellation of removal or to the admission of an inadmissible alien unless they qualify for a waiver.

Decisions on whether to exercise discretion must be made on a case-by-case basis. There are many stages in the immigration process in which discretion can be used, including when the government decides who will be the focus of an investigation; who will be stopped, questioned, arrested; whether the person will be detained; whether a Notice to Appear (NTA) will be issued and filed with the immigration court; whether to oppose relief sought by a respondent in court; whether to dismiss a proceeding; whether to grant deferred action or agree to a stay of removal; whether to agree to voluntary departure; whether to pursue an appeal; and, finally, whether to execute a final order of removal. Prosecutorial discretion applies in civil and administrative law as well as criminal law.[21]

As stated above, prosecutorial discretion applies to enforcement decisions, not to decisions on applications for immigration benefits. For example, a decision to issue an NTA against a noncitizen is subject to prosecutorial discretion. However, approval of an immigration benefit, such as naturalization or adjustment of status, is not subject to prosecutorial discretion.[22]

Legacy INS Memoranda

In 1999 and in 2000, legacy INS issued two memoranda addressing prosecutorial discretion. The first memo, issued by legacy INS General Counsel Bo Cooper, addressed questions on the nature of prosecutorial discretion, the reasons why enforcement agencies have prosecutorial discretion, the breadth of prosecutorial discretion,

---

[19] *See* INS Memorandum, J. Williams, "Unlawful Presence" (June 12, 2002), *published on* AILA InfoNet at Doc. No. 02062040 (*posted* June 20, 2002).

[20] INS Memorandum, *supra* note 14.

[21] *See Heckler v. Chaney,* 470 U.S. 821, 831 (1985); *see also Reno v. American-Arab Anti-Discrimination Committee, supra* note 7 (Court recognized that prosecutorial discretion applies to immigration enforcement activities).

[22] INS Memorandum, B. Cooper, "INS Exercise of Prosecutorial Discretion" (1999), *published on* AILA InfoNet at Doc. No. 00071171 (*posted* July 11, 2000).

CHAPTER 7 • PROSECUTORIAL DISCRETION

the limitations on the exercise of prosecutorial discretion, legacy INS exercise of discretion, and a discussion of how prosecutorial discretion relates to detention.[23]

In November 2000, legacy INS Commissioner Doris Meissner issued a second memorandum, which discusses legal and policy background relating to prosecutorial discretion, the principles of prosecutorial discretion, investigations and discretion, initiating and pursuing proceedings, and the process for deciding whether to exercise discretion.[24] U.S. Immigration and Customs Enforcement (ICE) has advised its officers to use the Meissner memorandum to guide them in their exercise of prosecutorial discretion in appropriate cases.[25] In discussing factors to take into account in deciding whether to exercise prosecutorial discretion in a case, the memorandum advises that the following should be considered:

- **Immigration status**: Lawful permanent residents generally warrant greater consideration. However, other noncitizens also may warrant favorable exercise of discretion, depending on the facts of the case.

- **Length of residence in the United States**: The longer a noncitizen has lived in the United States, the more inclined ICE will be to exercise discretion in the noncitizen's favor.

- **Criminal history**: The nature and severity of any criminal conduct as well as the time that has passed since the crime occurred must be considered. The sentence or fine imposed should be taken into account when making a finding regarding the seriousness of the offense. Additionally, the immigration officer should consider the age of the noncitizen at the time of the offense and whether he or she is a repeat offender.

- **Humanitarian concerns**: Such concerns include, but are not limited to, family ties in the United States, medical conditions affecting the noncitizen or his or her family, whether the noncitizen entered the United States at a young age, ties to the home country, extreme youth or advanced age, and home country conditions. For example, nursing mothers should be not be detained absent any statutory requirement or national security concern.[26]

- **Immigration history**: Noncitizens without a history of violating immigration laws deserve favorable consideration to a greater extent than those with such a history. The seriousness of the violations should be taken into account.

- **Likelihood of removing the noncitizen**: Whether the removal proceeding and final issuance of a removal order will likely result in the noncitizen's removal is a factor to consider.

---

[23] *Id.*

[24] INS Memorandum, *supra* note 14.

[25] ICE Memorandum, J. Myers, "Prosecutorial and Custody Discretion" (Nov. 7, 2007), *published on* AILA InfoNet at Doc. No. 07111263 (*posted* Nov. 12, 2007).

[26] *Id.*

- **Likelihood of achieving a law enforcement goal by other means**: Can the noncitizen's removal be effectuated by other quicker and more efficient means, such as voluntary departure or withdrawal of application for admission?
- **Whether the noncitizen is eligible or likely to be eligible for other relief**: It is relevant to consider whether there is an avenue for the noncitizen to legalize his or her status if not removed from the United States. However, the fact that the government cannot grant permanent relief should not mean favorable discretion should be withheld if warranted by other factors.
- **Effect of action on future admissibility**: The effect that removal may have on a noncitizen may vary—for example, time-limited as opposed to an indefinite bar to future admissibility—and may be considered.
- **Current or past cooperation with law enforcement authorities**: Current or past cooperation with law enforcement authorities weighs in favor of discretion.
- **Honorable U.S. military service**: Military service with an honorable discharge is considered a favorable factor.
- **Community attention**: Opinions in favor of or in opposition to the noncitizen's removal can be considered.
- **Resources available to DHS**: The resources available to the government to take enforcement action in a particular case, compared with the use of resources for other national or regional priorities, are appropriate to consider in determining whether to exercise discretion.

Not all of these factors will apply in all cases. In some cases, certain factors may deserve more weight than other factors. There also may be additional factors to consider that are not included in the list above. Each case must be decided on its own merits.

ICE Discretion—Detention and Removal Operations (DRO) Officers and Office of Investigations (OI) Officers

ICE officers have responsibility for the enforcement of immigration laws in the interior of the United States. They plan and conduct investigations of persons who may be subject to the criminal and administrative provisions of the Immigration and Nationality Act of 1952.[27] They are responsible for identifying noncitizens who may be removable from the United States. According to its strategic plan, ICE focuses its enforcement efforts on noncitizens who pose a threat to national security and public safety (criminal aliens), as well as on those who have not complied with removal orders. In carrying out its enforcement functions, ICE works through its attorneys in the chief counsels' offices across the country in processing removal of noncitizens.

During its enforcement of the immigration laws, ICE officers and attorneys must make a number of decisions about the arrest, detention, and disposition of a case. Depending on the circumstances, ICE officers can exercise discretion on who to stop,

---

[27] Pub. L. No. 82-414, 66 Stat. 163.

question, and arrest; how to initiate removal proceedings; whether to grant voluntary departure; and whether to detain a noncitizen pending a final decision.

ICE can exercise discretion at different stages of the process, including the initial contact with the noncitizen; apprehension; the charging phase; detention; removal proceedings; and the final removal of the noncitizen. Most discretion is exercised in the initial phases of the apprehension and removal process.[28] The primary goal of ICE officers is to initiate removal proceedings against any noncitizen they encounter who is subject to the grounds of removal. However, they are unable to do so for every noncitizen they encounter. The availability of detention space, the travel time to a noncitizen's location, and competing enforcement priorities affect their decision to initiate removal proceedings.[29]

The officers' ability to exercise discretion is limited in cases involving noncitizens who are targets of investigations, such as criminal noncitizens or fugitive noncitizens who have ignored final removal orders. However, officers do have discretion to process and apprehend noncitizens who are not the targets of investigations or who present humanitarian circumstances.[30] In such cases, they can exercise discretion by deciding to: (1) arrest the noncitizen and transport him or her to an ICE facility for processing; (2) issue an NTA by mail; or (3) schedule an appointment for the noncitizen to be processed at an ICE facility at a later date. For example, ICE officers often encounter friends or relatives of a target who are removable during an investigation. In such cases, if the person's case presents humanitarian concerns, ICE can decide not to arrest the person and choose to process at a later time. This may be appropriate in the case of a primary caregiver for small children.[31] ICE has issued guidelines advising its officers to release nursing mothers absent any statutory detention requirement or concerns relating to national security.[32] During the charging phase, most of ICE discretion appears to be related to the decision on whether to grant voluntary departure. Offices near the U.S. southwestern border issue a relatively high number of voluntary departure grants—equal or greater than the number of NTAs issued—than the rest of the country.[33] Once proceedings have been initiated, it may become more difficult to exercise discretion.

ICE Discretion—Chief Counsel's Offices

The ICE Office of the Principal Legal Advisor's Offices of Chief Counsel—the attorneys who are tasked with working with ICE officers in processing the removal of noncitizens—have authority to exercise prosecutorial discretion prior to the issuance

---

[28] Government Accountability Office Report to Congressional Requesters, *Immigration Enforcement: ICE Could Improve Controls to Help Guide Alien Removal Decision Making* (GAO-08-67, Oct. 2007).

[29] *Id.*

[30] *Id.*

[31] *Id.*

[32] ICE Memorandum, *supra* note 25.

[33] GAO Report, *supra* note 28, at 14.

of or in lieu of the NTA, after issuance and filing of an NTA, and after the issuance of a final removal order.

Prosecutorial Discretion Prior to or in Lieu of Issuance of NTA

Assistant chief counsel are advised to discourage the issuance of NTAs when there are other options available, such as administrative removal, crewman removal, or expedited removal. They also should discourage the issuance of an NTA in cases in which a person is eligible for a benefit that can be obtained outside of removal proceedings, or when the desired result is something other than a final order of removal.[34] Examples of such cases include the following:

Immediate relative of a military service person: An assistant chief counsel should consider not issuing an NTA when the noncitizen is an immediate relative of a military service member. Counsel are encouraged to analyze possible eligibility for citizenship under INA §328 [8 USC §1439] and INA §329 [8 USC §1440].[35]

Approvable I-130 Petition/I-485 Application for Adjustment of Status: When a noncitizen is the potential beneficiary of a clearly approvable I-130 petition and I-485 application for adjustment of status and there are no serious negative factors that would otherwise justify removal, permitting the noncitizen to process his or her status through the USCIS-adjudicated adjustment of status process is considered a cost-effective option as compared with proceeding in immigration court.[36]

Administrative Voluntary Departure: When a noncitizen is eligible for voluntary departure and is likely to depart, an assistant chief counsel should facilitate the grant of administrative voluntary departure or departure under safeguards.[37]

Failure to register under NSEERS: A noncitizen subject to the National Security Entry-Exit Registration System (NSEERS) who failed to timely register but is otherwise in status and has no criminal record should not be placed in removal proceedings if he or she has a reasonable excuse for failure to register. Reasonable excuses can include the noncitizen's hospitalization, his or her admission into a nursing home or extended care facility, or not being aware of the registration requirements.[38]

---

[34] ICE Memorandum, W. Howard, "Prosecutorial Discretion" (Oct. 24, 2005), *published on* AILA InfoNet at Doc. No. 06050511 (*posted* May 5, 2006).

[35] ICE Memorandum, M. Forman, "Issuance of Notices to Appeal, Administrative Orders of Removal, or Reinstatement of a Final Removal Order on Aliens with United States Military Service" (June 21, 2004), *published on* AILA InfoNet at Doc. No. 06051664 (*posted* May 16, 2006).

[36] ICE Memorandum, W. Howard, "Exercising Prosecutorial Discretion to Dismiss Adjustment Cases" (Oct. 6, 2005), *published on* AILA InfoNet at Doc. No. 05101360 (*posted* Oct. 13, 2005).

[37] ICE Memorandum, *supra* note 34.

[38] ICE Memorandum, V. Cerda, "Changes to the National Security Entry Exit Registration System (NSEERS)" (Jan. 8, 2004), *published on* AILA InfoNet at Doc. No. 06050512 (*posted* May 5, 2006).

NSEERS registrants: Prosecutorial discretion may be considered if an NSEERS registrant has a pending request or application for an immigration benefit, appears to be prima facie eligible for the benefit, and there is no adverse or disqualifying information in the case.[39]

Sympathetic humanitarian factors: Deferred action should be considered in compelling cases involving sympathetic humanitarian factors. Examples include cases in which the noncitizen has a U.S. citizen child with a serious medical condition or disability or cases in which the noncitizen or a close family member is undergoing treatment for a potentially life-threatening sickness.[40]

Prosecutorial Discretion After Issuance and Filing of NTA

Assistant chief counsel also have authority to exercise prosecutorial discretion after the issuance and filing of an NTA with the immigration court. There may be circumstances in the case that call for termination and dismissal of proceedings.[41] Additionally, counsel can resolve the case in immigration court by not opposing the requested relief, waiving appeal, making agreements to narrow the issues, or stipulating to the admission of certain evidence. There may be cases in which prosecutorial discretion should be considered for purposes of judicial economy or efficiency of process, or to promote the interests of justice. Examples of such cases include:

When relief is available: An assistant chief counsel should consider dismissing proceedings without prejudice when it appears that adjustment of status seems clearly approvable based on an I-130 or I-140 visa petition that appears appropriate for approval by USCIS.[42] Additionally, counsel should consider remanding a case to permit a noncitizen to pursue naturalization when he or she appears eligible.[43]

Humanitarian factors: Where a case presents compelling humanitarian factors as described above, an assistant chief counsel should consider exercising prosecutorial discretion to dismiss proceedings.[44]

Law enforcement assets and confidential informants: Federal, state, or local law enforcement often wish to have noncitizens remain in the United States for a period of time in order to help in an investigation or to testify at trial. A dismissal of the case, a grant of deferred action, a stay of removal, or administrative closure may be appropriate remedies to consider under these circumstances.[45]

---

[39] INS Memorandum, J. Williams, "Supplemental NSEERS Guidance for Call-In Registrants" (Jan. 8, 2003), *published on* AILA InfoNet at Doc. No. 03050141 (*posted* May 1, 2003).

[40] ICE Memorandum, *supra* note 34.

[41] 8 CFR §§239.2(c), 1239.2(c).

[42] ICE Memorandum, *supra* note 36.

[43] ICE Memorandum, *supra* note 34.

[44] *Id.*

[45] *Id.*

Prosecutorial Discretion After Hearing

After the close of the hearing and final decision of the immigration judge, assistant chief counsel have wide discretion to pursue different options. These include whether to file an appeal, what issues to appeal, how to respond to the respondent's appeal, and whether to seek a stay of decision or join in a motion to reopen. When the respondent's appeal brief is persuasive, the assistant chief counsel may consider joining that position and asking the Board of Immigration Appeals (BIA) to remand the case to the immigration judge, or to withdraw the government appeal and allow the immigration judge's decision to be final.

> **Joint untimely motions to reopen**: An assistant chief counsel should seriously consider exercising prosecutorial discretion and join in an untimely motion to reopen when the respondent would be eligible for adjustment of status or cancellation of removal except for the fact that the motion was filed beyond the 90-day limit under 8 CFR §1003.23 and when there are no serious criminal or immigration violations.[46]
>
> **Federal court remands to the BIA**: When pending federal court litigation presents weaknesses or pitfalls or when there are unusually sympathetic facts in a case and the BIA has authority to provide a remedy, appellate counsel should consider remanding the case to the BIA.[47]
>
> **In absentia orders**: Assistant chief counsel are encouraged to be flexible with cases when a noncitizen arrives late to court and faces an in absentia order. In such cases, counsel should consider requesting that the court either hold or reschedule the hearing for later in the day if the court is in session.[48]

After Issuance of Final Order—Motions to Reopen or Reconsider

Assistant chief counsel retain discretion after the issuance of a final order as well. For example, when a noncitizen has been deprived of an opportunity to obtain relief because of ineffective assistance of counsel, it is appropriate for counsel to join in or to not oppose a motion to reopen or motion to reconsider. When federal, state, or local law enforcement need a noncitizen as a witness, counsel should recommend that a stay of removal be granted and that the noncitizen be released under supervision.[49]

Conclusion

Prior to seeking deferred action or prosecutorial discretion, practitioners should speak with AILA members in the jurisdiction where a client's case is pending or where proceedings may be initiated. The memoranda mentioned in this chapter obviously pro-

---

[46] *Id.*; INS Memorandum, B. Cooper, "Motions to Reopen for Consideration of Adjustment of Status" (May 17, 2001), *reprinted in* 78 Interpreter Releases 1166 (July 16, 2001).

[47] *See* ICE Memorandum, *supra* note 34.

[48] *Id.*

[49] *Id.*

vide guidance to ICE officers and attorneys. However, it is helpful to know the local practices and the likelihood of success in your district before preparing the case.

In preparing your case for deferred action or the favorable exercise of prosecutorial discretion, make sure you have all the facts necessary to respond to ICE concerns or inquiries on the case. If your client's case is particularly compelling, you may want to contact a member of Congress to ask for his or her support. Additionally, you should consider creating an effective media strategy to publicize the case. However, you should make sure that media attention will not have an adverse effect on your client.

TABLE OF APPENDICES

Appendix A • Senate Rules of Procedure for Introducing
a Private Relief Bill (Immigration) 99

Appendix B • House Rules of Procedure for Private Immigration Bills 101

Appendix C • INS Operations Instructions on Private Bills............................109

Appendix D • Petition for Pardon After Completion of Sentence...................117

Appendix E • State Pardon Information 141

Appendix F • Private Immigration and Nationality Bills Introduced
and Laws Enacted, 77th Through 109th Congress 165

Appendix G • 9 FAM Appendix I..167

Bibliography 175

Appendix A

Subcommittee on Immigration, Border Security, and Citizenship

Rules of Procedure for Introducing a Private Relief Bill (Immigration)

(*as reprinted in* S. Prt. 108-58, U.S. Senate Comm. On the Judiciary, Legislative and Executive Calendar (Final Edition)), 108th Cong. (2005)

1. The introduction of a private bill does not act as a stay of deportation until the committee requests a departmental report. Requests for reports on private bills from the departments shall be made only upon written request addressed to the chairman of the subcommittee by the author of such bill. That request shall contain the following information:

   (a) In the case of an alien who is physically in the United States: The date and place of the alien's last entry into the United States; his or her immigration status at that time (visitor, student, exchange student, crewman, stowaway, illegal border crosser, etc.); his or her age; place of birth; address in the United States; and the location of the U.S. Consulate at which he or she obtained a visa, if any.

   (b) In the case of an alien who is physically outside of the United States: The alien's age; place of birth; address; and the location of the U.S. Consulate before which his or her application for a visa is pending; and the address of the relationship to the person primarily interested in the alien's admission into the United States.

   (c) In the case of an alien who is seeking expeditious naturalization: The date the alien was admitted to the United States for permanent residence; his or her age; and address in the United States.

2. The committee shall not address to the Attorney General communications designed to defer deportation of beneficiaries of private bills who have entered the United States as nonimmigrants, stowaways, in transit, deserting crewmen, or by surreptitiously entering without inspection through the land or sea borders of the United States.

   Exemption from this rule may be granted by the subcommittee if the bill is designed to prevent unusual hardship to the beneficiary or to U.S. citizens. However, no such exemption may be granted unless the author of the bill has secured and filed with the subcommittee full and complete documentary evidence in support of his or her request to waive the rule.

3. No private bill shall be considered if an adequate judicial or administrative remedy exists, or where court proceedings are pending for the purpose of adjusting or changing the immigration status of the beneficiary.
4. No favorable consideration shall be given to any private bill until the proper department has submitted a report.
5. Upon receipt of reports from the departments, private bills shall be scheduled for subcommittee consideration in the chronological order of their introduction, except that priority shall be given to bills introduced earliest in any previous Congresses.
6. Bills previously tabled shall not be reconsidered unless new evidence is introduced showing a material change of the facts known to the committee. In the event of a request for reconsideration the subcommittee shall, insofar as practicable, dispose of such request at the first meeting of the subcommittee following receipt of such request.

Material to Be Submitted by the Author

Supporting information shall be limited to three or four typewritten pages and must include an in-depth statement by the author setting forth the equities in the case and why an adequate judicial or administrative remedy is not available. Background material and other pertinent information, including character references, etc., are acceptable.

When a private immigration bill is recommended for favorable action, the supporting information is used for the Senate report and must be typewritten to be cut and pasted for printing. Therefore, do not send originals that you want returned. An important document, such as an original birth certificate, should be retained by the author—a copy will be sufficient for the subcommittee.

APPENDIX B

U.S. HOUSE OF REPRESENTATIVES

COMMITTEE ON THE JUDICIARY

SUBCOMMITTEE ON IMMIGRATION, CITIZENSHIP, REFUGEES, BORDER SECURITY, AND INTERNATIONAL LAW

ONE HUNDRED TENTH CONGRESS

RULES OF PROCEDURE AND STATEMENT OF POLICY FOR PRIVATE IMMIGRATION BILLS

COMMITTEE ON THE JUDICIARY

JOHN CONYERS, JR., Michigan, *Chairman*

HOWARD L. BERMAN, California
RICK BOUCHER, Virginia
JERROLD NADLER, New York
ROBERT C. SCOTT, Virginia
MELVIN L. WATT, North Carolina
ZOE LOFGREN, California
SHEILA JACKSON LEE, Texas
MAXINE WATERS, California
MARTIN T. MEEHAN,
  Massachusetts
WILLIAM D. DELAHUNT,
  Massachusetts
ROBERT WEXLER, Florida
LINDA T. SÁNCHEZ, California
STEVE COHEN, Tennessee
HANK JOHNSON, Georgia
LUIS V. GUTIERREZ, Illinois
BRAD SHERMAN, California
TAMMY BALDWIN, Wisconsin
ANTHONY D. WEINER, New York
ADAM B. SCHIFF, California
ARTUR DAVIS, Alabama
DEBBIE WASSERMAN SCHULTZ,
  Florida
KEITH ELLISON, Minnesota

LAMAR SMITH, Texas
F. JAMES SENSENBRENNER, JR.,
  Wisconsin
HOWARD COBLE, North Carolina
ELTON GALLEGLY, California
BOB GOODLATTE, Virginia
STEVE CHABOT, Ohio
DANIEL E. LUNGREN, California
CHRIS CANNON, Utah
RIC KELLER, Florida
DARRELL ISSA, California
MIKE PENCE, Indiana
J. RANDY FORBES, Virginia
STEVE KING, Iowa
TOM FEENEY, Florida
TRENT FRANKS, Arizona
LOUIE GOHMERT, Texas
JIM JORDAN, Ohio

PERRY APELBAUM, *Staff Director-Chief Counsel*
JOSEPH GIBSON, *Minority Chief Counsel*

SUBCOMMITTEE ON IMMIGRATION, CITIZENSHIP, REFUGEES, BORDER SECURITY, AND INTERNATIONAL LAW

ZOE LOFGREN, California, *Chairwoman*

LUIS V. GUTIERREZ, Illinois
HOWARD L. BERMAN, California
SHEILA JACKSON LEE, Texas
MAXINE WATERS, California
MARTIN T. MEEHAN,
  Massachusetts
WILLIAM D. DELAHUNT,
  Massachusetts
LINDA T. SÁNCHEZ, California
ARTUR DAVIS, Alabama
KEITH ELLISON, Minnesota

STEVE KING, Iowa
ELTON GALLEGLY, California
BOB GOODLATTE, Virginia
DANIEL E. LUNGREN, California
J. RANDY FORBES, Virginia
LOUIE GOHMERT, Texas

UR JADDOU, *Chief Counsel*
GEORGE FISHMAN, *Minority Counsel*

(II)

RULES OF PROCEDURE

1. All requests for consideration of a private immigration bill shall commence with a letter to the Chairman of the Subcommittee from the author of such bill outlining the relevant facts in the case and attaching thereto all pertinent documents. Documentation will not be accepted if submitted by anyone other than the author of the bill. The following must be submitted in triplicate:

(a) Date and place of birth of each beneficiary; addresses and telephone numbers of each beneficiary presently in the United States.

(b) Dates of all entries (legal and illegal) and departures from the United States, along with the type of visas used for admission; consulate where each beneficiary obtained a visa for entry to the United States; consulate where each beneficiary will be seeking a visa if one is made available.

(c) Status of all petitions and proceedings with the Department of Homeland Security, including nonimmigrant or immigrant petitions that have been filed by the beneficiaries or on their behalf.

(d) Names, addresses, and telephone numbers of interested parties in the United States.

(e) Names, addresses, dates and places of birth, and immigration or citizenship status of all close relatives.

(f) Occupations, recent employment records, and salaries of all beneficiaries.

(g) Copies of all immigration related letters to and from agencies of the United States.

(h) Copies of all administrative and judicial decisions involving the beneficiaries' case.

(i) A signed statement by each beneficiary, or the beneficiary's guardian, that he or she desires the relief sought by the bill.

(j) An explanation as to how the failure to obtain the relief sought in the private bill will result in extreme hardship to the beneficiary or each beneficiary's U.S. citizen spouse, parent or child.

(k) A signed statement by the author of the bill confirming that the author has met personally with the beneficiary or with members of the beneficiary's family

(l) In support of any private bill relating to adoption, the following additional information must accompany the request for Subcommittee action.

(1) Home-study of the prospective parents;

(2) Evidence of child support; and

(3) Statement detailing ages and occupations of natural parents and brothers and sisters.

(m) In support of a private bill on behalf of a doctor or nurse, the following additional information must accompany the request for Subcommittee action:

(1) Evidence of passage of the Federal Licensing Examination, or its equivalent, for doctors, and the Commission on Graduates of Foreign Nursing School Exam (CGFNS) for nurses.

(2) Evidence of employment by the doctor or the nurse in a health manpower shortage area, or a recommendation by a U.S. Government Agency indicating the doctor or nurse's services are needed.

(3) Evidence of substantial community ties over a long period of time. Extensive periods of employment give the Subcommittee some assurance there is every likelihood the doctor or nurse would remain employed in the area and provide medical services.

(4) Documentation as to a potential employer's efforts to recruit U.S. citizens for the position. Such information shall include salary levels of other doctors or nurses on staff and an explanation as to recruitment techniques on employment of the beneficiary.

(n) In support of a private bill waiving grounds of exclusion or deportation relating to criminal activity, the following addition documents, if available, will be required.

(1) All records relating to offenses, including state, and local police records; and

(2) An affidavit from the beneficiary describing his or her criminal record in full.

(o) Private bills concerning beneficiaries who are receiving medical treatment will require documentation as to the availability of similar medical treatment in the beneficiary's home country.

2. Each private bill must provide that the beneficiaries must apply for the benefits of the enacted law within a specified period of time, which shall be not

more than two years from the date of enactment of the private law.

3. No private bill shall be scheduled for Subcommittee action until all administrative and judicial remedies are exhausted.

4. The Subcommittee will not intervene in deportation proceedings and will not request stays of deportation on behalf of beneficiaries of private bills, except as indicated in Rule 5.

5. The Subcommittee may, at a formal meeting, entertain a motion to request that the Department of Homeland Security provide the Subcommittee with a departmental report on a beneficiary of a private bill. In the past, the Department of Homeland Security has honored requests for departmental reports by staying deportation until final action is taken on the private bill. Only those cases designed to prevent extreme hardship to the beneficiary or a U.S. citizen spouse, parent, or child will merit a request for a report.

6. The Subcommittee may request reports on private bills from appropriate Federal agencies or Departments and shall await receipt of such reports before taking final action.

7. Only the author of a private bill shall be permitted to testify before the Subcommittee on behalf of the private bill. All requests to testify shall be addressed in writing to the Chairman of the Subcommittee.

8. Action on a private bill shall not be deferred more than once due to the failure of the author to appear and testify at a duly noticed hearing.

9. The Subcommittee shall take no further action on a private bill that has been tabled by the full Judiciary Committee.

10. Each of the following types of private bills shall be subject to a point of order unless its consideration is agreed to by a two-thirds vote of the Subcommittee:

    (a) Bills not in compliance with these Rules.
    (b) Bills that waive the two-year foreign residence requirement for doctors.
    (c) Bills that waive any law regarding naturalization.

STATEMENT OF POLICY

In considering private immigration bills, the Subcommittee reviews only those cases that are of such an extraordinary nature that an exception to the law is needed. It is the policy of the Subcommittee generally to act favorably on only those private bills that meet certain precedents.

Members intending to introduce a private immigration bill are strongly encouraged to seek the technical drafting assistance of the Subcommittee staff (or the Office of Legislative Counsel) prior to introducing a private immigration bill. This will facilitate consideration of the bill by avoiding the need for Subcommittee amendments.

The following sets forth common types of private immigration bills and the criteria for reviewing them.

A. Adoption

Existing law provides for the immigration of foreign born adopted children if the adoption takes place while the child is under the age of 16 and (1) the child is an "orphan" as defined by immigration law, or (2) the child has resided with the adoptive parents two years. Favorable precedents exist if the child is young and there has been a longstanding parent-child relationship.

B. Doctors and Nurses

The Immigration and Nationality Act provides for the admission of foreign doctors and nurses who have passed certain exams prior to seeking immigrant status.

In past years, a number of private bills were introduced on behalf of foreign medical graduates. The legislative history relating to this group indicates many doctors enter the United States as nonimmigrants with the intention of remaining permanently. Legislation enacted in 1976 and 1977 sought to tighten the law requiring the return of such doctors to their home country.

The Subcommittee is dismayed to find that doctors who are beneficiaries of private laws often seek more lucrative employment upon gaining permanent residence, thereby leaving medically underserved areas without any medical assistance. Because of these experiences, the Subcommittee views doctor bills unsympathetically.

C. Drugs and Criminal Activity

In the case of a beneficiary who has been convicted of a deportable crime the Subcommittee will wish to review testimony and affidavits relating to the beneficiary's behavior subsequent to any criminal conviction. Such information is helpful in making a determination as to whether legislation will serve the best interests of the community. In this regard, letters of reference, bank records, and employment records are particularly helpful.

D. Medical Cases

The Subcommittee will be reluctant to schedule bills on behalf of persons who entered the United States for the purpose of seeking medical treatment. This type of admission is available to accommodate persons seeking advanced medical treatment in the United States. Many cases have come to the attention of the Subcommittee in which persons obtained admission to the United States for medical reasons and decided to try to stay here permanently. This undermines the intent of the original admission and jeopardizes continuance of the program.

The Subcommittee's reluctance to schedule such bills is based on the premise that persons may seek all available medical assistance while in the United States, but upon completion of any medical treatment the purpose of the visa expires and the alien must return home.

It is therefore the policy of the Subcommittee that advisory opinions be sought by the author from such organizations as the World Health Organization and the Pan American Health Organization as to the availability of adequate medical treatment in the alien's home country.

E. Deferred Action and Parole Cases

The Subcommittee will be reluctant to schedule any bill on behalf of an alien who is in "deferred" status or has been paroled into the United States indefinitely. It is the Subcommittee's understanding that the Department of Homeland Security reserves the conferral of such status to cases of a particularly compelling nature. In view of this, the Subcommittee will view such cases unsympathetically.

F. Waiver of Exclusions

1. HEALTH

All bills waiving the grounds of exclusion for mental or physical infirmities will require the posting of a bond. There are few favorable precedents for cases in this category. In order to obtain the best possible information, the Subcommittee will require all medical records as well as information from government agencies concerning possible public charge aspects of the case.

2. DRAFT EVADERS

There are few precedents for favorable action on behalf of aliens who seek permanent residency to avoid conscription. It will be the Subcommittee's policy to continue to view such bills unsympathetically.

3. FRAUD

The Subcommittee has been extremely reluctant to act favorably on cases involving visa fraud. It will be the policy of the subcommittee to adhere closely to precedents in such cases.

G. Naturalization

The Subcommittee will require that any bill expediting naturalization be accompanied by evidence indicating that such action would be in the national interest, as opposed to personal interest. There are few precedents for favorable action on bills waiving any naturalization requirements or granting posthumous or honorary citizenship. It is the Subcommittee's intent generally to view unfavorably legislation of this type. More appropriate mechanisms for rewarding individuals may be in the form of medals, awards, or ceremonies.

The Subcommittee is extremely concerned by requests to expedite citizenship on behalf of athletes seeking to compete in national, international, or Olympic games. The Subcommittee does not believe U.S. citizenship should be provided because of a person's athletic ability.

There are few instances of favorable action on behalf of individuals who renounce U.S. citizenship. The Subcommittee will adhere to precedents in such cases.

H. Bills Tabled in a Previous Congress

The Subcommittee has often been confronted with request for reconsideration of private bills that were tabled by the full Committee in previous Congresses. The Subcommittee believes that each bill is given sufficient review during the meetings of the Subcommittee and that authors are afforded ample time to present the merits of the case. Repetitious consideration of these cases detrimentally affects other private bills and reflects poorly on the integrity of the private bill process. For these reasons, the Subcommittee will be reluctant to reconsider its prior action absent new evidence or information not available at the time of initial consideration by the Subcommittee.

Appendix C

Immigration and Naturalization Service Operations Instructions on Private Bills

107.1. PRIVATE BILLS.

(a) General
A Service employee shall neither recommend the introduction of, nor draft, remedial private immigration or nationality legislation.

(b) Stay of deportation or voluntary departure pending introduction.
A stay of deportation or voluntary departure shall not be authorized solely to permit the introduction of a private bill or in anticipation of receiving a congressional committee request for a report on such a bill.

(c) When report requested by congressional committee.
Upon receipt of a request from the House or Senate Judiciary Committee for a report on a private bill relating to an immigration or nationality matter, a teletype message will be sent to the appropriate district office by the Private Bill Control Unit, Central Office. A copy of this message and the bill will be mailed to the appropriate district investigations branch. If the beneficiary appears to be an alien in the United States, a stay of deportation will generally be authorized.

If a private immigration bill received adverse action at any time and subsequently a new bill was introduced for the same purpose in the House or Senate, a request for a report from the Committee in which the new bill is pending will not be honored by the Service unless the adverse action on the earlier bill is reconsidered. A letter to this effect will be sent to the Committee, with a copy to the appropriate district office. If action to reconsider is taken, the usual teletype message will be sent concerning the new bill, indicating therein that the previous adverse action was reconsidered. When a field office finds in any case that adverse action had been taken on a private bill, and a teletype message concerning a new bill is received without mentioning reconsideration of the adversed bill, the Private Bill Control Unit should be contacted.

(d) When report not requested by congressional committee.
If a private immigration bill has been introduced for an alien who appears to be in the United States in other than a lawful immigrant status, but a request for a report from the House or Senate Judiciary Committee is not received within a reasonable period of time by the Private Bill Control Unit, the appropriate district office will be notified and furnished a copy of the bill; in such a case, an investigative report for Congress shall not be prepared nor should deportation be stayed because of the bill's introduction.

(e) Effect of introduction.
The introduction of a private bill seeking to adjust the status of an alien nonimmigrant in the United States to that of a lawful permanent resident shall be regarded as prima facie evidence of termination of his lawful nonimmigrant status, if not otherwise previously terminated. Deportation proceedings already commenced shall be carried forward to a final determination. If deportation proceedings have not already been instituted and the beneficiary was in lawful status as a B, C, D, or H nonimmigrant when the private bill was introduced, and either Judiciary Committee has requested a report on the bill, Form I-177, in duplicate, shall be sent to him by registered mail with return receipt requested or handed to him personally, if convenient; should the beneficiary fail, within thirty days from the date the form is received, to depart or to advise the Service that he does not desire to have his status adjusted through private legislation, an order to show cause shall be issued and deportation proceedings carried forward to a final determination. If the beneficiary advises the Service that he does not desire to have his status adjusted through private legislation, the regular investigation and private bill report shall not be prepared; instead, a report to the appropriate committee in letter form for the Commissioner's signature shall be forwarded immediately to the Private Bill Control Unit setting forth the details and reasons for the beneficiary's action. If a report on the bill is not requested, Form I-177A, in duplicate, shall be sent to him by registered mail with return receipt requested or handed to him personally, if convenient, and no report prepared.

If the beneficiary was maintaining status under section 101(a)(15)(A) or (G), or as a treaty trader under the Immigration Act, of 1924, as amended, when the private bill was introduced, the alien may be considered to have voluntary departure for the period the alien remains in that status; in such a case Form I-177 shall not be sent to the alien. If deportation proceedings have not already been instituted, but the beneficiary had terminated status as a lawful nonimmigrant when the private bill was introduced, an order to show cause shall be issued and deportation proceedings carried forward to a final determination upon the expiration of any outstanding voluntary departure time.

If the beneficiary was maintaining status under section 101(a)(15)(E), (F), (I), (J), or (M), Form I-177 shall not be sent to the alien and deportation proceedings shall not be instituted. Any such alien's application for extension of stay shall be denied unless the alien overcomes the presumption of termination of status raised by the bill's introduction. However, voluntary departure shall be granted in increments of one year, conditioned upon the alien's otherwise completely maintaining nonimmigrant status or upon abiding by the terms and conditions of the alien's exchange program. Generally, an exchange alien shall not be granted voluntary departure beyond the limits set forth in 22 CFR 63.23; also, see OI 242.10(b). Should the beneficiary fail to apply for additional voluntary departure time before the expiration of the last extension, the alien shall be interviewed, and, providing the alien is otherwise maintaining status, shall be granted voluntary departure under similar conditions. Other aliens of these classes who have already been placed under deportation proceedings solely because of the bill's introduction shall be granted extensions of voluntary departure or stays of deportation under like conditions.

Deportation proceedings shall not be instituted or reactivated in any case involving appealing humanitarian factors (see OI 103.1(a)(1)(ii)).

(f) Action by field office.

(1) Investigations Branch.
The mail copy of the teletype message shall be forwarded without index or file check directly to the Investigations Branch. If the Investigations Branch receives this copy of the teletype message before it receives the original, that branch will commence its action on the basis of that copy. When the Investigations Branch ascertains that the investigations "control office" function in relation to the private bill investigation is to be performed by any office other than the office to which the teletype message was addressed, the latter office shall transfer that function and send a copy of its teletype message or Form G-166 report to the Private Bill Control Unit. The private bill report shall be prepared and forwarded in accordance with outstanding investigations instructions.

In any private bill case involving citizenship or naturalization matters, the case is to be submitted to the Citizenship Section for determination as to whether the bill would accomplish the purpose for which it is intended. Suggestions for any changes it appears desirable to make in the bill in order to accomplish its intended purpose, where necessary, are to be included in the transmittal letter of the private bill report.

When a private bill which was introduced in successive Congresses for the same purpose is again reintroduced in the present one and a full report was made to the same branch of any preceding Congress, additional material information obtained from review of the file, new national agency checks, or interview of the beneficiary shall be furnished in a supplemental letter. If additional material information is not developed, a memorandum to that effect shall be addressed directly to the Private Bill Control Unit, stating the date of each of the new agency-check responses. When the previous full report was made to a different branch or to a previous Congress and thereafter the bill was not reintroduced in any succeeding Congress until the present one (i.e., a bill introduced in the 89th Congress or earlier was first reintroduced in the 91st), a new, complete report shall be submitted.

If a reintroduced bill is for a different purpose than one in the preceding Congress, a new, complete report shall be submitted.

(2) Deportation Branch.

(i) Initial departure date.
When a report has been requested by a congressional committee and a stay has been authorized by the Central Office, the date set for deportation or voluntary departure under a final order shall be February 1 of the next odd-numbered year. Thus, a bill introduced in the First or Second Session of a Congress would be authorized a stay to February 1 of the First Session of the next Congress.

(ii) Summary deportation.
The grant of a lesser period of time than that specified in subdivision (i) or the execution of the order of deportation when the beneficiary's continued presence here would

be contrary to the best interests of the United States is not precluded, since deportation may be effected notwithstanding the private bill; if the case falls in this category, the district director shall on the cover sheet note a summary of the facts, including Service ability to promptly effect departure, together with his recommendation, and forward the private bill report and the entire file to the regional office. If the regional office concurs, it shall include its comments on the cover sheet and forward the entire file to the Private Bill Control Unit, Central Office. After consulting with the committee and author of the bill, the Private Bill Control Unit will notify the appropriate district and regional offices of the decision and return the file. The foregoing procedure shall be followed at any time information is received which, in the opinion of the district director, warrants summary deportation.

(iii) Non-reintroduced bills.
If on February 2 of a new Congress notification of the reintroduction of a bill has not been received by the district office from the Private Bill Control Unit, prompt steps shall be taken to require the deportable former bill beneficiary's departure from the United States; however, the district director's discretionary authority to stay deportation or extend departure time may be exercised. The Private Bill Control Unit shall be advised of any stay or extension of departure time and of the closing action.

(iv) Adverse disposition.
When adverse action has been taken on a private bill which was introduced to adjust the immigration status of an alien who is in the United States, the Private Bill Control Unit will notify the appropriate district and regional offices and will usually direct that departure be effected by a specified date. Although every effort should be made to complete the action within the time specified, the district director's discretionary authority to stay deportation or extend departure time may be exercised. The Private Bill Control Unit shall be advised of any stay or extension of departure time and of the closing action.

(v) Notification of non-reintroduced bill or adverse disposition.
The alien and his attorney or other recognized representative shall be notified by letter when Congress has failed to approve, or has taken adverse action, on the private bill. If the alien is in a voluntary departure status, the letter should read substantially as shown below; the language in the first sentence will depend upon whether the 1961 and 1969 edition of Form G-386 was used when the alien was informed of the introduction of the bill:

You were previously notified that a private bill in your behalf was introduced in Congress and (you would be permitted to remain in the United States until February 1, 1969, or 30 days following adverse action on the bill, whichever occurred sooner) (you were granted an extension of time to depart voluntarily to February 1, 1969, or until adverse action was taken on the bill, whichever occurred sooner). You are now advised that (the 90th Congress adjourned without having approved the bill) (Congress has taken adverse action on the bill).

In view of the above, you are being granted until (date) to depart voluntarily from the United States. You must notify this office, Room No. , at least 7 days prior to the date of your departure of the arrangements you have made to depart, giving the date, place, and means of departure.

Failure to depart on or before the specified date will result in action being taken to effect your deportation.

If the deport part of an alternate order has taken effect, or a straight deportation order was issued, the wording of the letter should be similar to the following:

You were previously notified that a private bill in your behalf was introduced in Congress and (you would be permitted to remain in the United States until February 1, 1969, or 30 days following adverse action on the bill, whichever occurred sooner) (you were granted a stay of deportation until February 1, 1969, or until adverse action was taken on the bill, whichever occurred sooner). You are now advised that (the 90th Congress adjourned without having approved the bill) (Congress has taken adverse action on the bill).

As an order to deport you from the United States is still outstanding in your case, arrangements are being made for your deportation on or about (date). You should arrange your affairs accordingly. You will be informed at a later date as to the exact date and time to surrender to this Service for deportation.

The wording of the letter may be altered to meet local conditions or individual circumstances of a case. The date set for voluntary departure or deportation should be 30 days from that of the letter in cases where the 1961 edition of Form G-386 was sent to the alien upon introduction of the bill. If the 1969 edition of Form G-386 was used, a reasonable lesser or greater period for voluntary departure or deportation may be set, depending upon the facts in the individual case.

(g) Supplemental private bill report.
If, following the submission of the private bill report any material information is received or any material action is taken with respect to the beneficiary which might favorably or unfavorably affect the committee's consideration of the bill, the section in control of the file shall promptly transfer it to the Investigation Branch for the preparation of a supplemental report. When the information indicates that administrative relief is available or has been granted, or when the information is particularly adverse, the Private Bill Control Unit shall be notified immediately so that it can advise the committee informally and request that action be deferred pending transmittal of the supplemental report.

In order to ensure that supplemental information is submitted timely, the Investigations Branch shall maintain a call-up system to coincide with any pending action, i.e. hearing dates, anticipated adjudication completion dates, and visa availability dates and, at a minimum, the case shall be called-up and reviewed every six months.

(h) Notification of congressional action.

(1) Passage of one branch of Congress.

Upon the passage of a private bill in the first branch of Congress, the Private Bill Control Unit will send a copy of the act and the committee report to the appropriate district office. All procedures in progress shall continue since the bill may still not be enacted.

(2) Enactment of private law.
Upon the approval of a private bill by the President and receipt by the Private Bill Control Unit of copies of the private law affecting the immigration or nationality status of an individual, that unit will notify the appropriate district office of enactment. Thereafter, the appropriate field office shall, when the private law directs that permanent resident status be granted an alien beneficiary who is in the United States upon payment of the required visa fee, collect $150 and forward it to the Director, Office of Finance, Department of State, Washington, DC 20520; the letter of transmittal should refer to the private law number. Upon receipt of the fee, the field office shall prepare a Form I-181 which shall be placed in the Service file relating to the alien. Form I-357 shall be delivered to every alien who has been accorded permanent resident status. The date of delivery of Form I-357 shall be entered in the designated space on the record copy of Form I-181. If the private law directs a numerical reduction, a copy of Form I-181 shall be forwarded to the Director, Visa Office, Attention: Visa Control Office. If the alien is a nonimmigrant subject to central office control, the procedure in AM 2790 shall be followed. Form I-551 shall then be delivered to the alien.

Whenever the private law directs that permanent resident status be granted to an alien beneficiary who is in the United States, the employee who executes the Form I-181 in accordance with the above paragraph shall refer any person who requests a social security card, after such adjustment, to the nearest Social Security Office.

If the private law directs that permanent resident status be granted to an alien beneficiary who is in the United States and a visa fee is not required, the same record procedure shall be followed as in the case requiring a visa fee.

When the private law directs that an alien beneficiary be granted immediate relative or preference status for the purpose of procuring an immigrant visa, the field office shall send Form G-388 to the appropriate interested party; if a visa petition is required, but has not been filed, the interested party should be notified of the necessity for filing such a petition. If a public charge bond is required, the appropriate party, if in the United States, should be advised of the requirement and upon acceptance of a bond, the Director, Visa Office, Department of State, should be informed that the bond has been deposited.

If the private law directs that the pending deportation proceedings shall be terminated, the field office shall notify the beneficiary that such proceedings have been terminated by reason of the enactment of the private law. When the private law grants some other benefit or waiver under the immigration or nationality laws, the field office shall notify the beneficiary or interested party thereof and offer appropriate advice and assistance.

The Service shall not institute subsequent exclusion or deportation proceedings against an alien beneficiary of a private law which granted him the status of a permanent resident or which terminated deportation proceedings in his case on grounds based solely on facts contained in the Judiciary Committees' reports on the bill.

APPENDIX D

Petition for Pardon After Completion of Sentence

Please read the accompanying instructions carefully before completing the application. Type or print the answers in ink. Each question must be answered fully, truthfully, and accurately. If the space for any answer is insufficient, you may complete the answer on the optional continuation page or on a separate sheet of paper and attach it to the petition. You may attach any additional documentation that you believe is relevant to your petition. The submission of any material, false information is punishable by up to five years' imprisonment and a fine of not more than $250,000. 18 U.S.C. §§ 1001 and 3571.

To The President of the United States:

The undersigned petitioner prays for a pardon and in support thereof states as follows:

1. **Full name:** _____
              First   Middle   Last

   Address: _____
            Number Street   City   State Zip Code

   Telephone Number: _____ **Social Security No.** _____
                           (area code)

   Date and place of birth: _____

   Sex: _____ **Height:** _____ **Weight:** _____ **Hair Color:** _____ **Eye Color:** _____

   State in full every other name by which you have been known, including the name under which you were convicted, the reason for your use of another name, and the dates during which you were so known (*i.e.*, include your maiden name, name by a former marriage, aliases, and nicknames).

   _____

   _____

   Are you a United States citizen?   ☐ yes ☐ no
   If you are not a U.S. citizen, state your nationality and your alien registration number. If you are a naturalized U.S. citizen, state the date and place of your naturalization.

   _____

   Have you ever applied for a presidential pardon before?   ☐ yes ☐ no
   If yes, state the date you applied for pardon, and the date you were notified of the final disposition of the petition.

   _____

   _____

United States Department of Justice
Office of the Pardon Attorney
Washington, D.C. 20530

January 2002

Offense(s) For Which Pardon Is Sought

Under the Rules Governing Petitions for Executive Clemency, a minimum waiting period of five years after completion of sentence is required before you become eligible to apply for a presidential pardon. The waiting period begins on the date of release from confinement. If the conviction resulted in probation or a fine with no term of imprisonment, the waiting period begins on the date of sentencing. Please see paragraph 3 of the Information and Instructions on Pardons.

2. Petitioner was convicted on a plea of _____ in the United States District
   (guilty, not guilty, nolo contendere)

   Court for the _____ District of _____ of the crime of:
   (Northern, Western, etc.)   (identify state)

   _____
   (State specific offense; provide citation of statute(s) violated, if known)

   and was sentenced on _____, _____ to ☐ imprisonment for _____,
                        (month/day) (year)

   ☐ probation/supervised release for _____, ☐ a fine of $ _____, and ☐ restitution

   of $ _____. Petitioner was _____ years of age when the offense was committed.

3. Petitioner began service of the sentence of (☐ imprisonment ☐ probation) on _____, _____;
                                                                              (month/day) (year)

   was released on _____, _____ from _____; began service of
                   (month/day) (year)   (Federal institution)

   probation/supervised release on _____, _____; and completed the sentence on
                                   (month/day) (year)

   _____, _____. Petitioner (☐ did ☐ did not) appeal the conviction.
   (month/day) (year)

4. Indicate the date(s) on which the fine or restitution was paid. If the fine or restitution has not been paid in full, explain why, and state the remaining balance.

   _____
   _____
   _____
   _____

5. If you appealed your conviction or sentence, provide the date of the decision(s) by the Court of Appeals and, if applicable, the Supreme Court. Also provide citations to any published judicial opinion(s), and a copy of any unpublished opinion(s), if available.

   _____
   _____
   _____
   _____

Petition for Pardon After Completion of Sentence

APPENDIX D • PETITION FOR PARDON AFTER COMPLETION OF SENTENCE

6. **Provide a complete and detailed account of the offense for which you seek pardon.** You are expected to describe in your own words the relevant factual circumstances of the offense. Do not simply repeat the description of the offense contained in the indictment or presentence report, or rely on criminal code citations alone. If the conviction resulted from a plea agreement, you should describe the full extent of your involvement in the criminal conduct, in addition to the charge(s) to which you pled guilty. If you need more space, use the optional continuation page.

Prior and Subsequent Criminal Record

7. Aside from the offense for which you seek pardon, **have you ever been arrested, taken into custody, held for investigation or questioning, charged by any law enforcement authority, or convicted in any court, either as a juvenile or an adult, for any other incident?**

☐ yes ☐ no

For each such incident, state the following: the date, the nature of the charge, the relevant facts, the law enforcement authority involved, the location, and the disposition of the incident. You must list every violation, including traffic violations that resulted in an arrest or criminal charge, such as driving under the influence. You are expected to describe in your own words the relevant factual circumstances of each incident. Any omission will be considered a falsification. If you need more space, use the optional continuation page.

APPENDIX D • PETITION FOR PARDON AFTER COMPLETION OF SENTENCE

Biographical Information

8. **Current marital status:** ☐ Never Married ☐ Married ☐ Divorced ☐ Widowed ☐ Separated

   For each marriage, state the following: name of spouse, date and place of spouse's birth, date and place of marriage, and, if applicable, date and place of divorce, and current or last known address and telephone number of your current and each former spouse. If you need more space, use the optional continuation page.

   _____ _____
   name of spouse   date/place of birth

   _____ _____
   full address, including zip code telephone number, including area code

   _____ _____
   date/place of marriage   date/place of divorce

   _____ _____
   name of spouse   date/place of birth

   _____ _____
   full address, including zip code telephone number, including area code

   _____ _____
   date/place of marriage   date/place of divorce

9. (a) **List your children by name and furnish the date and place of birth for each:**
   If you have no children, indicate that the question is not applicable. If you need more space, use the optional continuation page.

   _____ _____
   name of child   date/place of birth

   _____ _____
   name of child   date/place of birth

   _____ _____
   name of child   date/place of birth

   _____ _____
   name of child   date/place of birth

   (b) **If you have minor children, but do not have custody of one or more of them, indicate whether and to whom you pay child support, whether your payments are current, and, if not, the reason for your failure to pay and any agreement you have made to satisfy your payment obligation.**

   _____
   _____
   _____

   (c) **If the other parent of any child listed above is not your spouse or former spouse,** identify the child, and state the name, address, and telephone number of the other parent.

   _____
   _____

10. List the complete address of all schools you have attended since your conviction, beginning with the most recent and working backward. Indicate the type of degree or diploma received or anticipated, and give the name of an instructor, counselor, or other school official who knows you well. If you need more space, use the optional continuation page. If you have not attended any schools since your conviction, indicate that the question is not applicable.

School		From (month/year)	To (month/year)
Number and Street		Degree	Month/year awarded
City		State	Zip Code
Name of school official		Telephone number of school official	

Residences

11. Provide the full address of every place you have lived since the conviction or release from incarceration, beginning with the present and working backward. *All time periods must be accounted for.* List the physical location of your residence; do not use a post office box as an address. If you lived in an apartment complex, list your apartment number. If you need more space, use the residence continuation page.

Date you moved to present address (month/year):	Number and Street		Apartment Number
	City	State	Zip Code

From (month/year):	Number and Street		Apartment Number
To (month/year):	City	State	Zip Code

From (month/year):	Number and Street		Apartment Number
To (month/year):	City	State	Zip Code

From (month/year):	Number and Street		Apartment Number
To (month/year):	City	State	Zip Code

From (month/year):	Number and Street		Apartment Number
To (month/year):	City	State	Zip Code

APPENDIX D • PETITION FOR PARDON AFTER COMPLETION OF SENTENCE 123

Employment History

12. List all periods of employment and unemployment since the conviction or release from incarceration, beginning with the present and working backward. *All time periods must be accounted for.* List all full and part-time work, self-employment, and any periods of unemployment. For any period of unemployment, indicate your means of support. For additional employments, use the employment history continuation page.

Present Employer			Telephone (include area code)
Date you began this employment (month/year):	Number and Street		
	City	State	Zip Code
Type of business	Position	Supervisor	Supervisor's telephone number

Employer			Telephone (include area code)
Began (month/year):	Number and Street		
Ended (month/year):	City	State	Zip Code
Type of business	Position	Supervisor	Supervisor's telephone number

Employer			Telephone (include area code)
Began (month/year):	Number and Street		
Ended (month/year):	City	State	Zip Code
Type of business	Position	Supervisor	Supervisor's telephone number

(a) Since your conviction, have you been fired or left a job following allegations of misconduct or unsatisfactory job performance? ☐ yes ☐ no

(b) Have you ever failed to list your conviction, or any other arrest or conviction, on any employment or other application where such information was requested? ☐ yes ☐ no

If you answered yes to either of the above questions, provide the employer's name, address and telephone number, and explain fully below. If you need more space, use the optional continuation page.

_____

_____

_____

Substance Abuse and Mental Health Information

13. (a) Have you ever used any illegal drug or abused prescription drugs or alcohol? ☐ yes ☐ no

If yes, identify the drugs used, the dates of drug or alcohol abuse, and the frequency of such use. If you need more space, use the optional continuation page.

_____
_____
_____
_____
_____
_____

(b) Have you ever been involved in the illegal manufacture, sale, or distribution of drugs, other than the offense for which you seek pardon? ☐ yes ☐ no

If yes, provide complete details and dates of your involvement. If you need more space, use the optional continuation page.

_____
_____
_____
_____
_____
_____

(c) Have you ever sought or participated in counseling, treatment, or a rehabilitation program for drug use or alcohol abuse? ☐ yes ☐ no

If yes, specify the dates of treatment or counseling, and provide the full name, address, and telephone number of the treatment facility and of the doctor, counselor or other treatment provider.

_____
_____
_____
_____
_____
_____

(d) **Have you ever consulted with a mental health professional (psychiatrist, psychologist, or counselor), or with another health care provider, concerning a mental health-related condition?** ☐ yes ☐ no

If yes, specify the nature of the condition, the dates of treatment, the type of treatment, and the full name, address, and telephone number of the counselor or treatment provider.

_____
_____
_____
_____
_____
_____
_____

Civil and Financial Information

14. (a) **Are you currently in default or delinquent in any way in the payment or discharge of any debt or financial obligation imposed upon you?** ☐ yes ☐ no

If yes, state the amount of the debt, the full name, address, and telephone number of the creditor, the reason for the failure to pay, and the terms of any agreement you have made to satisfy the obligation. If you need more space, use the optional continuation page.

_____
_____
_____
_____
_____
_____

(b) **Have any liens (including federal or state tax liens) been filed against you?** ☐ yes ☐ no

If yes, state the amount of the lien, the full name, address, and telephone number of the lien holder, the reason the lien was imposed, the current status of the lien, and the terms of any agreement you have made to satisfy the obligation. If you need more space, use the optional continuation page.

_____
_____
_____
_____
_____
_____

(c) **Have you ever been named as a party in a civil lawsuit?** ☐ yes ☐ no
If yes, state the full name, address, and telephone number of any other party to the lawsuit, the court in which it was filed, the case number, the nature of the dispute, and the final disposition, including the terms of any settlement agreement. If you need more space, use the optional continuation page.

_____
_____
_____
_____
_____
_____

(d) **Have you ever filed for the discharge of your debts in bankruptcy?** ☐ yes ☐ no
If yes, state the court in which the petition was filed, the case number, the amount of debt sought to be discharged, the final disposition of the action, and the date of disposition. If you need more space, use the optional continuation page.

_____
_____
_____
_____
_____
_____

(e) **Do you have pending any judicial or administrative proceedings with the federal, state, or local governments?** ☐ yes ☐ no
If yes, state the full name, address and telephone number of the relevant authority involved, the jurisdiction in which the proceeding is pending, the case number, the nature of the dispute, and the current status of the matter. If you need more space, use the optional continuation page.

_____
_____
_____
_____
_____
_____
_____

Petition for Pardon After Completion of Sentence

Military Record

15. (a) Have you ever served in the armed forces of the United States? ☐ yes ☐ no

Dates of service: _____ Branch(es): _____

Serial number: _____ Type of discharge: _____

Decorations (if any): _____

(b) If you were other than honorably discharged, describe in detail the factual circumstances surrounding your discharge. If you need more space, use the optional continuation page. Attach a copy of your separation papers (Form DD-214), if available.

_____
_____
_____
_____
_____
_____
_____
_____
_____

(c) While serving in the armed forces, did you receive non-judicial punishment, or were you the defendant in any court-martial? ☐ yes ☐ no

If yes, state fully the nature of the charge, the relevant facts, the disposition of the proceedings, the date thereof, and the name and address of the authority in possession of the records thereof. If you were convicted of an offense by court-martial, with respect to each conviction, provide a copy of the court-martial promulgating order and the information that is required in questions 2 through 6 of this application. If you need more space, use the optional continuation page.

_____
_____
_____
_____
_____
_____
_____
_____
_____
_____
_____
_____

Civil Rights and Occupational Licensing

16. Have you ever applied for the restoration of your state civil rights (*i.e.*, a state pardon, a certification of restoration of civil rights, or a certificate of discharge)? ☐ yes ☐ no

    If yes, indicate whether the application was granted or denied, and attach a copy of your application and the document(s) evidencing the state's action.

    _____

17. (a) Have you ever applied for the removal of your state firearms disabilities? ☐ yes ☐ no

    If yes, indicate whether the application was granted or denied, and attach a copy of your application and the document(s) evidencing the state's action.

    _____

    (b) Have you ever applied for the removal of your federal firearms disabilities? ☐ yes ☐ no

    If yes, indicate whether the application was granted or denied, and attach a copy of your application and the document(s) evidencing the federal government's action.

    _____

18. (a) Have you ever been denied any type of business or professional license, had any such license revoked, or had reinstatement of any such license denied? ☐ yes ☐ no

    If yes, attach a copy of the document(s) evidencing the action, including your application and any explanation of the reasons for the action. If not available, provide the name, address, and telephone number of the authority taking the action, the nature of the license, the disposition of your request, and the date of disposition.

    _____
    _____
    _____
    _____

    (b) Have you ever been granted any type of business or professional license or received the reinstatement of any such license that had been revoked? ☐ yes ☐ no

    If yes, attach a copy of the document(s) evidencing the action, including your application and any explanation of the reasons for the action. If not available, provide the name, address, and telephone number of the authority taking the action, the nature of the license, the disposition of your request, and the date of disposition.

    _____
    _____
    _____
    _____
    _____

Petition for Pardon After Completion of Sentence

Charitable and Community Activities

19. Describe any charitable or civic activities in which you have been engaged, or other contributions you have made to the community, since your conviction. In this regard, you may include the names of any organizations in which you have participated, the time periods of your participation, your role in these activities, and the name, address, and telephone number of a person associated with each organization who is familiar with your involvement. If you need more space, use the optional continuation page.

Reasons for Seeking Pardon

20. State your reasons for seeking a pardon. Please refer to paragraph 4 of the Information and Instructions on Pardons, which indicates that a pardon is ordinarily a sign of forgiveness, not vindication. If you need more space, use the optional continuation page.

Petition for Pardon After Completion of Sentence

APPENDIX D • PETITION FOR PARDON AFTER COMPLETION OF SENTENCE

Certification and Personal Oath

    I hereby certify that all answers to the above questions and all statements contained herein are true and correct to the best of my knowledge, information, and belief. I understand that any intentional misstatements of material facts contained in this petition may cause adverse action on my petition for pardon, in addition to subjecting me to any other penalties provided by law.

    In petitioning the President of the United States for pardon, I do solemnly swear that I will be law-abiding and will support and defend the Constitution of the United States against all enemies, foreign and domestic, and that I take this obligation freely and without any mental reservation whatsoever, So Help Me God.

Respectfully submitted this _____ day of _____ (month), _____ (year).

_____
(signature of petitioner)

Subscribed and sworn before me this _____ day of _____ (month), _____ (year).

_____
Notary Public

(SEAL)

My commission expires: _____

**Continuation Page for
Petition for Pardon After Completion of Sentence**

Residences

From (month/year):	Number and Street		Apartment Number
To (month/year):	City	State	Zip Code

From (month/year):	Number and Street		Apartment Number
To (month/year):	City	State	Zip Code

From (month/year):	Number and Street		Apartment Number
To (month/year):	City	State	Zip Code

From (month/year):	Number and Street		Apartment Number
To (month/year):	City	State	Zip Code

From (month/year):	Number and Street		Apartment Number
To (month/year):	City	State	Zip Code

From (month/year):	Number and Street		Apartment Number
To (month/year):	City	State	Zip Code

From (month/year):	Number and Street		Apartment Number
To (month/year):	City	State	Zip Code

Petition for Pardon After Completion of Sentence

**Continuation Page for
Petition for Pardon After Completion of Sentence**

Employment History

Employer			Telephone (include area code)
Began (month/year):	Number and Street		
Ended (month/year):	City	State	Zip Code
Type of business	Position	Supervisor	Supervisor's telephone number

Employer			Telephone (include area code)
Began (month/year):	Number and Street		
Ended (month/year):	City	State	Zip Code
Type of business	Position	Supervisor	Supervisor's telephone number

Employer			Telephone (include area code)
Began (month/year):	Number and Street		
Ended (month/year):	City	State	Zip Code
Type of business	Position	Supervisor	Supervisor's telephone number

Employer			Telephone (include area code)
Began (month/year):	Number and Street		
Ended (month/year):	City	State	Zip Code
Type of business	Position	Supervisor	Supervisor's telephone number

Petition for Pardon After Completion of Sentence

**Optional Continuation Page for
Petition for Pardon After Completion of Sentence**

Answers to Other Questions

Question #   *Response:*

Petition for Pardon After Completion of Sentence

Optional Continuation Page for
Petition for Pardon After Completion of Sentence

Answers to Other Questions

Question #   Response:

Petition for Pardon After Completion of Sentence

Character Affidavit
on behalf of

_____
(print or type name of petitioner)

In support of the application of the above named petitioner to the President of the United States for pardon, I, _____,
(Print or type name of affiant)

residing at _____,
Number   Street   City   State   Zip Code

_____, whose occupation is _____;
Telephone No. (Include area code)

certify that I have personally known the petitioner for _____ years. Except as otherwise indicated below, petitioner has behaved since the conviction in a moral and law-abiding manner. My knowledge of petitioner's reputation, conduct and activities, including whether the petitioner has been arrested or had any other trouble with public authorities and has been steadily employed, is as follows:

_____
_____
_____
_____
_____
_____
_____
_____
_____

     I do solemnly swear that the foregoing information is true and correct to the best of my knowledge, information, and belief.

_____
(Signature of Affiant)

Subscribed and sworn to before me this _____ day of _____, _____.
                                                                                      (month)   (year)

(SEAL)

                                              Notary Public: _____

                                              My commission expires: _____

CHARACTER AFFIDAVIT
on behalf of

_____
(print or type name of petitioner)

In support of the application of the above named petitioner to the President of the United States for pardon, I, _____,
(Print or type name of affiant)

residing at _____,
Number   Street   City   State   Zip Code

_____, whose occupation is _____,
Telephone No. (include area code)

certify that I have personally known the petitioner for _____ years. Except as otherwise indicated below, petitioner has behaved since the conviction in a moral and law-abiding manner. My knowledge of petitioner's reputation, conduct and activities, including whether the petitioner has been arrested or had any other trouble with public authorities and has been steadily employed, is as follows:

_____
_____
_____
_____
_____
_____
_____
_____
_____

I do solemnly swear that the foregoing information is true and correct to the best of my knowledge, information, and belief.

_____
(Signature of Affiant)

Subscribed and sworn to before me this _____ day of _____, _____.
(month)   *(year)*

(SEAL)

Notary Public: _____

My commission expires: _____

Character Affidavit
on behalf of

_____
(print or type name of petitioner)

In support of the application of the above named petitioner to the President of the United States for pardon, I, _____,
(Print or type name of affiant)

residing at _____,
Number   Street   City   State   Zip Code

_____, whose occupation is _____,
Telephone No. (include area code)

certify that I have personally known the petitioner for _____ years. Except as otherwise indicated below, petitioner has behaved since the conviction in a moral and law-abiding manner. My knowledge of petitioner's reputation, conduct and activities, including whether the petitioner has been arrested or had any other trouble with public authorities and has been steadily employed, is as follows:

_____
_____
_____
_____
_____
_____
_____
_____

I do solemnly swear that the foregoing information is true and correct to the best of my knowledge, information, and belief.

_____
(Signature of Affiant)

Subscribed and sworn to before me this _____ day of _____, _____.
                                                        (month)   *(year)*

(SEAL)

Notary Public: _____

My commission expires: _____

Authorization for Release of Information

Carefully read this authorization to release information about you, then complete, sign and date it in ink.

I authorize any investigator, special agent, or other duly accredited representative of the Federal Bureau of Investigation, the Department of Defense, and any other authorized Federal agency, to obtain any information relating to my activities from schools, residential management agents, employers, criminal justice agencies, retail business establishments, courts, or other sources of information. This information may include, but is not limited to, my academic, residential, achievement, performance, attendance, disciplinary, employment history, criminal history, arrest, conviction, including the presentence investigation report, if any, medical, psychiatric/psychological, health care, and financial and credit information.

I understand that, for financial or lending institutions and certain other sources of information, a separate specific release may be needed (pursuant to their request or as may be required by law), and I may be contacted for such a release at a later date.

I further authorize the Federal Bureau of Investigation, the Department of Defense, and any other authorized Federal agency, to request criminal record information about me from criminal justice agencies for the purpose of determining my suitability for a government benefit.

I authorize custodians of records and sources of information pertaining to me to release such information upon request of the investigator, special agent, or other duly accredited representative of any Federal agency authorized above regardless of any previous agreement to the contrary. I understand that the information released by records custodians and sources of information is for official use by the Federal Government only for the purposes of processing my application for a government benefit, and may be redisclosed by the Government only as authorized by law.

Copies of this authorization that show my signature are as valid as the original release signed by me. This authorization is valid for three (3) years from the date signed.

Signature (sign in ink)		
Full Name (type or print legibly)		Date Signed
Other Names Used		
Street Address		
City	State	Zip Code
Home Telephone Number (include area code)	Social Security Number	

Authorization for Release of Information   *January 2002*

APPENDIX E
STATE PARDON INFORMATION

ALABAMA

Pardon Authority and Process: Board of Pardon and Parole exercises the pardon power.[1] The board's administration and procedure are governed by Ala. Code §§15-22-20 to 15-22-40. Information regarding the pardon application and process can be obtained from the Alabama Board of Pardon and Parole website at *www.paroles.state.al.us.* In fiscal year 2004, the Board of Pardon and Parole granted 71% of all applications filed.[2]

Eligibility: A person is eligible for a pardon upon completion of sentence, or completion of at least three years of permanent parole, unless the pardon is sought on grounds of innocence.[3]	*Effect:* A state pardon does not relieve civil and political disabilities unless it expressly states so in the pardon.[4] The Board may grant a full pardon that restores all rights, or it may grant a pardon with restrictions.	*Contact:* Cynthia Dillard Executive Director Alabama Board of Pardons and Parole P.O. Box 302405 Montgomery, AL 36130 Tel: (334) 242-8700 Fax: (334) 242-1809 *cynthia.dillard@alabpp.gov* *www.paroles.state.al.us*

ALASKA

Pardon Authority and Process: Pardon power, with the exception of impeachment cases, rests with the governor.[5] The governor is authorized to refer applications to the Board of Parole for investigation, but is not bound by the board's advice.[6] There are no formal regulations governing the pardon process. The Board has posted a guide on its website, Executive Clemency in Alaska—An Informational Booklet for Prospective Applicants.[7] The Alaska Board of Pardons grants very few pardon applications.[8]

Eligibility: A person is eligible for a pardon two years after completion of sentence.	*Effect:* A pardon has the effect of setting aside the conviction, so the person is no longer considered convicted; however, the conviction does remain on the record. Alaska pardons do not ordinarily restore gun rights. Therefore, it is not considered a full pardon for immigration law purposes.	*Contact:* Kathy Matsumoto Executive Director 550 West 7th Ave., Suite 601 Anchorage, AK 99501 Tel: (907) 770-6310 Fax: (907) 770-6308 *www.correct.state.ak.us/corrections/parole/*

---

[1] Ala. Const. amend. 38.

[2] M. Love, *Relief from Collateral Consequences of a Criminal Conviction: A State-by-State Resource Guide*, Alabama-4 (2006).

[3] Ala. Code §15-22-36(c).

[4] *Id.*

[5] Alaska Const. art. III, §21; Alaska Stat. §33.20.070.

[6] Alaska Stat. §33.20.080(a).

[7] *See www.correct.state.ak.us/corrections/parole.* Click on Clemency Handbook.

[8] M. Love, *supra* note 2, at Alaska-2.

ARIZONA		
\multicolumn{3}{l}{*Pardon Authority and Process:* The authority to grant pardons rests with the governor, except in cases involving treason or impeachment. This authority may be restricted by statute.[9] By statute, no pardon may be granted unless it has first been recommended by the Board of Executive Clemency.[10] Information regarding the pardon process can be found at Ariz. Rev. Stat. §13-401 *et seq.* and is available on the state's website at *www.azsos.gov/public_services/Title_05/5-04.pdf* and at the State's Legislature website at *www.azleg.state.az.us/ArizonaRevisedStatutes.asp*. Pardon applications are granted sparingly.[11] }		
Eligibility: A person is eligible to seek a pardon at any time after release from prison, if the conviction has not been vacated or set-aside.	*Effect:* A pardon absolves the person of all legal consequences of the crime.[12]	*Contact:* Duane Belcher, Senior Chairman Board of Executive Clemency 1645 West Jefferson, Suite 101 Phoenix, AZ 85007 Tel: (602) 542-5656 duane.belcher@aboec.state.az.us www.azboec.gov/

ARKANSAS		
Pardon Authority and Process: The authority to grant pardons rests with the governor, who has full clemency power.[13] By statute, all applications are first referred to the Board of Parole, which is required to investigate each case and submit a recommendation to the governor.[14] The governor is not bound by the Board's recommendation. Procedures relating to the pardon process can be found on the Board's website at *www.arbop.org*. During 2003 and 2004, between 40 to 50% of all pardon applications were granted.[15]		
Eligibility: A person can apply for a pardon upon release from prison or sentence. There are no restrictions on eligibility.	*Effect:* A pardon restores eligibility to serve on a jury, but not to hold public office.[16] It removes any conviction-related obstacles to licensing and employment. With the exception of a few serious offenses, automatic expungement follows the grant of a pardon.[17] The pardon must specifically restore firearms privileges.	*Contact:* Arkansas Parole Board Tamara Salaam, Board Coordinator Two Union National Plaza Bldg. 105 West Capitol, Suite 500 Little Rock, AR 72201 Tel: (501) 682-3850 Fax: (501) 682-3860

---

[9] Ariz. Const. art. V, §5.

[10] Ariz. Rev. Stat. §31-402A.

[11] M. Love, *supra* note 2, at Arizona-2, 3.

[12] *See* 68 Ariz. Op. Att'y Gen. 17.

[13] Ark. Const. art. VI, §18.

[14] Ark. Code Ann. §§16-39-204(a), (b).

[15] M. Love, *supra* note 2, at Arkansas-3.

[16] Ark. Code Ann. §§16-93-301, 16-93-302, 16-93-303.

[17] Ark. Code Ann. §16-90-605(a).

CALIFORNIA

Pardon Authority and Process: The power to pardon rests exclusively with the governor, who may request investigation and recommendation from the Board of Parole Hearings.[18] For those persons who reside in the state, the pardon process generally starts with an application for certificate of rehabilitation in the county of residence.[19] Convicted persons who reside outside of the state, or who may be ineligible for a certificate of rehabilitation (*e.g.*, sex offenders) may apply directly to the governor.[20] Under Governor Schwarzenegger, only three pardons have been granted.[21]

Eligibility: A person applying for a certificate of rehabilitation may do so after completion of the period of rehabilitation which runs from release from prison or release on probation. Five years of residence in California plus four years for serious offenses and two years for less serious offenses is required before seeking the certificate.[22] Pardon applications are accepted only if 10 years have passed from the date of discharge from parole or probation.[23]	*Effect:* A pardon does not act to seal or expunge a record of conviction. It does restore civil rights and removes occupational bars.[24] The right to possess a firearm is restored except when the underlying offense involved the use of a dangerous weapon.[25]	*Contact:* Board of Parole Hearings P.O. Box 4036 Sacramento, CA 95812-4036 Tel: (916) 445-1539 www.cdcr.ca.gov/Divisions_Boards/BOPH/index.html

COLORADO

Pardon Authority and Process: The authority to grant pardons rests with the governor, with the exception of treason or impeachment.[26] Clemency power is governed by Colo. Rev. Sta. §§16-17-101, 102. The governor is advised by the Colorado Executive Clemency Advisory Board, consisting of unpaid volunteers. Only a small number of pardons have been granted in recent years.[27]

Eligibility: Pardon applications generally cannot be made until 10 years after the completion of sentence.	*Effect:* A pardon restores firearm privileges, and removes legal disabilities, including employment disqualifications.	*Contact:* Office of the Governor 136 State Capitol Denver, CO 80203-1792 Tel: (303) 866-2471 Fax: (303) 866-2003

---

[18] Cal. Const. art. V, §8(a); Cal. Penal Code §§4800, 4812-13.

[19] Cal. Penal Code §§4852.06, 4852.13, 4852.19, 4852.21.

[20] For information on the pardon process before the governor, see *www.cdcr.ca.gov/Divisions_Boards/BOPH/docs/apply_for_pardon.pdf*.

[21] M. Love, *supra* note 2, at California-4.

[22] Cal. Penal Code §4852.21.

[23] See www.cdcr.ca.gov/Divisions_Boards/BOPH/ docs/apply_for_pardon.pdf.

[24] Cal. Penal Code §§4852.15, 4853.

[25] Cal. Penal Code §4852.17.

[26] Colo. Const. art. IV, §7.

[27] M. Love, *supra* note 2, at Colorado-2.

CONNECTICUT

Pardon Authority and Process: The authority to grant pardons rests with the State Board of Pardons and Paroles.[28] An application for a pardon must be made to the Board. Hearings are not required for certain misdemeanors and minor felonies.[29] The Board grants about 25% of pardon applications.[30]

Eligibility: A person is eligible to seek a pardon for certain crimes five years after completion of sentence.[31]	Effect: A pardon relieves all legal disabilities. The Board may grant a conditional or absolute pardon. An absolute pardon results in the automatic erasure of court records relating to the offense.	Contact: Rasa Pakalnis Hearing Coordinator Board of Pardons and Paroles 55 West Main Street, Suite 520 Waterbury, CT 06702 Tel: (203) 805-6643 Fax: (203) 805-6652 ct.bpp@po.state.ct.us www.ct.gov (search for Board of Pardons and Paroles)

DELAWARE

Pardon Authority and Process: The authority to pardon rests with the governor, except for impeachment; however, the governor cannot grant a pardon without a recommendation from the majority of the Board of Pardons. He or she is not bound to accept the Board's recommendation.[32] An application for a pardon should be in writing and sent to the office of the secretary of state, who acts as the secretary of the Board of Pardons.[33] Rules governing the pardon process are available on the Board's website at *http://pardons.delaware.gov/information/pardrule.shtml*. Instructions for filing a pardon application can be found at *http://pardons.delaware.gov/services/pardinst.shtml*. Delaware has a high grant rate of pardons.[34]

Eligibility: The Board requires that the applicant wait three to five years after completion of the sentence, depending on the seriousness of the offense, unless the applicant can demonstrate a legitimate hardship should he or she have to wait.	Effect: The granting of an unconditional pardon fully restores all civil rights to the person.[35]	Contact: Delaware Board of Pardons Judy Smith, Assistant Secretary of State's Office 401 Federal Street, Suite 3 Dover, DE 19901 Tel: (302) 739-4111 Fax: (302) 739-7654 judy.smith@state.de.us http://pardons.delaware.gov/

---

[28] Conn. Gen. Stat. §54-124a(f).

[29] Conn. Gen. Stat. §54-124a(j)(2).

[30] M. Love, *supra* note 2, at Connecticut-2.

[31] Conn. Gen. Stat. §54-124a(j)(2).

[32] Del. Const. art. VII, §1.

[33] *See http://pardons.delaware. gov/services/pardinst.shtml.*

[34] M. Love, *supra* note 2, at Delaware-4.

[35] Del. Code Ann. tit. 11, §4364.

APPENDIX E • STATE PARDON INFORMATION

DISTRICT OF COLUMBIA

Pardon Authority and Process: The president of the United States has the authority to pardon persons who have been convicted under the D.C. Code. The mayor has limited authority to pardon violations of municipal ordinances.[36] Pardons are rarely granted in the District of Columbia.[37] The pardon process is the same as that for federal offenses as described in chapter 5 of this book.

Effect and Eligibility: The eligibility and effect of a presidential pardon are the same as described in chapter 5 of this book.

FLORIDA

Pardon Authority and Process: The authority to grant pardons rests with the governor, with the exception of treason or impeachment.[38] Under the Florida constitution, the governor may grant full or conditional pardons with the approval of two members of the cabinet.[39] The governor and three members of his or her cabinet constitute the Clemency Board. The Office of Clemency conducts the daily business of the Clemency Board. Information regarding the application procedure and rules governing pardons can be found on the Clemency Board's website at *https://fpc.state.fl.us/Clemency.htm*. There is no publicly available information on the number of pardons granted.

Eligibility: An applicant for a pardon must wait 10 years following the completion of sentence prior to applying.[40]	*Effect:* A full pardon unconditionally releases the person from punishment and forgives guilt. A pardon may also be made conditional.[41]	*Contact:* The Office of Executive Clemency 2601 Blair Stone Road, Building C Tallahassee, FL 32399-2450 Tel: (850) 488-2952 Toll free: (800) 435-8286 Fax: (850) 488-0695 *clemencyweb@fpc.state.fl.us* *https://fpc.state.fl.us/Clemency.htm*

---

[36] D.C. Code §1-307.76.

[37] M. Love, *supra* note 2, at District of Columbia-1.

[38] Fla. Const. art. IV, §8(a).

[39] *Id.*

[40] Fla. Rules of Executive Clemency, 5E.

[41] Fla. Rules of Executive Clemency, 4A.

GEORGIA		
Pardon Authority and Process: The power to pardon rests with the Board of Pardons and Paroles; however, it can be precluded from issuing a pardon or superseded by the legislature in cases involving recidivists and persons serving life sentences.[42] The governor is expressly prohibited from exercising authority over pardons.[43] Information on the pardon application and process can be found on the Board of Pardons and Paroles website at *www.pap.state.ga.us/opencms/opencms/*. Between 35% and 50% of pardon applications are approved by the Board.[44]		
Eligibility: An applicant for a pardon must wait five years after completion of sentence before applying.	*Effect:* A full pardon relieves all disabilities resulting from the conviction.[45]	*Contact:* State Board of Pardon and Paroles Pardon Administration Unit 4th Floor, East Tower 2 Martin Luther King, Jr., Dr. S.E. Atlanta, GA 30334 Tel: (404) 657-9350 Pardon_Administration@pap.state.ga.us www.pap.state.ga.us/opencms/opencms/

HAWAII		
Pardon Authority and Process: The power to pardon rests with the governor,[46] who may seek the recommendation of the Hawaii State Paroling Authority.[47] There is no statutory process for adjudicating pardon applications, but the governor asks the paroling authority and the attorney general for advice and recommendation.[48] A copy of the pardon application is available on the paroling authority's website at *http://hawaii.gov/psd/attached-agencies/hpa/Pardon-application2.pdf/view*. The paroling authority receives between 100 and 200 applications a year. In fiscal year 2005, it received 180 applications and the governor granted 32 pardons.[49]		
Eligibility: An applicant may apply for a pardon upon completion of sentence.	*Effect:* A pardon relieves all legal disabilities and prohibitions.	*Contact:* Hawaii Paroling Authority Paroles and Pardon Administrator 1177 Alakea Street, Ground Floor Honolulu, HI 96813 Tel: (808) 587-1340 Fax: (808) 587-1282 http://hawaii.gov/psd/attached-agencies/hpa

---

[42] Ga. Const. art. IV, §2, para. II.

[43] Ga. Code Ann. §42-9-56.

[44] M. Love, *supra* note 2, at Georgia-3.

[45] Ga. Code Ann. §42-9-54.

[46] Haw. Const. art. V, §5.

[47] Haw. Rev. Stat. §353-72.

[48] *Id.*

[49] M. Love, *supra* note 2, at Hawaii-2.

IDAHO

Pardon Authority and Process: The Idaho Commission of Pardons and Parole is vested with the authority to grant pardons, except in cases of treason and impeachment, subject to legislative limitations on its power and manner of proceeding.[50] The governor must approve the Commission's recommendation in cases involving murder, voluntary manslaughter, rape, kidnapping, lewd and lascivious conduct with a child, or manufacture or delivery of a controlled substance, before the pardon becomes effective. In these cases, the Commission's decision acts as a recommendation to the governor.[51] Information relating to the pardon application can be found on the Idaho Commission of Pardons and Parole website at *www2.state.id.us/parole/pardons.htm*. Administrative rules governing the pardon process are also available on the website. Twenty to 30 pardon applications are received annually and about two-thirds of those are approved.[52]

Eligibility: For nonviolent felony and misdemeanor offenses, an applicant must wait three years after completion of sentence before applying for a pardon. If the conviction is for a violent crime or a sex offense, the applicant must wait five years before applying.[53]	*Effect:* A pardon relieves all legal disabilities.	*Contact:* Commission of Pardons and Parole Olivia Craven, Executive Director P.O. Box 83720 Statehouse Mail Boise, ID 83720-1807 Tel: (208) 334-2520 www2.state.id.us/parole/pardons.htm

ILLINOIS

Pardon Authority and Process: Pardon power rests with the governor.[54] By statute, the Illinois Prisoner Review Board (PRB) is authorized to review and makes recommendations to the governor on pardon applications.[55] However, the PRB authority to review and recommend does not limit the governor's pardon power.[56] Guidelines on executive clemency, including information regarding the pardon application and the parole process, are available from the PRB website at *www.state.il.us/prb/docs/exclemexg.pdf*. The PRB receives between 500 to 600 pardon petitions each year. As of February 2006, the governor had denied 524 applications and granted 63, representing a grant rate of 8.3%.[57]

Eligibility: A person can apply for a pardon upon completion of sentence.	*Effect:* A pardon relieves all legal disabilities.	*Contact:* Illinois Prisoner Review Board 319 East Madison, Suite A Springfield, IL 62701 Tel: (217) 782-7273 Fax: (217) 524-0012 www.state.il.us/prb/docs/exclemexg.pdf

---

[50] Idaho Const. art. IV, §7.

[51] Idaho Code §20-240.

[52] M. Love, *supra* note 2, at Idaho-3.

[53] Idaho Code §18-310(3).; *see* Rules of the Commission of Pardons and Parole, Rule 550-01(a), (b).

[54] Ill. Const. art. V, §12.

[55] 730 Ill. Comp. Stat. 5/3-3-1(a)(3).

[56] *Id.*

[57] M. Love, *supra* note 2, at Illinois-3.

INDIANA

Pardon Authority and Process: The authority to pardon rests with the governor, but he or she may not grant a pardon without the advice and consent of the parole board.[58] The parole board is authorized to review all applications and make recommendations to the governor.[59] An application for a pardon should be filed with the parole board, which will conduct an investigation into the merits of the case. Rules governing the pardon process can be found at Ind. Code §§11-9-2-1 and 11-9-2-2. Indiana has a high pardon grant rate.[60]

Eligibility: Applicants must wait five years after completion of sentence before applying for a pardon.	*Effect:* A pardon removes all disabilities, acts to wipe out guilt, and becomes grounds for judicial expungement.[61]	*Contact:* Indiana Parole Board Indiana Government Center South 302 West Washington Street, Room E-321 Indianapolis, IN 46204 Tel: (317) 232-5673 www.in.gov/indcorrection/paroleboard.htm

IOWA

Pardon Authority and Process: Pardon power rests with the governor, except in cases of treason or impeachment.[62] The Iowa Board of Parole is authorized to review applications and make recommendations to the governor.[63] A person may apply either to the governor or to the Board of Parole.[64] Information on the pardon process can be contained in Board of Parole Rules 14.3, 14.4, and 14.5, available on its website at *www.bop.state.ia.us/*, and in the instructions to the clemency application found at *www.governor.iowa.gov/administration/clemency.php*. From 1998 through 2004, 238 applications for pardon were filed and 52 were granted.[65]

Eligibility: An application for a pardon can be submitted at any time following the conviction.[66] However, it is the policy of the governor's office to require at least 10 years from the completion date of the sentence before granting a pardon.[67]	*Effect:* A full and unconditional pardon restores all rights to the applicant.	*Contact:* James Larew, General Counsel Governor's Office State Capitol Building Des Moines, IA 50319 Tel: (515) 281-5211 www.governor.iowa.gov/administration/clemency.php

---

[58] Ind. Const. art. 5, §17.

[59] Ind. Code §§11-9-2-1 to 11-9-2-3.

[60] M. Love, *supra* note 2, at Indiana-3.

[61] *Kelley v. State*, 185 N.E. 453 (Ind. 1933).

[62] Iowa Const. art. IV, §16; Iowa Code §§914.1–914.7.

[63] Iowa Code §914.3(1).

[64] Iowa Code §914.2.

[65] M. Love, *supra* note 2, at Iowa-5.

[66] Iowa Code §914.2.

[67] *See* executive clemency application at *www.governor.iowa.gov/administration/clemency.php*.

KANSAS

Pardon Authority and Process: The authority to grant a pardon rests with the governor.[68] He or she is required to seek a recommendation from the Kansas Parole Board but is not bound to follow it.[69] Rules governing the application for pardons and the process can be found at Kan. Stat. Ann. §§22-3701(1)–(4) and Kan. Admin. Regs. §45-900-1(c). The Kansas Parole Board also posts instructions on the pardon process on its website at *www.dc.state.ks.us/kpb/clemency*. Pardons are rarely granted in Kansas.[70]

Eligibility: There are no eligibility restrictions. An applicant may apply for a pardon upon completion of sentence.	*Effect:* Generally, a pardon removes all disabilities imposed under state law. It does not erase or expunge convictions.	*Contact:* Kansas Parole Board Libby Scott, Administrator 900 SW Jackson, Suite 425-S Topeka, KS 66612 Tel: (785) 296-3469 Fax: (785) 296-7949 *www.dc.state.ks.us/kpb/clemency*

KENTUCKY

Pardon Authority and Process: The authority to pardon rests with the governor,[71] and he or she may ask the Kentucky Parole Board to investigate applications for pardons and make recommendations.[72] However, the governor is not bound by the recommendation of the Parole Board.[73] Pardon applications are made to the Parole Board, which forwards eligible applications to the governor. The application is then sent to the prosecutor for review and recommendation. After that review, the applicant is asked to submit three reference letters.[74] In 2001, the Kentucky legislature directed the Department of Corrections to implement procedures for restoration of a simplified process for restoration of civil rights, including pardons.[75] It appears, however, that the department has not yet done so. Pardons are rarely granted in Kentucky.[76]

Eligibility: An applicant for a pardon must wait seven years after completion of sentence before applying.	*Effect:* A full pardon relieves all legal disabilities; however, a pardon may limit the rights being restored.	*Contact:* Charles A. Wilkerson, Executive Director Kentucky Parole Board P.O. Box 2400 Frankfort, KY 40602-2400 Tel: (502) 564-3620 Fax: (502) 564-8995 *charles.wilkerson@ky.gov* *http://justice.ky.gov/parolebd/*

---

[68] Kan. Const. art. 1, §7.

[69] Kan. Stat. Ann. §22-3701(4).

[70] M. Love, *supra* note 2, at Kansas-2.

[71] Ky. Const. §§77, 150.

[72] Ky. Rev. Stat. Ann. §439.450.

[73] *Id.*

[74] M. Love, *supra* note 2, at Kentucky-2, -3.

[75] Ky. Rev. Stat. Ann. §196.045.

[76] M. Love, *supra* note 2, at Kentucky-4.

LOUISIANA

Pardon Authority and Process: The governor may pardon convicted persons after receiving a favorable recommendation from the Board of Pardons.[77] The rules governing the pardon application and process can be found on the Board of Pardons' website at *www.corrections.state.la.us/offices/Pardon/boardofpardons.htm*. The Board of Pardons hears between 25 to 30 cases of pardons and commutations every two months and denies approximately 75 percent of the applications.[78]

Eligibility: An applicant for a pardon may apply upon completion of sentence, including having paid court costs.[79]	Effect: If a person receives a full pardon by the governor upon recommendation by the Board of Pardons, he or she is restored to the status of innocence.	Contact: Board of Pardons 504 Mayflower St., Building 6 Baton Rouge, LA 70802 Tel: (225) 342-5421 Fax: (225) 342-2289 *www.corrections.state.la.us/offices/ Pardon/boardofpardons.htm*

MAINE

Pardon Authority and Process: The governor has the power to pardon except in cases of impeachment,[80] and is assisted by a nonstatutory Board of Executive Clemency.[81] Instructions regarding the pardon application and process can be found on the secretary of state's website at *www.maine.gov/sos/cec/boards/pardons.htm*. Between January 1, 2003, and August 1, 2004, 262 applications for pardon were filed, and 11 applications were granted.[82]

Eligibility: An applicant for a pardon must wait five years after completion of sentence before applying.	Effect: A pardon acts to remove all legal disabilities.	Contact: Pardon Clerk Office of the Secretary of State 101 State House Station Augusta, ME 04333-0101 Tel: (207) 624-7752 *www.maine.gov/sos/cec/boards/pardons.htm*

---

[77] La. Const. art. IV, §5(E)(1); La. Rev. Stat. Ann. §15:572(A).

[78] M. Love, *supra* note 2, at Louisiana-4.

[79] La. Rev. Stat. Ann. §15:572(A).

[80] Me. Const. art. V, pt. 1 §11.

[81] *See www.maine.gov/sos/cec/boards/pardons.htm*.

[82] M. Love, *supra* note 2, at Maine-2.

MARYLAND

Pardon Authority and Process: The authority to pardon is vested in the governor, except in cases of impeachment.[83] The Maryland Parole Commission investigates and provides recommendations to the governor, if requested. However, the recommendations are not binding.[84] Applications for pardons are submitted to the Maryland Parole Commission. If the applicant is eligible for a pardon, the Commission will direct the Division of Parole and Probation to carry out an investigation.[85] After completion of the investigation, the Commission will make its recommendation to the governor.[86] Instructions regarding the pardon application and process can be found on the State of Maryland website, Frequently Asked Question—Pardons, *www.dpscs.state.md.us/aboutdpscs/FAQmpc.shtml#pardon*. From 2003 to 2006, Maryland granted a significant number of pardons.[87]

Eligibility: A person convicted of a misdemeanor must wait until five years after completion of sentence and be crime free during that period before seeking a pardon. A person convicted of a felony must wait 10 years after completion of sentence and be crime free during that period before applying.[88]	*Effect:* A pardon relieves all disabilities imposed because of the conviction.	*Contact:* Maryland Parole Commission 6776 Reisterstown Rd., Suite 307 Baltimore, MD 21215-2343 Tel: (410) 585-3200

MASSACHUSETTS

Pardon Authority and Process: With the exception of impeachment cases, pardon power rests with the governor, who may grant a pardon only upon the advice and consent of the governor's council.[89] Information regarding the pardon application and process are available on the State of Massachusetts's website, under the Executive Clemency Unit section of the parole board's page at *www.mass.gov*.[90] In the past, Massachusetts governors have been generous in granting pardons; however, fewer pardons have been granted in recent years.[91]

Eligibility: An applicant convicted of a felony may seek a pardon 15 years after completion of sentence. An applicant convicted of a misdemeanor may apply 10 years after conviction or sentence.	*Effect:* A pardon relieves all disabilities and eradicates the conviction.	*Contact:* Julie Ching Pease, Paralegal Executive Clemency Unit Massachusetts Parole Board 12 Mercer Road Natlick, MA 01760 Tel: (508) 650-4500 /-4542 Fax: (508) 650-4599 *Julie.pease@state.ma.us* *www.mass.gov*

---

[83] Md. Const. art. II, §20.

[84] Md. Code Ann. §7-206(3)(ii).

[85] Md. Regs. Code tit. 12, §08.01.16(B).

[86] *See* Annual Report Fiscal Year 2002—Maryland Parole Commission, at 12, available on the State of Maryland's website at *www.dpscs.state.md.us/publicinfo/publications/pdfs/mpc2002AnnualReport.pdf*.

[87] M. Love, *supra* note 2, at Maryland-4, -5.

[88] *See* Frequently Asked Questions—Pardons, available on the State of Maryland's website at *www.dpscs.state.md.us/aboutdpscs/FAQmpc.shtml#pardon*.

[89] Mass. Const. pt. 2, ch. II, sec. I, art. VIII.

[90] *See* Executive Clemency Guidelines, issued by Governor Deval L. Patrick (May 21, 2007), available on the State of Massachusetts's website, under the Executive Clemency Unit section of the parole board's page at *www.mass.gov*.

[91] M. Love, *supra* note 2, at Massachusetts-4, -5.

MICHIGAN

Pardon Authority and Process: The power of pardon rests with the governor, with the exception of impeachment cases.[92] The governor is required to obtain a recommendation in an application for pardon from the Parole Board but is not bound by it.[93] Rules governing the pardon application and process can be found at Mich. Comp. Laws §§791.243 and 791.244. The application for pardon can be found on the website of the Michigan Parole Board on the State of Michigan's website at *www.michigan.gov*. Pardons are rarely granted in Michigan.[94]

Eligibility: An applicant for a pardon may apply upon completion of sentence.	*Effect:* A pardon relieves the applicant of all disabilities and erases his or her guilt.	*Contact:* Michigan Parole Board Pardons and Commutations Coordinator P.O. Box 30003 Lansing MI 48909 Tel: (517) 373-6391

MINNESOTA

Pardon Authority and Process: The governor, the attorney general, and the chief justice of the supreme court constitute the Board of Pardons, which has the power to grant pardons.[95] The director of corrections acts as the secretary of the Board and carries out investigations and makes recommendations to the Board.[96] Rules relating to the pardon application and process can be found at Minn. Stat. §§638.01 to 638.08 and Minn. R. 6600.0200 to 6600.1100. The latter are available at *www.revisor.leg.state.mn.us/arule/6600/*. In 2006, 27 applications for pardon were filed. Twelve were granted and another 12 were denied. Three were not considered because the Board refused to waive the waiting period.[97]

Eligibility: Applicants who have committed crimes of violence must wait 10 crime-free years from completion of sentence prior to seeking a pardon. Applicants who have committed nonviolent crimes must wait five crime-free years from completion of sentence before applying. The waiting period can be waived.	*Effect:* A pardon relieves all legal disabilities.	*Contact:* Randy Harnett Minnesota Board of Pardons 1450 Energy Park Dr., Suite 200 Saint Paul, MN 55108-5219 Tel: (651) 361-7178 Fax: (651) 603-6770 *randy.hartnett@state.mn.us*

---

[92] Mich. Const. art. 5, §14.

[93] Mich. Comp. Laws §§791.243, 791.244.

[94] M. Love, *supra* note 2, at Michigan-4.

[95] Minn. Const. art. V, §7; Minn. Stat. §638.01–.08.

[96] Minn. Stat. §638.075.

[97] Minnesota Board of Pardons—Annual Report to the Legislature 2006 Activity (Apr. 2007), available at *www.doc.state.mn.us/publications/legislativereports/documents/BOP2006report.pdf*.

APPENDIX E • STATE PARDON INFORMATION

MISSISSIPPI

Pardon Authority and Process: The governor has full clemency authority,[98] and the Parole Board has exclusive authority to investigate pardon cases at the governor's request.[99] All pardon applicants must post notice of their application in a newspaper in the county of conviction 30 days prior to filing with the governor, setting forth the reasons why the pardon should be granted.[100] Cases are then forwarded to the Parole Board for investigation prior to final action by the governor on the application.

Eligibility: Applicants are required to wait seven years after completion of sentence prior to requesting a pardon.	*Effect:* A pardon restores all civil rights.	*Contact:* State of Mississippi Parole Board 201 West Capitol Street, Suite 800 Jackson, MS 39201 Tel: (601) 354-7716

MISSOURI

Pardon Authority and Process: The power to pardon rests with the governor, with the exception of treason or impeachment cases.[101] All applications must be referred to the Board of Probation and Parole for investigation and recommendation, but the governor is not bound by the Board's recommendation.[102] Information regarding the pardon application and process are available on the Executive Clemency section on the website of the Board of Probation and Parole at *www.doc.mo.gov/division/prob/ExecClem.htm*. There is a low grant rate for pardons in Missouri.[103]

Eligibility: Applicants must wait three years after completion of sentence before applying for a pardon.	*Effect:* A pardon relieves all legal disabilities.	*Contact:* Board of Probation and Parole 1511 Christy Drive Jefferson City, MO 65101 Tel: (573) 751-8488 Fax: (573) 751-8501 *www.doc.mo.gov/division/prob/ExecClem.htm*

---

[98] Miss. Const. art. 5, §124.

[99] Miss. Code Ann. §§47-7-5(3), 47-7-31.

[100] Miss. Const. art. 5, §124.

[101] Mo. Const. art. IV, §7.

[102] Mo. Rev. Stat. §217.800(2).

[103] M. Love, *supra* note 2, at Missouri-3.

MONTANA

Pardon Authority and Process: The power to pardon rests with the governor.[104] The governor may only issue a pardon after recommendation of the Board of Pardons and Parole, except in capital cases; however, he or she is not required to accept the recommendation.[105] The rules governing the pardon application and process can be found at Mont. Code Ann. §§46-23-301 to 46-23-307 and at Mont. Admin. R. 20-25-901 to 20-25-904. The administrative rules are available on the Board's website at *www.mt.gov/bopp/adminrules/default.asp*. In 2002, three pardons were granted and 16 denied. In 2003, five were granted and 21 denied. In 2004, four pardons were granted and 16 denied. Statistics on pardon grants and denials are available on the Board's website.

Eligibility: An applicant for a pardon may apply upon completion of sentence.	*Effect:* A pardon relieves all legal disabilities.	Contact: Montana Board of Pardons and Parole Craig Thomas, Executive Director 300 Maryland Avenue Deer Lodge, MT 59722 Tel: (406) 846-1404 Fax: (406) 846-3512 *crthomas@mt.gov* *www.mt.gov/bopp/*

NEBRASKA

Pardon Authority and Process: The power to grant a pardon rests with the Board of Pardons, which is composed of the governor, the secretary of state and the attorney general.[106] Information on the pardon application and process can be found in the Instructions and Policy and Procedure Guidelines available on the Board of Pardons website at *www.pardons.state.ne.us/pardons.html*. During the past several years, about half of all pardon applications were granted.

Eligibility: An applicant with a felony conviction must wait 10 years after completion of sentence before seeking a pardon. An applicant with a misdemeanor conviction must wait three years after completion of sentence before applying.	*Effect:* A pardon restores all civil rights lost as a result of conviction.	Contact: Nebraska Board of Pardons P.O. Box 94754 Lincoln, NE 68509-4754 Tel: (402) 479-5726 Fax: (402) 471-2453 *sfauver@dcs.state.ne.us*

---

[104] Mont. Const. art. VI, §12.

[105] Mont. Code Ann. §§46-23-104(1), 46-23-301(3).

[106] Neb. Const. art. IV, §13; Neb. Rev. Stat. §§83-1, -126; Neb. Rev. Stat. §83-170(10) (scope of pardon power).

NEBRASKA

Pardon Authority and Process: Under the Nevada constitution, the governor is granted short-term clemency powers.[107] Full clemency power rests with a panel consisting of the governor, the justices of the supreme court, and the attorney general.[108] This group has been constituted as the Board of Pardons Commissioners.[109] A majority of the Board can grant a pardon, but the governor must be part of that majority.[110] Information on the pardon application and process are found at Nev. Rev. Stat. §231.020 *et seq.* and in the Nev. Admin. Code ch. 213, §020 *et seq.* Information is also available on the Board of Pardons Commissioners' website at *www.pardons.nv.gov/*.

Eligibility: Pardons are generally not considered until a significant period of time has passed since completion of sentence.	Effect: A full and unconditional pardon removes all legal disabilities.	Contact: Board of Pardons Commissioners 1445 Old Hot Springs Rd. #108B Carson City, NV 89711 Tel: (775) 687-8278 *www.pardons.nv.gov/*

NEW HAMPSHIRE

Pardon Authority and Process: With the exception of impeachment cases, the pardon power rests with the governor.[111] He or she must exercise this authority with the advice of an executive council.[112] The governor is required to obtain a supporting majority vote of the executive council before granting a pardon. Information on the pardon application and process are contained in N.H. Rev. Stat. Ann. §§4:21 to 4:28. Pardons are rarely granted in New Hampshire.[113]

Eligibility: An applicant for a pardon can apply at the completion of sentence.	Effect: A pardon relieves all disabilities.	Contact: Richard S. Carey Assistant Attorney General Department of Justice 33 Capitol Street Concord, NH 03301 Tel: (603) 271-3658 Fax: (603) 271-2110 *robert.carey@doj.nh.gov*

NEW JERSEY

Pardon Authority and Process: With the exception of treason and impeachment cases, the power to pardon rests with the governor.[114] The governor may refer pardon applications to the New Jersey State Parole Board for investigation and recommendation.[115] The governor is not required to accept the Board's recommendation. New Jersey has a low grant rate of pardons.

Eligibility: An applicant for a pardon can apply upon completion of sentence.	Effect: A pardon relieves all legal disabilities.	Contact: N.J. Department of Criminal Justice 25 Market Street; P.O. Box 080 Trenton, NJ 08625-0080 Tel: (609) 984-6500 Fax: (609) 292-3508

---

[107] Nev. Const. art. 5, §13.

[108] Nev. Const. art. 5, §14.

[109] Nev. Rev. Stat. §213.010(1).

[110] Nev. Const. art. 5, §14.

[111] N.H. Const. pt. 2, art. 52.

[112] *Id.*

[113] M. Love, *supra* note 2, at New Hampshire-2.

[114] N.J. Const. art. 5, §2, cl. 1.

[115] N.J. Stat. Ann. §2A:167-7.

NEW MEXICO

Pardon Authority and Process: The pardon power rests exclusively in the governor.[116] The New Mexico Parole Board is authorized to investigate requests for parole at the request of the governor.[117] Information regarding the pardon application and process are available in the Executive Clemency Guidelines, which can be found on the State of Mexico's website at *www.governor.state.nm.us/MEDIA/PDF/ExecClemencyGuidelines.pdf*. From 1995 until 2002, approximately five percent of applications were granted.[118]

Eligibility: Applicants must wait a period of five to 10 years following completion of sentence, depending on the seriousness of the offense.	*Effect:* A pardon restores all civil rights, but firearms rights must be specifically requested.	*Contact:* Pardons/Paroles Office of the Governor State Capitol Building Santa Fe, NM 87501 Tel: (505) 476-2200 www.governor.state.nm.us/pardon.php?mm=6

NEW YORK

Pardon Authority and Process: The power to pardon rests with the governor, with the exception of impeachment and treason cases.[119] The board of parole may advise the governor on applications if requested.[120] The Executive Clemency Bureau within the Division of Parole screens applications for eligibility, receives materials relating to pardon applications, and maintains correspondence.[121] For information regarding pardon application and process, see the New York State Parole Handbook (2007), which is available at *http://parole.state.ny.us/Handbook.pdf*. Pardons are rarely granted in New York.[122]

Eligibility: Pardons are considered as follows: when there is overwhelming evidence of innocence; to relieve a disability imposed upon conviction from disabilities (this is rarely used though because of a remedy available through the Certificate of Good Conduct or Relief); or to prevent deportation or permit re-entry to the United States. An applicant may apply upon completion of sentence.	*Effect:* A pardon relieves all legal disabilities. It acts to set aside a judgment of conviction when based on innocence.	*Contact:* Executive Clemency Bureau New York Division of Parole 97 Central Avenue Albany, NY 12206 Tel: (518) 473-9672 http://parole.state.ny.us/Clemency.asp

---

[116] N.M. Const. art. V, §6; N.M. Stat. Ann. §31-13-1(C).

[117] N.M. Stat. Ann. §31-21-17.

[118] M. Love, *supra* note 2, at New Mexico-3.

[119] N.Y. Const. art. 4, §4.

[120] N.Y. Exec. Law. §259-c.

[121] New York State Parole Handbook, §9 (2007), available at *http://parole.state.ny.us/Handbook.pdf*.

[122] M. Love, *supra* note 2, at New York-2.

APPENDIX E • STATE PARDON INFORMATION

NORTH CAROLINA

Pardon Authority and Process: Pardon power rests with the governor.[123] The Post Release Supervision and Parole Commission can assist the governor in investigating pardon applications at his or her request.[124] The governor's Office of Executive Clemency processes all applications for pardons. Information regarding the pardon application and process is available on the Executive Clemency webpage at *www.doc.state.nc.us/clemency/*. Pardons are rarely granted in North Carolina.[125]

Eligibility: An applicant for a pardon may apply upon completion of sentence.	*Effect:* A pardon relieves all legal disabilities.	*Contact:* Governor's Clemency Office 4294 Mail Service Center Raleigh, NC 27699-4294 Tel: (919) 715-1695 Fax: (919) 715-8623 *clemency@ncmail.net*

NORTH DAKOTA

Pardon Authority and Process: With the exception of treason and impeachment cases, pardon power rests with the governor.[126] The governor is advised by a Pardon Advisory Board.[127] Information on the pardon application and process can be found in the Pardon Advisory Board's policies and procedures, available at *www.nd.gov/docr/parole/pardon_policy.htm*. The rules are also set forth in N.D. Cent. Code §§12-55.1-05, 12-55.1-07, 12-55.1-08, and 12-55.1-09. In 2004, two pardons were granted out of 21 applications filed.[128]

Eligibility: An applicant for a pardon can apply upon completion of sentence.	*Effect:* A pardon relieves all legal disabilities.	*Contact:* Pardon Clerk Field Services Division Pardon Advisory Board P.O. Box 5521 Bismarck, ND 58506-5521 Tel: (701) 328-6192 *www.nd.gov/docr/parole/pboard/pardon_board.htm*

---

[123] N.C. Const. art. III, §5(6).

[124] N.C. Gen. Stat. §143B-266(a).

[125] M. Love, *supra* note 2, at North Carolina-2.

[126] N.D. Const. art. 5, §7.

[127] N.D. Cent. Code §12-55.1-02.

[128] M. Love, *supra* note 2, at North Dakota-2.

OHIO

Pardon Authority and Process: With the exception of treason and impeachment cases, the power to pardon rests with the governor.[129] Applications for clemency must be made in writing to the Adult Parole Authority, which investigates and makes recommendations to the governor on every application; however, the recommendation is not binding.[130] Information regarding pardon applications and process can be found on the website of the Ohio Department of Rehabilitation and Correction at *www.drc.state.oh.us/web/ExecClemency.htm*. From 1998 through 2004, approximately 21 percent of applications were granted.

Eligibility: An applicant may seek a pardon upon completion of sentence.	*Effect:* A pardon relieves all legal disabilities.	*Contact:* Ohio Parole Board 1050 Freeway Drive North Columbus, Ohio 43229 Tel: (614) 752-1200 www.drc.state.oh.us/web/ExecClemency.htm

OKLAHOMA

Pardon Authority and Process: A pardon can be granted by the governor but only with the favorable recommendation from a majority of the Pardon and Parole Board.[131] Information on the pardon application and process can be found on the Pardon and Parole Board's website at *www.ppb.state.ok.us*. The grant rate for pardons in Ohio is high. About 80 percent of applications were approved from 1996 through 2006.

Eligibility: An applicant for a pardon must wait five years from completion of sentence before applying.	*Effect:* A pardon relieves all legal disabilities, except that firearms privileges are separately and specifically restored.	*Contact:* Office of General Counsel First National Center 120 N. Robinson Ave., Suite 900W Oklahoma City, OK 73102-7436 Tel: (405) 602-5863 www.ppb.state.ok.us

OREGON

Pardon Authority and Process: The power to pardon rests exclusively with the governor.[132] However, the governor may not pardon applicants for crimes that the law permits a court to set aside.[133] For information on the pardon application and process, visit the website of the Criminal Justice Policy Foundation at *www.cjpf.org/clemency/Oregon.html*. The rules governing pardons can be found at Or. Rev. Stat. §§144.650(1) and 144.650(4). Pardon grant rates are low in Oregon; however, during his first two years in office, Governor Kulongoski issued three pardons for immigration purposes.[134]

Eligibility: Depending on the type of crime, an applicant for a pardon must wait either three years or 10 years after judgment before applying for a pardon.	*Effect:* A pardon relieves all legal disabilities.	*Contact:* Office of the Governor 160 State Capitol 900 Court Street, NE Salem, OR 97301-4047 Tel: (503) 378-3111 Fax: (503) 378-4863 www.cjpf.org/clemency/Oregon.html

---

[129] Ohio Const. art. III, §11.

[130] Ohio Rev. Code Ann. §2967.07.

[131] Okla. Const. art. VI, §10.

[132] Or. Const. art. V, §14; Or. Rev. Stat. §144.649.

[133] Or. Rev. Stat. §137.225.

[134] M. Love, *supra* note 2, at Oregon-2.

APPENDIX E • STATE PARDON INFORMATION

PENNSYLVANIA

Pardon Authority and Process: The governor has the power to pardon but may not act without a favorable recommendation from a majority of the Board of Pardons.[135] Information regarding the pardon application and process can be found at 37 Pa. Code §§81.221, 81.225, 81.226, 81.227, 81.263, and 81.301. The application and instructions can be found on the Board of Pardons' website at *http://sites.state.pa.us/PA_Exec/BOP/*. Between 10 and 20 percent of all pardon applications filed from 2000 to 2005 were granted.[136]

Eligibility: Applicants for a pardon may apply while still in prison and when released.	*Effect:* A pardon relieves all legal disabilities.	*Contact:* Board of Pardons 333 Market Street; 15th Floor Harrisburg, PA 17126-0333 Tel: (717) 787-2596 Fax: (717) 772-3135 *http://sites.state.pa.us/PA_Exec/BOP/*

PUERTO RICO

Pardon Authority and Process: The governor has exclusive power to pardon.[137] The parole board may make a nonbinding recommendation to the governor. The pardon process is carried out by the Puerto Rico Board of Parole. Information on the pardon application and process can be found on the Criminal Justice Policy Foundation website at *www.cjpf.org/clemency/PuertoRicoEnglish.html*.

Eligibility: Policy during the past several administrations has required a five-year wait following completion of sentence prior to application.	*Effect:* A pardon relieves all legal disabilities.	*Contact:* Board of Parole P.O. Box 40945, Minillas Station San Juan, PR 00940-945 Tel: (787) 754-8115 ext. 327 or 240 *www.cjpf.org/clemency/PuertoRicoEnglish.html*

RHODE ISLAND

Pardon Authority and Process: With the exception of treason and impeachment cases, pardon power rests with the governor.[138] There is no formal process for seeking a pardon. Applications should be sent to the office of the governor. Information relating to the pardon application and process can be found on the Criminal Justice Policy Foundation website at *www.cjpf.org/clemency/RhodeIsland.html*.

Eligibility: An applicant for pardon can apply upon completion of sentence.	*Effect:* A pardon relieves all legal disabilities.	*Contact:* Office of the Governor State House, Room 115 Providence, RI 02903-1196 Tel: (401) 222-2080 Fax: (401) 222-8096

---

[135] Pa. Const. art. 4, §9(a).

[136] M. Love, *supra* note 2, at Pennsylvania-3.

[137] P.R. Const. art. IV, §4.

[138] R.I. Const. art. 9, §13.

SOUTH CAROLINA

Pardon Authority and Process: Although the governor has the authority to grant reprieves and commute sentences, pardon power is vested by statute in the Probation, Parole, and Pardon Board.[139] Information regarding the pardon application and process is contained in S.C. Code Ann. §§24-21-30, 24-21-50, 24-21-990, 24-21-950(A)(1), and 24-21-960(B). Information on pardons can also be found on the Department of Probation, Parole and Pardon Board's website at *www.dppps.sc.gov/apply_for_a_pardon.html*. The Probation, Parole and Pardon Board generally grants about 60 percent of all applications.[140]

Eligibility: An applicant can apply for a pardon upon completion of sentence, including payment of all fines and restitution.	Effect: A pardon relieves all legal disabilities.	Contact: Department of Probation, Parole and Pardon Services 2221 Devine Street, Suite 600 P.O. Box 50666 Columbia, SC 29250 Tel: (803) 734-9220 Fax: (803) 734-9440 www.dppps.sc.gov/apply_for_a_pardon.html

SOUTH DAKOTA

Pardon Authority and Process: There are two types of pardons in South Dakota. The governor may grant pardons independently under the South Dakota Constitution.[141] The governor may also delegate by executive order advisory authority to the Board of Pardons and Parolees.[142] When the governor seeks advice from the Board, the Board receives the pardon application, investigates the case, and refers the case back to the governor with a non-binding recommendation.[143] Information on the pardon process is available on the State of South Dakota Department of Corrections' website at *www.state.sd.us/corrections/FAQ_Clemency.htm*. The application is available at *www.state.sd.us/corrections/Executive%20Clemency%20Pardon%20Application52007.pdf*. South Dakota has a grant rate of approximately 50 percent.[144]

Eligibility: An applicant for a pardon can file an application upon completion of sentence.	Effect: A pardon relieves all legal disabilities.	Contact: Board of Pardons and Parole South Dakota Penitentiary 1600 North Drive P.O. Box 5911 Sioux Falls, SD 57117-5911 Tel: (605) 367-5040 Fax: (605) 367-5115 www.state.sd.us/corrections/parole.htm

---

[139] S.C. Const. art. IV, §14; S.C. Code Ann. §24-21-920.

[140] M. Love, *supra* note 2, at South Carolina-3.

[141] S.D. Const. art. 4, §3.

[142] S.D. Codified Laws §24-14-1. *See also Doe v. Nelson,* 680 N.W. 2d 302 (S.D. 2004) (South Dakota has "two prong" pardon system).

[143] S.D. Codified Laws §§24-14-1 to 24-14-5.

[144] M. Love, *supra* note 2, at South Dakota-5.

APPENDIX E • STATE PARDON INFORMATION

TENNESSEE

Pardon Authority and Process: With the exception of impeachment and treason cases, pardon power rests with the governor,[145] who may be advised by the Board of Probation and Parole.[146] However, the governor is not bound by the Board's advice. Rules governing the pardon process are contained in the Rules of the Tennessee Board of Parole ch. 1100-1-1-.15(1)(d) and (f). Information on the pardon application and process is available on the Tennessee Board of Probation and Parole's section on Executive Clemency at *www2.tennessee.gov/bopp/bopp_bo.htm#EXECUTIVE%20CLEMENCY%20SECTION*. In the past, Tennessee has had a grant rate of less than 10 percent.[147]

Eligibility: An applicant can seek a pardon upon completion of sentence.	*Effect:* A pardon has limited legal effect in Tennessee. A person who receives a pardon that restores full rights of citizenship can petition the court for restoration.[148]	*Contact:* Board of Probation and Parole Board Operations Division 404 James Robertson Pkwy, Suite 1300 Nashville, TN 37243 Tel: (615) 741-2001 Fax: (615) 741-5337

TEXAS

Pardon Authority and Process: The governor may only grant a pardon with the affirmative written recommendation from a majority of the members of the Board of Pardons and Paroles.[149] Information regarding the pardon application and process is available on the Board of Pardons and Paroles' website at *www.tdcj.state.tx.us/bpp/exec_clem/exec_clem.html*. In fiscal year 2003, 238 applications were filed, 76 were recommended favorably by the Board, and the governor granted 67.[150]

Eligibility: An applicant for pardon can apply upon completion of sentence.	*Effect:* A pardon relieves all legal disabilities.	*Contact:* Texas Board of Pardon and Paroles Executive Clemency Section 8610 Shoal Creek Boulevard Austin, TX 78757 Tel: (512) 406-5852 Fax: (512) 467-0945 *www.tdcj.state.tx.us/bpp/exec_clem/exec_clem.html*

---

[145] Tenn. Const. art. 3, §6; Tenn. Code Ann. §40-27-101.

[146] Tenn. Code Ann. §§40-28-104(a)(10), 40-28-128.

[147] M. Love, *supra* note 2, at Tennessee-5.

[148] Tenn. Code Ann. §40-29-105(c).

[149] Tex. Const. art. 4, §11(b).

[150] M. Love, *supra* note 2, at Texas-3.

UTAH		
Pardon Authority and Process: The power to pardon is vested in the Board of Pardons and Parole.[151] The rules governing the pardon procedure are available at *www.rules.utah.gov/publicat/code/r671/r671-315.htm*. Additionally, the procedures are governed by Utah Admin. Code §§671-304, 671-305, and 671-315. The Board receives between three to five requests a year and granted only 10 from 1996 to 2006.[152]		
Eligibility: A person may seek a pardon five years after completion of sentence.	*Effect:* A pardon relieves all legal disabilities.	*Contact:* Board of Pardons and Paroles 448 East Winchester Street, Suite 300 Murray, UT 84107 Tel: (801) 261-6464 Fax: (801) 261-6481 *bopinfo@utah.gov* *http://bop.utah.gov/*

VERMONT		
Pardon Authority and Process: Pardon power is vested exclusively with the governor.[153] At the governor's request, the Parole Board may investigate pardon applications and act in an advisory capacity.[154] Information on pardons is available from the Vermont Parole Board Manual, ch. 5 (May 9, 2006), available on the Parole Board's website at *www.doc.state.vt.us/about/parole-board/pb-manual*. About 10 percent of pardons are granted.[155]		
Eligibility: An applicant must wait 10 years after completion of sentence before applying for a pardon.	*Effect:* A pardon relieves legal disabilities.	*Contact:* Office of the Governor 109 State Street, Pavilion Montpelier, VT 05609-0101 Tel: (802) 828-3333

---

[151] Utah Const. art. VII, §12; Utah Code Ann. §77-27-5(4).

[152] M. Love, *supra* note 2, at Utah-2.

[153] Vt. Const. chap. II, §20.

[154] Vt. Stat. Ann. tit. 28, §453.

[155] M. Love, *supra* note 2, at Vermont-1.

VIRGINIA

Pardon Authority and Process: The governor has the power to grant full pardons or limited restoration of rights.[156] At the request of the governor, the Parole Board can investigate requests for pardons and make recommendations.[157] Information on the pardon application and process can be found on the website of the secretary of the commonwealth at *www.commonwealth.virginia.gov/JudicialSystem/Clemency/pardons.cfm*. In 2003, there were 231 requests for pardons and 12 were granted, including one to avoid deportation. Three pardons were granted in 2003. As of June 2005, Governor Warner had granted 37 pardons during his first 30 months in office.[158]

Eligibility: Generally, an applicant must first have his or her rights restored through the restoration of rights procedure and wait five years after completion of sentence before seeking a pardon.	*Effect:* A pardon can relieve legal disabilities. However, it does not restore the right to possess a firearm, which must be done through the courts.	*Contact:* Patricia Tucker, Director of Extradition and Clemency Office of the Secretary of the Commonwealth P.O. Box 2454 Richmond, VA 23218-2454 Tel: (804) 692-0105 *www.commonwealth.virginia.gov/JudicialSystem/Clemency/pardons.cfm*

WASHINGTON

Pardon Authority and Process: Pardon power is vested in the governor,[159] who may seek advice from the State Clemency and Pardons Board.[160] Information on the pardon application and process can be found at the webpage of the Criminal Justice Policy Foundation at *www.cjpf.org/clemency/Washington.html*. Pardons are rarely granted in Washington.[161]

Eligibility: An applicant may seek a pardon upon completion of sentence.	*Effect:* A pardon relieves all legal disabilities.	*Contact:* Clemency and Pardons Board Office of the Governor Legislative Building P.O. Box 40002 Olympia, WA 98504-0002 Tel: (360) 753-6780 Fax: (360) 753-4110

WEST VIRGINIA

Pardon Authority and Process: The power to pardon is vested exclusively in the governor.[162] The governor does not consider any pardon application without recommendation from the parole board. Pardons are very rarely granted in West Virginia.[163]

Eligibility: An applicant can apply upon completion of sentence.	*Effect:* A pardon relieves legal disabilities but does not restore firearms privileges, which must be done through the courts.	*Contact:* Office of the Governor 1900 Kanawha Boulevard, E. Charleston, WV 25305 Tel: (888) 438-2731

---

[156] Va. Const. art. V, §12.

[157] Va. Stat. Ann. §§53.1-136(5), 53.1-231.

[158] M. Love, *supra* note 2, at Virginia-3.

[159] Wash. Const. art. III, §9.

[160] Wash. Rev. Code §§9.94A.880, 9.94A885, and 10.01.120.

[161] M. Love, *supra* note 2, at Washington-3.

[162] W.Va. Const. art. IV, §1.

[163] M. Love, *supra* note 2, at West Virginia-1.

WISCONSIN

Pardon Authority and Process: With the exception of impeachment and treason cases, the governor has exclusive authority to pardon.[164] The governor is advised by a nonstatutory Pardon Advisory Board. Information on the pardon application and process can be found on the State of Wisconsin's website at *www.wi-doc.com/PDF_FIles/Doyle%20Pardon%20Packet.pdf.* Pardons are rarely granted in Wisconsin.[165]

Eligibility: An applicant for a pardon must generally wait five years after completion of sentence before applying; however, this period of time may be waived in extraordinary circumstances.	Effect: A pardon relieves all legal disabilities.	Contact: Office of the Governor Pardon Advisory Board Room 115; East State Capitol P.O. Box 7863 Madison, WI 53707 Tel: (608) 266-1212

WYOMING

Pardon Authority and Process: The power to pardon rests with the governor.[166] Procedures for pardons are described in Wyo. Stat. Ann. §§7-13-803 to 7-13-806. Pardons are rarely granted in Wyoming.[167]

Eligibility: An applicant must wait 10 years after completion of sentence before applying.	Effect: A pardon relieves legal disabilities.	Contact: Attorney General's Office 123 Capitol; 200 West 24th Street Cheyenne, WY 82002 Tel: (307) 777-7841 Fax: (307) 777-6869

---

[164] Wis. Const. art. V, §6.

[165] M. Love, *supra* note 2, at Wisconsin-1.

[166] Wyo. Const. art. 4, §5.

[167] M. Love, *supra* note 2, at Wyoming-2.

APPENDIX F

PRIVATE IMMIGRATION AND NATIONALITY BILLS INTRODUCED AND LAWS ENACTED 77TH THROUGH 109TH CONGRESS

Congress	Bills Introduced	Laws Enacted	Congress	Bills Introduced	Laws Enacted
109th Congress	41	0	92nd Congress	2,866	62
108th Congress	39	3	91st Congress	6,266	113
107th Congress	85	6	90th Congress	7,293	218
106th Congress	121	19	89th Congress	5,285	279
105th Congress	67	9	88th Congress	3,647	196
104th Congress	27	2	87th Congress	3,592	544
103rd Congress	50	4	86th Congress	3,069	488
102nd Congress	71	11	85th Congress	4,364	927
101st Congress	127	7	84th Congress	4,474	1,227
100th Congress	194	20	83rd Congress	4,797	753
99th Congress	347	15	82nd Congress	3,669	729
98th Congress	454	33	81st Congress	2,811	505
97th Congress	728	42	80th Congress	1,141	121
96th Congress	902	83	79th Congress	429	14
95th Congress	1,024	138	78th Congress	163	12
94th Congress	1,023	99	77th Congress	430	22
93rd Congress	1,085	63			

* Source: U.S. Department of Homeland Security, *Yearbook of Immigration Statistics: 2003*, Table 51, available at *www.dhs.gov/xlibrary/assets/statistics/yearbook/2003/Table51.xls*.

** Note: The numbers for the 108th and 109th Congress represent that number of reports requested by Congress from ICE (as opposed to the number of bills introduced).

APPENDIX G

U.S. Department of State Foreign Affairs Manual Volume 9 - Visas

9 FAM APPENDIX I, 500 GENERAL GUIDELINES REGARDING PRIVATE BILLS

(TL:VISA-496; 11-21-2002)
(Office of Origin CA/I/O/L/R)

9 FAM APPENDIX I 501 BACKGROUND

(TL:VISA-496; 11-21-2002)

Private immigration legislation is an effort to provide extraordinary relief after all administrative remedies under the INA have been exhausted. Based on the information submitted, the Congressional Committees must decide whether such circumstances merit passage of a private law which in effect, would exempt the beneficiary from a provision of the law applicable to all other visa applicants or would confer a benefit to which the alien would not otherwise be entitled. It is the Department's experience that Members of Congress, when making an exception to the general immigration laws, examine each private bill very carefully to determine whether there is sufficient equity in the merits of the case. A fully documented background investigation would not only alert these Members to any relevant facts which might otherwise surface subsequent to the bill proceedings being completed but could also substantiate the necessity of passing the private bill. *Although most beneficiaries of private bills are in the United States, and frequently have been for some time, it is rare that posts will be asked to provide a bill report. However, instructions are being provided in case a post is asked to prepare one.*

9 FAM APPENDIX I 502 GENERAL INFORMATION POST SHOULD INCLUDE IN A BILL REPORT

(TL:VISA-167; 05-23-1997)

A report from the post concerning a private bill case should provide the Senate and House Judiciary Committees all available information relating to the beneficiary of the private legislation. The report should not only verify the reasons for which a visa was denied (or could otherwise not be issued) in

U.S. Department of State Foreign Affairs Manual Volume 9 - Visas

an individual case, but should also touch on matters which relate to the merits of the case and should contain any other pertinent information which may be of help to the Committees in weighing the equities of the private bill. However, while the Committees expect the report to provide detailed facts relevant to their final determination on the private legislation, posts should make no recommendation or observation on the merits of the private bill as such. If the files contain information of which the Committees should be made aware, but which does not belong in the official report, the consular officer should forward such information in a separate communication to the Department (CA/VO/L/R).

9 FAM APPENDIX I 503 DEPARTMENT REQUEST FOR INFORMATION

(TL:VISA-496; 11-21-2002)

When the Department is requested to provide a private bill report, it is generally on very short notice. Often the bill is coming before the Committee in the next day or two. Thus, when a Departmental request for a private bill report is received, the consular officer shall promptly determine whether the visa files contain the necessary information to prepare a report as outlined in this chapter. In some cases, it will be necessary to interview the beneficiary of the private bill to obtain the pertinent data. If the alien's address is not available, the post must so inform the Department for follow-up through the sponsor of the bill in obtaining the information. When preparing the report, the consular officer shall reexamine the validity of any previous visa refusal to determine whether subsequently enacted legislation would provide the same relief as passage of the private bill.

9 FAM APPENDIX I 504 PREPARING THE REPORT

(TL:VISA-274; 05-09-2001)

The report should be transmitted to the Department either by fax, e-mail or cable. Posts should provide as much information about the beneficiary and any visa application the beneficiary has made. The report should include:

(1)   The private bill (S or HR) number;

(2)   Biographical data regarding the beneficiary (See 9 FAM Appendix I, 509);

(3) Any known relationship to a U.S. citizen or Legal Permanent Resident;

(4) A complete report regarding any nonimmigrant or immigrant visa application made by the beneficiary (See 9 FAM Appendix I, 511);

(5) Results of local police and other agencies' name checks, whether negative or not (See 9 FAM Appendix I, 506);

(6) Any information known regarding any hardship of the beneficiary that might result in the denial of the visa;

(7) Any known grounds of ineligibility applicable to the beneficiary (See 9 FAM Appendix I, 507); and

(8) Any relief which might be available to the beneficiary that would permit the issuance of a visa, either now or in the future.

9 FAM APPENDIX I 505 SUBMITTING THE MEMORANDUM OF INFORMATION

(TL:VISA-496; 11-21-2002)

Prompt submission of private bill reports is important, as the period during which the Congress is in session and in which it can complete action on private legislation is very limited. *Some sort of response to the Department's request must be made immediately.* If a full report cannot be made, posts must *advise the Department of* the reason(s) for the delay and when a full report might be expected.

9 FAM APPENDIX I 506 CLEARANCE PROCEDURES

(TL:VISA-496; 11-21-2002)

a. Clearance procedures for private bill cases are identical to those for any immigrant visa case and must include checks with other posts. To avoid delay in submitting a report because of an incomplete investigation, the report should include a statement to the effect that the results of the investigation will be forwarded at a later date.

b. When the investigation is completed, the post should forward its results telegraphically, *by e-mail or by fax* for the Department to transmit to the

> U.S. Department of State Foreign Affairs Manual Volume 9 - Visas
>
> appropriate Committee.
>
> c. In cases in which the beneficiary of a private bill has been convicted of a criminal offense, the consular officer must submit a copy of the conviction, with translation if necessary, together with the charges brought against the alien, the applicable provisions of the law, and the judgment of the court.
>
> d. Consular officers are reminded, however, that whether or not a record of the beneficiary exists in the post's file, they must conduct a check of the local police and clearance sources and submit the results, negative or not, to the Department.
>
> # 9 FAM APPENDIX I 507 GROUNDS OF INELIGIBILITY
>
> *(TL:VISA-496; 11-21-2002)*
>
> a. When a private bill provides relief from a ground of ineligibility, the report should state whether the pending private bill would remedy all known disqualifications for which the beneficiary might be refused a visa and, if not, the other grounds for which ineligibility exists. In this connection, the consular officer shall make every effort to ascertain whether other grounds of ineligibility may exist, to avoid embarrassment resulting from additional grounds coming to light after enactment of the bill which would make the beneficiary still ineligible to receive an immigrant visa.
>
> b. When submitting a report on a bill waiving a drug or criminal conviction, the consular officer must furnish:
>
>   (1) Complete transcripts of the conviction's related court proceedings;
>
>   (2) Any other record relating to the offense(s) including state and local police records;
>
>   (3) An affidavit from the beneficiary describing any criminal record in full, and
>
>   (4) Any other information available at the post.
>
> c. In the case of a bill that would provide relief from grounds of a drug conviction, the consular officer must also submit the court transcript indicating the exact amount of drug possession at the time of arrest. If such information is not available to the consular officer, because the beneficiary is not residing abroad or because the courts will not disclose

such information, the report must include a statement to that effect and indicate whether the documents may be made available through direct request from the beneficiary. A certified copy of all documents and their translation must be submitted to the Department.

9 FAM APPENDIX I 508 MEDICAL EXAMINATION

(TL:VISA-274; 05-09-2001)

a. A beneficiary of a private bill is required to undergo a medical examination. If the beneficiary refuses to comply, the consular officer must indicate this fact in the report. A copy of the medical report, and its translation if in a language other than English, must be submitted only if the report shows a medical ground of ineligibility. In such a case, the report by the examining physician must include:

  (1)   Whether the condition affects the alien's employability;

  (2)   Type(s) and results of treatments, if applicable;

  (3)   How the alien gets along with others; and

  (4)   Any other observations that have a bearing on the prognosis of the particular condition.

b. In cases involving mental grounds of ineligibility, the report must also include the date of the last known attack or other manifestation of mental affliction and a statement of the prognosis of the case.

c. In cases where the beneficiary's medical condition would prevent the alien from earning a living, the consular officer must provide information as to whether arrangements have been made by relatives to provide for the beneficiary's room, board, adequate medical insurance and any other necessities in connection with the medical impairment after arrival in the United States, and whether the relatives have provided for the alien in the past in the form of monetary contributions, etc.

d. If it appears that arrangements for the medical examination will delay submission of the report, the consular officer shall submit a preliminary report covering all other aspects of the case with a statement that the results of the examination will be transmitted at a later date. Submitting copies of negative medical findings is not necessary, but the report must include a statement to the effect that no diseases or defects were disclosed.

U.S. Department of State Foreign Affairs Manual Volume 9 - Visas

9 FAM APPENDIX I 509 BIOGRAPHICAL DATA

(TL:VISA-167;   05-23-1997)

Biographical data concerning a beneficiary of a private bill should contain:

(1)   The beneficiary's name (including aliases, maiden, professional or religious name, or variant spellings);

(2)   Date and place of birth;

(3)   Place of residence;

(4)   Marital status and, if divorced, duration of marriage or previous marriage(s);

(5)   Children, if any, and their date(s) and place(s) of birth and present residence;

(6)   Background data (including, but not limited to, schooling, professional or vocational training or experience, military service, standing in the community);

(7)   Circumstances which led to existing disqualification;

(8)   Previous action taken on visa application, if any, including ground(s) for refusal;

(9)   General health conditions, including the date and results of medical examination;

(10) Family ties in the United States and/or abroad; and

(11) Claimed purpose of entry into the United States and length of intended stay if a nonimmigrant visa was previously issued to the beneficiary

9 FAM APPENDIX I 510 ADOPTION CASES

(TL:VISA-167;   05-23-1997)

a. When a private bill would accord the beneficiary the status of a child, the report should include:

(1)   A specific statement regarding the adoption proceedings (instituted, pending or completed);

(2) The applicable adoption law in the beneficiary's country; and

(3) Whether the adoptive parent(s) and the child have met and the two-year period of legal custody and residence with adoptive parent(s) has been fulfilled.

b. Three certified copies of the foreign adoption decree, and translation, if applicable, must be furnished. Evidence of support of the beneficiary, in the form of canceled checks, letters, and clothing, if any, should also be noted as it could favorably affect Congressional determination.

c. Furthermore, in cases where the results of the medical examination show an affliction or disability, the report shall indicate that all pertinent details relating to the affliction or disability have been provided to the adoptive parents and that they have elected to pursue the processing of the visa application to completion.

9 FAM APPENDIX I 511 BENEFICIARY RESIDING IN THE UNITED STATES

(TL:VISA-496; 11-21-2002)

In most instances, the beneficiary of a private bill is in the United States. In cases where the beneficiary entered the United States in a nonimmigrant status, the report must provide the purpose of entry, length of stay, and any statement as to the necessity to return abroad after a visit to the United States as these appear on the visa application. The members of the Senate and House Judiciary Committees place great importance on this information in determining whether the beneficiary had intended all along to obtain immigrant status by circumventing standard immigrant visa procedures.

9 FAM APPENDIX I 512 ENACTMENT OF PRIVATE LEGISLATION

(TL:VISA-274; 05-09-2001)

a. Upon receipt of notification of enactment of a private bill permitting issuance of a visa, the post shall immediately request the beneficiary to appear at the consular office for final interview and issuance of the visa. Consular officers must bear in mind that, unless the bill provides otherwise, the beneficiary must apply for and be issued a visa within two years from enactment of the bill or lose the relief provided by the private law. Consular officers must assure that the beneficiary is aware of this

U.S. Department of State Foreign Affairs Manual Volume 9 - Visas

requirement at the time of the scheduling of the visa interview.

b. The telegraphic communication should form the basis for issuing the visa, provided a confirmation of a petition approval (unless such requirement has been waived by the private legislation) has also been received from INS. The consular officer shall telegraphically inform interested Members of Congress that the visa has been issued and clearly indicate the number of the private bill or law and the name of the beneficiary. An information copy must be sent to the Department and slugged "Attention: Private Bill Staff - CA/VO/L/R.

BIBLIOGRAPHY

Books

M. Love, *Relief from the Collateral Consequences of a Criminal Conviction: A State-by-State Resource Guide* (2006)

U.S. House of Representatives, *A History of the Committee on the Judiciary 1813–2006* (2006)

B. Maguire, *Immigration—Public Legislation and Private Bills* (1997)

A. Hinds, *Hinds' Precedents of the House of Representatives of the United States* (1907)

Articles

M. Mantel, "Private Bills and Private Laws," 99 *Law Libr. J.* 87 (Winter 2007)

A. Gallagher, "Remedies of Last Resort: Private Bills and Pardons," 06-02 *Immigration Briefings* (Feb. 2006)

K. Griffith, "Perfecting Public Immigration Legislation: Private Immigration Bills and Deportable Lawful Permanent Residents," 18 *Geo. Immigr. L.J.* 273 (Winter 2004)

M. Wishnie, "Immigrants and the Right to Petition," 78 *N.Y.U. L. Rev.* 667 (May 2003)

R. Hopper, "Private Bills and Deferred Action: A New Look at Old Remedies," *Immigration & Nationality Law Handbook* 471 (AILA 1999–2000 Ed.).

R. Hopper and J. Osuna, "Remedies of Last Resort: Private Bills and Deferred Action," 97-06 *Immigration Briefings* (June 1997)

A. Steiner, "Remission of Guilt or Removal of Punishment? The Effects of a Presidential Pardon," 46 *Emory L.J.* 959 (Spring 1997)

Reports

Government Accountability Office, Immigration Enforcement—ICE Could Improve Controls to Help Guide Alien Removal Decision Making (2007)

M. Lee, Private Immigration Legislation (CRS Report Feb. 28, 2007)

V. Heitshusen, The Legislative Process on the Senate Floor: An Introduction (CRS Report Dec. 8, 2006)

M. Lee, Private Immigration Legislation (CRS Report Aug. 9, 2005)

R. Beth, Private Bills: Procedure in the House (CRS Report Oct. 21, 2004)

C. Johnson, How Our Laws Are Made, H. Doc. No. 108-93 (June 20, 2003)

SUBJECT-MATTER INDEX

A

A nonimmigrant status, 35
Abscam scandal (1978), 7
Adjustment of status, 42, 92, 93
Adoption cases, 10, 25, 38–39, 42, 43–48
Age-out cases, 43–48
Aggravated felonies and pardons, 63, 64
Alabama pardon provisions, 141
Alaska pardon provisions, 141
Alien Registration Act of 1940, 11
Antiterrorism and Effective Death Penalty Act of 1996, 2
Application for relief requested, time limit for, 24
Arizona pardon provisions, 142
Arkansas pardon provisions, 142
ATF (Bureau of Alcohol, Tobacco and Firearms), 67
Athletes, 27, 42
Attorneys representing potential beneficiaries of private bills, 29–30, 60
Automatic stay of removal, 24

B

Board of Immigration Appeals (BIA)
    constitutional arguments over pardons before, 70–71
    remands to, 94
Bureau of Alcohol, Tobacco and Firearms (ATF), 67
Bush, George W., 75–76

C

California pardon provisions, 143
Carlesi v. New York (1914), 69
Carter, Jimmy, 64
Chief Counsel's Offices, Office of the Principal Legal Advisor (ICE), 91–94
Children
    See also Adoption cases; Age-out cases
    born abroad, 13
Chinese crewmen, 7, 14, 28
Citizenship
    honorary citizenship, 27
    private bills granting, 41, 56–57
    renunciation of, 27, 42
Clemency. *See* Pardons
Clinton, Bill, 74
Colorado pardon provisions, 143
Communists, 11, 13
Confidential informants, 93
Confidentiality of pardon files, 83
Congressional hearings on presidential pardon power, 74
Congressional Record, publication of private bills in, 15
Congressional rules. *See* House rules; Senate rules
Connecticut pardon provisions, 144
Constitution, U.S.
    art. I, sec. 8, cl. 1, 5
    art. II, sec. 2, 69, 73
Constitutionality of immigration pardon provision, 67–70
Cooper memo on prosecutorial discretion, 88–89
Criminal exclusion, waiver of, 11, 26, 38, 42, 52–54
Cuban Adjustment Act of 1966, 13
Cuban nationals, 13
Customs and Border Protection (CBP), 33

D

Death of sponsor cases, 49–52
Deferred action, 85–87
    no appeal of refusal to grant, 87
Delaware pardon provisions, 144
Dellinger memo (1995) on presidential pardons, 67–68
DHS. *See* Homeland Security Department
Displaced Persons Act of 1948, 10
Displaced persons and refugees from World War II, 41
District of Columbia pardon provisions, 145
Doctors and nurses, 25–26, 42
DOJ. *See* Justice Department
Domestic violence, 64
DOS. *See* State Department
Draft dodgers, 13
    Vietnam War dodgers, pardon by Carter, 64, 74–75
    waivers for those seeking to avoid military service in their home countries, 42
Drug offenses
    pardon of, 63–64, 78, 80
    waiver of. *See* Criminal exclusion, waiver of

E

E nonimmigrant status, 36
Employment authorization, 33–34
Enactment of private bills, 39
    notification of, 36
English requirement, 13
Exclusion laws, 11–12
Executive branch's role, 31–39
Executive Order No. 11967, 64
Exhaustion of remedies, 24
Expungement of criminal record, 74–75

F

F nonimmigrant status, 36
Family relief cases, 20, 33, 48–49, 92
FBI investigation prior to pardon, 80
Felonies, pardons of. *See* Pardons
Firearms disabilities, 66–67
First Amendment, 5
Florida pardon provisions, 145
Foreign Affairs Manual provisions, 167–74
Form G-388, 36
Form I-130, 92, 93
Form I-140, 93
Form I-181, 36
Form I-357, 36
Form I-485, 92
Form I-765, 33
Fraud, 27, 42, 78
Freedom of Information Act, 85

G

G nonimmigrant status, 35
Garland, Ex parte (1866), 68, 69
Georgia pardon provisions, 146
German nationals and presidential vetoes of private bills, 32
Government Printing Office, 16
Gubernatorial pardons. *See* Pardons
Gulf War. *See* Persian Gulf War evacuees

H

Hardship criteria, 20, 21, 43
Hawaii pardon provisions, 146
Health exclusion, waiver of, 11, 42
Homeland Security Department (DHS), 31, 33–36
　deferred action, 87
　notification of enactment of private bill, 36
Honorary citizenship, 27
House Judiciary Committee, 21, 35, 36
House Private Calendar, 14, 22
House rules, 14, 21–27, 101–8
　evolution of (1954-1988), 19–21
　precedential considerations, 22–23, 41
　procedure, 23–24
　Rule 4, 20, 21
House Subcommittee on Immigration, Citizenship, Refugees, Border Security, and International Law, 21, 23–24
　See also House rules
Humanitarian factors, 93
Hurricane Katrina, 86

I

I nonimmigrant status, 36
ICE. *See* Immigration and Customs Enforcement
Idaho pardon provisions, 147
Illegal Immigration Reform and Immigrant Responsibility Act of 1996, 2
Illinois pardon provisions, 147
Immigration and Customs Enforcement (ICE), 15–16, 33
　Operations Instructions (legacy INS), 34–36, 85, 109–15
　prosecutorial discretion and, 89–91
　reports to subcommittees, 24, 29, 34
　role of, 34
Immigration and Nationality Act of 1952 (INA), 8, 10, 11, 25, 63
Immigration and Naturalization Service (INS)
　legacy memoranda on prosecutorial discretion, 88–90
　legacy INS Operations Instructions, 34–36, 85–86, 109–15
　opposition to a private bill, 31
　reports to subcommittees, 20
In absentia orders, 94
Indiana pardon provisions, 148
Ineligibility, relief from grounds of, 38
INS. *See* Immigration and Naturalization Service
Internal Security Act of 1950, 11
Iowa pardon provisions, 148

J

J nonimmigrant status, 36
Justice Department (DOJ)
　on detained noncitizens, 73
　Office of the Pardon Attorney, 76–77, 79–80

K

Kansas pardon provisions, 149
Kennedy, Edward, 19
Kentucky pardon provisions, 149
Knote v. U.S. (1877), 68, 69
Kwai Chiu Yuen v. INS (1969), 70

L

Langer, William D., 6–7
Lobbying Disclosure Act of 1995, 59
Loss of citizenship, 12
Louisiana pardon provisions, 150

M

M nonimmigrant status, 36
Mahler v. Eby (1924), 70
Maine pardon provisions, 150
Mansfield, Michael J., 28
Maryland pardon provisions, 151
Massachusetts pardon provisions, 151
Medical care, cases of people seeking in U.S., 26, 42, 54–55, 93
Medical examination of beneficiary of private bill, 38

© 2008 American Immigration Lawyers Association

Subject-Matter Index

Medical personnel, 25–26, 42
Meili family, 58
Meissner memo on prosecutorial discretion, 89
Michigan pardon provisions, 152
Minnesota pardon provisions, 152
Mississippi pardon provisions, 153
Missouri pardon provisions, 153
Mistake of law, 57–58
Mondale, Walter, 74
Montana pardon provisions, 154
Motions to reopen or reconsider, 94

N

Narcotic Control Act of 1956, 63
National Origins Quota Act of 1924, 8
National Security Entry-Exit Registration System (NSEERS), 92–93
Naturalization, 12–13, 27, 42, 56–57
Nebraska pardon provisions, 154–55
New Hampshire pardon provisions, 155
New Jersey pardon provisions, 155
New Mexico pardon provisions, 156
New York pardon provisions, 156
Noonan; U.S. v. (1990), 74
North Carolina pardon provisions, 157
North Dakota pardon provisions, 157
Notice to Appear (NTA), 88, 92–93

O

Occupations, 10
Office of Congressional Relations (OCR), 34
Office of Immigration Statistics, 15
Office of Investigations (ICE), 34, 90–91
Office of the Pardon Attorney (DOJ), 76–77, 79–80
Office of the Principal Legal Advisor (ICE), 34
  Chief Counsel's Offices, 91–94
Ohio pardon provisions, 158
Oklahoma pardon provisions, 158
Olympic athletes, 27, 42
Operations Instructions (legacy INS), 34–36
  deferred action, 85–86
  text of, 109–15
Oregon pardon provisions, 158

P

Pardon Clause, 69, 73
Pardons, 2, 63–72
  confidentiality of files, 83
  constitutional arguments before BIA, 70–71
  constitutionality of immigration pardon provision, 67–70
  federal, 73–83
  full and unconditional, 65–67
  historical background and statistics, 75–76
  limited grounds applicable, 63
  no due process rights, 73
  Office of the Pardon Attorney, role of, 76–77, 79–80
  Petition for Pardon After Completion of Sentence, 79, 117–39
  petition procedures and requirements, 79–80
  preparing application for, 81–83
  processing of, 76–83
  standards for consideration of petitions, 78–79
  state provisions, 141–64
  U.S. attorney, role of, 77
Pasha v. Gonzales (2005), 71
Pennsylvania pardon provisions, 159
Persian Gulf War evacuees, 42, 59
Petition for Pardon After Completion of Sentence, 79, 117–39
Political cases, 58–59
Posner, Richard, 71
Posthumous citizenship, 42
Precedential considerations, 22–23, 41–59
  adoption, children, and age-out cases, 43–48
  criminal issues, 52–54
  death of sponsor cases, 49–52
  family relief cases, 48–49
  medical issues, 54–55
  mistake of law, 57–58
  political cases, 58–59
  practice tips and strategies, 59–61
  waiver of naturalization and citizenship requirements, 56–57
Preference system, 8–10
Presidential action on private bills, 15, 31
  vetoes, 31–33
Presidential pardons. *See* Pardons
Principal Legal Advisor. *See* Office of the Principal Legal Advisor (ICE)
Private immigration bills, 5–17
  controversy surrounding, 6–7
  defined, 5
  documentation required, 23, 28–29
  enactment of, 39
  Foreign Affairs Manual provisions, 167–74
  historical background of, 1, 7–13
  implementation of enacted bill, 36
  introduction's effect on immigration status, 35–36
  notification of enactment of, 36
  number of, 7–8
  procedure, 13–15
    See also House rules; Senate rules
  purpose of, 1, 6
  reports. *See* Immigration and Customs Enforcement (ICE); State Department (DOS)
  researching, 15–17
  rules governing. *See* House rules; Senate rules
  statistics (77th through 109th Congress), 165
Prosecutorial discretion, 85–95
  after hearing, 94
  after issuance and filing of NTA, 93
  after issuance of final order, 94

© 2008 American Immigration Lawyers Association

current procedures, 87–88
deferred action, 85–87
defined, 88
prior to or in lieu of issuance of NTA, 92–93
Puerto Rico pardon provisions, 159

Q

Quota Act of 1921, 1, 8
Quota laws and preference system, 8–10, 41

R

Realty Co.; U.S. v. (1896), 5–6
Reconsideration of private bills, 22
Refugee Relief Act of 1953, 10
Relative status, 9
Remands to BIA, 94
Removal of noncitizens due to prior criminal convictions, 73
Removal proceedings, 24
    See also Stay of removal
    cancellation of, 36
    commencement of, 36
Reports. *See* Immigration and Customs Enforcement (ICE)
Residence requirements, 12, 13
Rhode Island pardon provisions, 159
Rodino, Peter W., Jr., 6
Roosevelt, Franklin, 32

S

Scott, Hugh D., 28
Senate Calendar of Business, 14
Senate Judiciary Committee, 28, 35, 36
Senate rules, 7, 14, 28–30, 99–100
    evolution of (1954-1988), 19–21
    procedure, 28–30
Senate Subcommittee on Immigration, Refugees and Border Security, 28
    See also Senate rules
Serial Set Index (Congressional Information Service), 16
Sexual battery, pardon for, 64
Sheepherders, 10
Simpson, Alan, 19
Smith Act (Alien Registration Act) of 1940, 11
South Carolina pardon provisions, 160
South Dakota pardon provisions, 160
State
    federal vs. state felony convictions, 66–67
    pardon provisions, 141–64
State Department (DOS), 36–38
    reports by, 36–37
Statutes at Large, publication of private laws in, 16
Stay of deportation, 20
    private bills for, 6–7, 9, 29
Stay of removal, 24–25, 31

when Congress requests report on private bill, 35
Suh, Matter of (2003), 71
Supremacy Clause, 69

T

Tennessee pardon provisions, 161
Texas pardon provisions, 161
Thomas (Library of Congress website), 16
Time limit for application for relief requested in private bill, 24
Treaty trader status, 35

U

U visas, 86
U.S. v. See name of opposing party
U.S. attorney, role in pardon process, 77
U.S. Citizenship and Immigration Services (USCIS), 33
    on deferred action, 86–87
U.S. Government Printing Office, 16
Utah pardon provisions, 162

V

Vermont pardon provisions, 162
Victims of crime
    contacting during deciding on pardon, 74, 80
    U visas for, 86
Vietnam War draft resisters, pardon by Carter, 64, 74–75
Violent crimes, pardon for, 64, 78
Virginia pardon provisions, 163
Voluntary departure, 92

W

Waiver of exclusions, 9, 11, 41
    for health and criminal grounds for fiancés, 9
    for naturalization. *See* Naturalization
Waiver of grounds of inadmissibility, 27
War brides and children of U.S. citizen military personnel, 41
Washington pardon provisions, 163
Wei Jingsheng, 42, 58–59
West Virginia pardon provisions, 163
Whistleblower protection, 58
Wilding, Michael, 12
Wisconsin pardon provisions, 164
Work authorization, 33–34
Wyoming pardon provisions, 164

Y

Yearbook of Immigration Statistics, 15